Building a Peaceful Society

Creative Integration of Peace Education

A volume in
Peace Education
Ian Harris, Edward J. Brantmeier, and Jing Lin, *Series Editors*

Peace Education

Ian Harris, Edward J. Brantmeier, and Jing Lin
Series Editors

Building a Peaceful Society

Creative Integration of Peace Education

Laura L. Finley

Barry University

INFORMATION AGE PUBLISHING, INC.
Charlotte, NC • www.infoagepub.com

Library of Congress Cataloging-in-Publication Data

Finley, Laura L.
 Building a peaceful society : creative integration of peace education /
Laura L. Finley.
    p. cm. – (Peace education series)
 Includes bibliographical references.
 ISBN 978-1-61735-457-1 (hardcover) – ISBN 978-1-61735-456-4 (pbk.) –
ISBN 978-1-61735-458-8 (e-book)
 1. Conflict management–Social aspects. 2. Violence–Prevention. 3.
Crime prevention. 4. Peace–Social aspects. 5. Peace–Study and teaching.
I. Title.
 HM1126.F56 2011
 303.6'90973–dc22

                                                                    2011012502

Printed in the United States of America

Contents

Acknowledgements and Dedication

While surely there will be important individuals I miss here, I will make my best effort to thank all of those who helped make this dream a reality.

I am thrilled to have been given the opportunity to write this book, as peace, and peace education, is my passion. I thank Edward Brantmeier and Ian Harris, editors of this series of books, as well as Information Age Press, for accepting my proposal and for helping me adjust it so that it (hopefully) offers something unique to the field. I especially thank Jing Lin, the editor who worked with me throughout this process and who gave me such positive and useful feedback.

In addition, I think it is important to acknowledge those who have most influenced me and nurtured my academic and activist development. I thank my mentor, Dr. Sue Caulfield of Western Michigan University, for it was under her loving guidance that I began to develop my own peacemaking perspective. Although we are not personally acquainted beyond perhaps a passing hello at academic conferences, I also wish to acknowledge those who have shaped my peacemaking thinking in general. In no particular order: Riane Eisler, the late Elise Boulding, Evelyn Ang, Paulo Freire, Johann Galtung, Alfie Kohn, Paul Loeb, Marshall Rosenberg, and many more. In particular, thanks to all those involved with the Peace and Justice Studies Association, a tremendous organization of which I am excited to be a part. Specific to my field of criminology, I want to acknowledge the peacemaking criminology pioneers Richard Quinney, Hal Pepinsky, Sue Caulfield, Larry

Building a Peaceful Society, pages ix–x
Copyright © 2011 by Information Age Publishing

Tifft, Dennis Sullivan, Howard Zehr, Gordon Bazemore, and all the other amazing folks.

Many others helped shape this book. My great colleagues at Barry University—Gary Grizzle, Lisa Konczal, Luigi Esposito, Fernando Perez, Victor Romano, and our ever-organized and happy departmental assistant Chrissie Chiarella. I also thank our wonderful sociology and criminology students, who give me inspiration and continue to excite new ideas. Thanks go out also to the wonderful Broward County, Miami-Dade County, and Palm Beach County teachers, who are teaching peace every day and who have allowed me to present in their classes and schools. Special kudos to the Broward Schools Office of Prevention Programs for advancing peace in the schools and beyond.

On a more personal level, none of my academic or activist work would have happened were it not for the loving support of my husband, Peter. Although my constant search for additional projects likely infuriates him, his belief in me has never failed. A huge thank-you goes to my beautiful peace-loving daughter, Anya. At 7, your energy and enthusiasm to do good in the world is a continual inspiration. You amaze me, make me laugh, and remind me daily that peacemaking is a journey that begins in our homes. This book is dedicated to you.

Finally, I wish to acknowledge and honor my colleague, Somy Ali, the kindest living embodiment of peace that I know. I am a board member of her nonprofit, No More Tears, which assists victims of domestic violence. Somy gives all she can—financially, emotionally, and in every other way—to help women and children so that they can live in peace. Although it may be small, I am dedicating 50 percent of the proceeds from the sale of this book to No More Tears to help her with that incredible work.

Preface

We see everything that's going wrong
with the world and those who lead it.
We just feel like we don't have the means
to rise above and beat it.
So we keep waiting,
waiting on the world to change

Waiting on the World to Change
—John Mayer

Several years ago, I worked as a trainer for a domestic-violence agency. Shortly after I was hired, the agency developed a new Department of Social Change, charged with coordinating prevention efforts in the community. I was thrilled to be offered the exciting opportunity to lead what sounded like a truly progressive program. One project involved creating a "kit" that we would disseminate to community groups so they could then teach local groups about domestic and dating violence and promote healthy relationships. We were to create the kit and provide training for community leaders on how to use it. I was charged with creating the kit and instructional manual. The first draft I showed my supervisor incorporated a number of peace education activities and images related to peace, as I saw the endeavor to be one of peace-building in the community. I was both shocked and dismayed when my supervisor told me to eliminate all references to peace, as "that was for the antiwar people."

Building a Peaceful Society, pages xi–xvii
Copyright © 2011 by Information Age Publishing
All rights of reproduction in any form reserved.

The experience I just described was an "aha" moment for me. As I have written elsewhere (Finley, 2010), "I realized this was more than a one-time concern with one individual. Rather, it was reflective of a larger problem in the field—a disjuncture between the goals of the anti-domestic movement and its structures and methods." I began to see that this was true of other organizations and other institutions. It made me realize that, many times, those groups and institutions that can and should be helping make peace do not see their work in that light. I began to think about the implications of that. It seems to assume that peace is not possible, as it is not defined as the goal. How can violence be prevented—by social services, by law enforcement, by courts, etc.—when we automatically assume that it is inevitable? And how do we move these groups to see that their work can be, has to be, peace education? These thoughts lead me to contemplate writing this book.

As I was writing this book, the 2010 Global Peace Index (GPI), compiled by Vision of Humanity (www.visionofhumanity.org), was released. The United States ranked 85 out of 149. This was not surprising to me, but yet is still disturbing. The rankings are made up of 23 indicators, including perceived criminality, number of homicides, jailed population, military expenditures, disrespect for human rights, and more. Clearly, we have much work to be done. Violence is endemic in U. S. culture. It is built into our structures and institutions. As Rynne (2008) explained,

> The myth of redemptive violence in which our culture is enmeshed is the belief that, when one is really up against it, only might can bring deliverance. When push comes to shove, most people believe, the only logical thing is to push back. One has every right to defend one's self, one's property, one's family, one's nation. End of story. The way to maintain power is to carry a big stick and not be afraid to use it when you have to. Otherwise you just invite attack. This is undoubtedly the conventional wisdom and the way of the world. (p. 2)

Yet all is not lost. Wonderful peace education programs are being implemented in schools and universities. More than 300 colleges give degrees of certificates in peace-building or peace studies. Activists across the globe are working on making social change for human betterment. Structural and institutional violence are insidious, but not unchangeable. Through careful analysis, discourse, strategic planning, inclusive collaborations, creativity, and perseverance, peace can and will prevail.

Readers may be wondering what I can offer that is unique, given the many great books on peace, peace education, nonviolence, and related topics. Although I profess no great intellect, I believe my perspective is somewhat different than most authors who have written on peace education.

I am a humanist sociologist, a peacemaking criminologist, a community peace and human rights activist, a lifelong educator, an athlete, a wife, and a mother. Each of these statuses allows me a vantage point from which to examine violence and peace, and each is included, in some way, in this book. I am also a hopeful, creative, and excitable person. Although these qualities sometimes have drawbacks (like when I think it is a good idea to write two books simultaneously!), I feel as though they have served me well. It is my hope that these qualities come through in this book and inspire passion about peace education—any time, anywhere, any way.

Sociology has much to offer to the study of violence and peace. As Weber (2006) explained, "Sociology can contribute to an in-depth understanding of the larger social forces that shape our communities and individual lives" (p. 161). That is, rather than seeing violence, and peace, as rooted solely in the individual, a sociological approach helps us see that violence is institutionalized and structured in society. As Iadicola and Shupe (1999) explained, a sociological view helps point out that violence is "a pattern of behavior that emanates fundamentally from the very organization of society" (p. 4).

Too often, however, sociologists use their skills in academe only. In the zeal to be considered a "real science," sociologists promoted a field dominated by "university-based, value-neutral scientists" (Dale & Kalob, 2006, p. 123). Even today, many sociologists are discouraged or even prohibited from engaging in activism. As Dale and Kalob (2006) explained,

> Staying in the ivory tower is simply not enough . . . an intellectual craft has its place, of course, but it is small comfort to the millions of people who die every year from hunger and war and who cry out for justice and peace. They and all the others suffering in our world are reaching out to us. We are well educated, privileged, relatively comfortable, and generally caring and compassionate. We are well placed in our society to make a difference in our communities and beyond. (p. 119)

A growing humanistic and liberation sociology has emerged from this call. These are sociologists who are devoted to understanding and helping alleviate conditions of oppression, exploitation, and domination (Feagin & Vera, 2001). Humanist sociology is built on several core premises: (a) all people share a common humanity and have inherent dignity and worth; (b) human beings are interdependent and should act toward one another with respect (vs. mere tolerance), mutual care, and compassion; (c) all people should have the freedom and opportunity to pursue their aspirations and to develop their full potential as individual human beings; (d) all people should enjoy equal rights, most of which are articulated in the *Universal Declaration of Human Rights*; (e) all human affairs, not just political ones, should be based on genuine democracy; (f) all people have the right to a safe, healthy environment and are obligated to practice environmental stewardship and ecological sustainability; and (g) people should address or resolve conflicts without resorting to violence (Dale & Kalob, 2006, pp. 138–139). I would place myself in this camp. I believe that social critique and analysis are essential, yet must also be coupled with social action and activism. Our words must be translated into action that helps humanity. This can certainly occur inside the classroom, but must not remain exclusively there (Adarkar & Keiser, 2007; Alexander & Carlson, 1999; Baker, Martin, & Pence, 2008; Bar-Tal & Rosen, 2009; Brown & Morgan, 2008; Fountain, 1999; Galtung, 1996; Jenkins, 2007; Nava, 2001; Nelson, Van Slyk, & Cardella, 1999; O' Brien, 1997; Page, 2007).

Most criminologists do not engage in the study of peace. As Ruggiero (2005) explained, criminology is largely concerned with explaining why people commit crime rather than why most do not. As such, its focus tends to be on the negative, not on the positive. Until relatively recently, the field paid little attention to the crimes of the powerful. As a result, criminology has long left state crime untouched and undertheorized. The default effect of this is that it has reinforced the status quo. Peacemaking criminology emerged in response to this critique. It is a criminology devoted to humane policies that decrease human suffering and maximize human potential. Peacemaking criminology looks for alternatives to the traditional criminal justice system, which in many ways does as much harm as crime itself (Fuller, 1998; Pepinsky & Quinney, 1991; Wozniak, 2002). I consider myself a peacemaking criminologist. And, like other peacemaking criminologists, I realize that my work in the classroom is but one venue to make social change. Following Pepinsky (2006), I see the creative integration of not just peace themes but peace processes as a work in progress.

Throughout my life, I have always been a good student. That is, I got good grades. But as I grew older and gained additional degrees, I began to wonder whether I was smart or simply compliant. Did I earn good grades because of my intellect and abilities, or was it because I did what was asked of me? And what was I really *doing* with any of that? Granted, I was teaching high school social studies, but was that enough to change any of the social inequalities I was learning about? As an undergraduate, I excused myself from engaging in community projects because I was an athlete on scholarship, which ate up a lot of time. I told myself, as many do and as John Mayer's lyrics show us, that this was enough (Dalai Lama, 2005). As Palmer (1998) pointed out, schooling today is full of paradoxes. We separate head from heart, facts from feelings, theory from practice, and teaching from learning. Emphasis is on the cognitive realm and, even more narrowly, on specific disciplines that are separated from one another (Gardner, 1999a). In the 20th century, we have "trained people to use their minds sharply but have largely neglected to cultivate their hearts and souls with love and compassion" (Lin, 2006, p. xi). Higher education, too, generally expects students to learn in similar ways—passive lecture; spit-back testing; and little, if any, student voice or opportunity to engage in community betterment (Finley, 2004a). I was schooled in this system and under this worldview. Activism was not for me but rather for those crazy marchers or wild bra-burners. Instead of taking action, I let life act on me.

Today, I am devoted to making a difference in my community. I feel as though I do this in my position as a professor, but that is no longer enough for me. I now realize that teaching peace cannot end when the semester does but must extend into my life in other ways. I am a volunteer board member of several organizations devoted to peace, human rights, and women's rights. I get involved in local human rights actions and have helped sponsor events and numerous awareness campaigns about a variety of social issues. Today, I realize that my lifelong involvement in sports has been personally beneficial and that sport, despite all its current problems, can be a form of peace education. And perhaps my most important role as a peace educator is that as mother to Anya, is 7 years old. I see that through each institution I am involved with, I can make linkages, collaborations, and promote peace. And, most importantly, it is my unique perspective and creative ideas that contribute to a collective movement. Each one of us has a unique perspective and creative ideas to share—it is that potential that must be tapped.

I have found creativity to be one of the most important forces for social change. Little happens when we do the same thing over and over and expect the same results—isn't that how Albert Einstein supposedly defined insanity? That is why I have woven the thread of creativity throughout this book, including beginning each chapter with a significant song lyric.

This book begins by examining violence. The Introduction first discusses the three levels of violence: interpersonal, institutional, and structural. It focuses largely on explaining the concept of structural violence, first articulated by Johan Galtung, and institutional violence, as those are the focus of the book. Peace education to address structural and institutional violence is not as common as that which addresses more microlevel violence, like conflict resolution and peer mediation programs. This book discusses why, illustrating how U. S. society is dominator modeled (Eisler, 1987) or based on adversarialism. The dominator model is a militaristic one. The United

States, in essence, is a society built on preparation for war and warmaking. It values the same qualities that are esteemed in the military: authority, obedience, power over others, masculinity, and competition. This model is packaged and "sold" to us as though it was not only normal but the only way that society can function. The dominator model permeates throughout three levels: structures, methods, and content. These are all discussed in the chapter, and examples are provided to highlight how this model often precludes the integration of peacemaking perspectives into society.

Chapter 1 begins by articulating what peace means, as it is only by clearly defining the goal that we can begin to move toward achieving it. It then provides an overview of the many varieties of peace education, showing how these can help devise an alternate model—what Eisler (1987) called a partnership model or what Fellman (1998) called a mutuality model. The chapter discusses what that model looks like at all three levels (structure, methods, and content). It also introduces the importance of creativity and highlights how it is essential in helping integrate peace education for a peaceful society.

Chapters 2 through 7 are all structured similarly in that they begin by providing a brief critical analysis of institutional violence in specific institutions. The second half of each chapter offers alternate ways to view the social issues discussed, to structure the institutions involved, and to incorporate concepts of peacemaking and peace education. Chapter 2 addresses policing/law enforcement, chapter 3 discusses courts and corrections, and chapter 4 addresses prevention programs. These were all selected because of my academic and activist background in criminology and sociology. Chapter 5 discusses nonprofits, NGOs, and social services. I have worked in these areas for some time, so draw on the academic literature as well as my personal experience to highlight the promise of partnership and how the dominator model has prevailed. As a lifelong athlete and a scholar of sport sociology, I show in chapter 6 that while sport is far from perfect, it has great potential to make social change and peace. Chapter 7 provides creative examples of peace education—what Fellman (1998) called "seeds of mutuality"—in areas where there has been significant conflict, in corporations and in families.

Chapter 8 sums things up and provides recommendations for moving forward. It highlights the importance of creativity in establishing and implementing peace education that truly addresses structural and institutional violence. Appendix A shares some of my favorite resources for education about and for positive peace, including books, Web sites, and films. Appendix B provides some of my favorite ideas, most of which can be integrated into a variety of institutions.

As Paulo Freire (1974) said, "To surmount the situation of oppression, people must first critically recognize its causes, so that through transforming action they can create a new situation, one which makes possible the pursuit of a fuller humanity" (p. 47). It is my hope that this book can show anyone the importance of peace education. Further, I hope that this book inspires readers to see that we can all teach about and for peace. And, when we use our creativity, nothing can stop us from creating the world we want.

INTRODUCTION
Violence and the Dominator Model

The present curriculum, I put my fist in 'em
Eurocentric every last one of 'em.
See right through the red, white and blue disguise

Take the Power Back
—Rage Against the Machine

The purpose of this Introduction is to identify the types of violence that exist in society and to highlight why they are so prevalent. It first provides an overview and definitions of violence, describing interpersonal, institutional, and structural forms. It next situates these forms of violence as part of Eisler's (1987) dominator model, which is a warmaking or militaristic model, that influences our structures, processes, and content. As the lyrics above illustrate, this model influences our educational system as well as many other societal institutions. The dominator model is hegemonic, thus we find it difficult to see alternate ways of thinking. This leads us to a number of "mind traps," which prohibit us from making social change toward a more peaceful world.

The goal of this book is to inspire creative ways to integrate peacemaking into "nontraditional" institutions. Before we can do so, however, it is essential to analyze the current system. As the late Howard Zinn (2007)

Building a Peaceful Society, pages xix–xxxvii
Copyright © 2011 by Information Age Publishing
xix

explained, it is important to search history in a way that will awaken our consciousness about injustices and inequalities. Zinn (2007) noted that, "America's future is linked to how we understand our past" (p.11). Following Zinn (2007), this examination of violence and domination in U.S. institutions is intended to help identify where, when, and how we can emphasize peacemaking instead. Once we understand issues of "power, oppression, privilege, and social stratification," as Lin, Brantmeier, and Bruhn (2008, p. xv) noted, we can craft peace education that is "positive, integrative, restorative, generative, and transformative" (p. xiv).

Number 85: The Global Peace Index

As noted in the Preface, the 2010 Global Peace Index ranked the United States number 85 out of 149 nations. This ranking is an attempt to measure the elements of positive peace (discussed in chapter 1) and includes measures that assess violence in many forms and at many levels. The GPI uses 32 indicators to measure peacefulness, which are divided into three broad categories: measures of ongoing domestic and international conflict, measures of societal safety and security, and measures of militarization. The measures of domestic and international conflict included the number of external and internal conflicts fought, estimated number of deaths from organized external conflict and organized internal conflict, the level of organized internal conflict, and relations with neighboring countries. Ten indicators were used to measure societal safety and security: perception of societal criminality, number of refugees and displaced persons as a percentage of the population, political instability, level of respect for human rights, potential for terrorist acts, number of homicides per 100,000 people, level of violent crime, likelihood of violent demonstrations, number of jailed population per 100,000 people, and number of internal security officers and police per 100,000 people. Militarization was assessed through eight indicators: military expenditure as a percentage of GDP, number of armed services personnel per 100,000 people, volume of imported conventional weapons per 100,000 people, volume of exported conventional weapons per 100,000 people, budget support for UN peacekeeping missions, aggregate number of heavy weapons per 100,000 people, ease of access to small arms and light weapons, and military capability and sophistication (Institute for Economics & Peace, 2010a). The GPI was first calculated in 2007, and researchers sadly noted that there was improvement on only four indicators in the 4 years: access to weapons of minor destruction, respect for human rights, potential for terrorist acts, and military expenditure as a percentage of GDP.

The United States ranked poorest on internal organized conflict and number of deaths from internal conflict, number of displaced persons, political instability, number of armed services personnel per 100,000 people, imports of major conventional weapons, and funding for UN peacekeeping missions. The United States was given a score of 1 out of 5 on each of these measures. In 2009, the United States spent $965 billion on current military and an additional $484 billion on past military, according to the War Resister's League. In all, 54 percent of total federal income tax funds are devoted to a military purpose. Department of Defense spending plus expenditures on nuclear weapons in the United States equaled the total military spending of the next 15 countries (Where your income tax $ really goes, 2009).

Additionally, the 2010 GPI report identified other societal and economic correlates. These included the functioning of the government and the degree of established checks and balances, electoral processes, freedom of press, government corruption, international openness (including imports and exports, foreign investment, visitors, and migration), gender equality, regional integration, education (including spending, primary and secondary school enrollment, enrollment in higher education, and adult literacy), and health and well-being. In all, the GPI researchers found that society measured low not only on peacefulness but also on other indicators of societal well-being. The least peaceful countries had high levels of governmental corruption, a lack of respect for human rights, poor relations with neighboring countries, lower levels of educational participation, lack of acceptance of the rights of others, and inequitable distribution of resources. The United States has much work to be done on some of these correlates. Women constitute only 16.8 percent of Congress, and gender inequality was ranked at .74 percent. Freedom of the Press was given a ranking of 4/100, and only 5.7 percent of GDP was allotted for education.

As of February 2010, 33 violent conflicts were occurring across the globe. Military expenditure totaled $1,531 billion, according to the Stockholm International Peace Research Institute. Military spending in the United States accounted for 54 percent of the increase in overall spending between 2008 and 2009. Global violence in all its forms has been estimated to cost $28.27 trillion dollars over a 4-year period (Institute for Economics & Peace, 2010b). Given that the United States is the world's largest economy, GPI researchers noted it has the most to gain economically by becoming more peaceful.

The GPI is a great tool to measure violence in a variety of forms. It is a creative way to gauge our planet's progress in making peace. Too often, people think of violence as interpersonal only; that is, they envision acts of personal aggression from one person to another, such as a gang fight, rape by a stranger, or domestic violence. This is a very basic definition of violence and one that fails to consider the bulk of what happens in a given society. Iadicola and Shupe (1999) explain why it is essential to understand violence in all its forms:

> If we focus only on the lowest levels of violence, we see the trees but miss the forest of which they are a part. In doing so, we fail to understand the forces beyond the individual actors who are in their personal drama of violence. This is how we generally view the violence in our society as we look for defects in the individual actors or their immediate social situation. We fail to understand and see how the violence that is committed at the highest levels by those with the greatest power manifests itself in the violence of those with least power in the society and the world. (p. 46)

Defining Violence

Iadicola and Shupe (1999) defined violence as "any action or structural arrangement that results in physical or nonphysical harm to one or more persons" (p. 26). This definition includes six important points: (a) Actions or structural arrangements must be willfully or deliberately committed or condoned; (b) violence can be intended or unintended; (c) violence may be justified or unjustified; (d) violence and its harmful effects address both physical and psychological well-being; (e) violence may or may not be recognized as such by the recipient, the actor, or both; (f) this definition of violence is universal.

In regard to Iadicola and Shupe's (1999) first and second points, this definition of violence recognizes that harmful effects might not be the intended goal, but violence occurs when harm is the result. "Violence is defined as legitimate or illegitimate as it relates to whether it furthers or threatens the social structures in the society... those who are more powerful in the society have greater ability to commit legitimate violence and the violence they commit is more likely to be defined as legitimate, thus not problematic" (p. 41). As Pilisuk (2008) explained, "violence is evident where any life is harmed or ended through the behavior or the negligence of other people... it may be direct, as when one uses a gun or bomb to destroy others, or structural, as when patterns of land ownership and land use by distant corporate entities result in the starvation of children who live on that land" (p. x). An example of unintentional violence is the Ford Pinto case, in which the poorly designed gas tank sometimes exploded upon collision. Although Ford surely did not intend for anyone to die or even to be hurt, their actions were willful and the result was violence (Iadicola & Shupe, 1999). The state is allowed to define the type of violence that is justified. Thus, war and other international acts of aggression, like the current debacles in Iraq and Afghanistan, may be defined as necessary and justified, while the actions of other individuals in society are considered unlawful and unjustified. Likewise, capital punishment—which is nothing more than the state giving itself permission to kill—is still considered justified in the United States (Fuller, 1998).

Building on Iadicola and Shupe's definition, violence occurs at three different levels: interpersonal, institutional, and structural or societal. Interpersonal violence was defined above. Institutional violence is violence that occurs by the action of societal institutions and their agents. Sociologists generally look at five major societal institutions: economy, politics, family, religion, and education (Iadicola & Shupe, 1999). Structural violence is violence that occurs in the context of establishing, maintaining, extending, reducing or as a consequence of the hierarchical ordering of categories of people in a society" (Iadicola & Shupe, 1999, p. 33). All forms of violence and oppression are linked together, as "violence stems from, and is legitimized by, situations of oppression" (James et al., 2003, p. 129).

Structural Violence

The largest portion of violence in our society is structural violence (Gil, 1999) generated or committed by agents of the state and corporate economic organizations. Ultimately, violence and the threat of violence are forms of power used to control people's behavior. "Violence takes place within the context of the social structures in which we live our lives. Violence is a form of power that is an instrument for the maintenance of social structures in the society" (p. 37). Much of this structural violence is directed against the poor, against minorities, and against women and children (Farmer, 1996; Madriz, 2001; Rousseau & Rousseau, 1999). It is a way to maintain inequalities that benefit some over others. "Whole populations are being held hostage in poverty, sickness, addiction, and brutality against one another" (Quinney, 2001, p. ix).

Globalization has worsened structural violence. Pilisuk (2001) noted how globalization places corporations ahead of people, which has exacerbated poverty, effected tremendous environmental damage, and diminished peoples' sense of agency and control. He commented, "As corporations become the social group commanding major portions of the waking day, the mechanism that assures interactive behavior is not *caring*, but rather *marketability*" (p. 3). Americans generate more than 4.6 pounds of garbage, on average, each day. About one fifth of the world's population—some 1.2 billion people—experience water scarcity. Half the world's population lives on less than $2.50 per day. We lose more than 7 million hectares of trees a year, or 20,000 hectares (almost 50,000 acres) each day. This is equivalent to an area twice the size of Paris each day, or 33 football fields each minute. Without thinking, we buy items made in sweatshops, or electronics or jewelry that continue to fuel conflicts in the Democratic Republic of Congo, Sierra Leone, Rwanda, Burundi, and Uganda. U.S.-based multinational companies exploit the land and the people in their quest for profits. The petroleum industry has been responsible for some of the worst offenses. Texaco (now Chevron) spent almost three decades between 1964 and 1992 extracting oil from the Amazonian forest in a chunk of land three times the size of Manhattan. Texaco dumped toxic water and carcinogens like benzene, cadmium, and mercury. In Nigeria, Shell Oil began extracting petroleum in Ogoniland in 1958, destroying the land. When the Ogoni began to organize to fight for their rights and the land, led by environmental activist Ken Saro-Wiwa, Shell and the Nigerian government were not pleased. They arranged for Ken and several other activists to be arrested and tried on trumped up charges, and Saro-Wiwa was hung on November 10, 1995 (Leonard, 2010).

As I write this, the oil spill from BP's Transocean Deepwater Horizon platform, which killed 11 workers when it exploded on April 20, 2010, is FINALLY being cleaned up, although the damage is far from over. The link to former Vice President Dick Cheney's old company Halliburton is clear. Halliburton was in charge of the cementing process, which involves plugging holes in the pipeline seal by pumping cement into it from the rig. Haliburton had been implicated for its shoddy cementing work in another spill in Australia ("Haliburton may be culprit," 2010).

The most visible indicators of structural violence are the differential rates of mortality, morbidity, and incarceration rates among groups in the same society (Dohrenwend et al., 1992; Gallagher, 2008; Link, Lennon, & Dohrenwend, 1993; Thoits, 1981; Ulbrich,Warheit, & Zimmerman, 1989). Dr. Paul Farmer (2004) has noted that the suffering and illness of the powerless in developing countries, particularly Haiti, is the result of political and economic injustices.

Violence is more likely within hierarchical social structures, which involve "ranking of people in terms of specific identifiable attributes that allow one category of people to possess more power in social interaction than another category of people" (Iadicola & Shupe, 1999, p. 39). The United States has the greatest income inequality of any developed nation besides Singapore (Moyers, 2010). A 2008 study found that the top .01% of American families (14,000) hold 22.2 percent of wealth. The bottom 90 percent, or over 133 million people, control just 4 percent of the nation's wealth. The top 25 percent of U.S. households own 87 percent of America's wealth, while the bottom 25 percent owns no wealth at all (Hill, 2010). The gender/pay gap in 2009 was still large, with women earning just 77 cents to a man's dollar, which totals more than $10,600 less that a woman brings home annually simply because of her sex (Kelley, 2010). Inequality is even greater when race and ethnicity are considered. United for a Fair Economy (UFE) publishes an annual "State of the Dream" report, which tallies economic inequality by race in the United States. The 2010 report noted that in December 2009, the unemployment rate for blacks was 16.2 percent, the highest in 27 years, and much higher than the 9 percent for whites. Blacks earn 62 cents for every dollar of white income, and Latinos earn 68 cents. Blacks and Latinos are 2.9 times and 2.7 times more likely, respectively, to live in poverty than whites. Further, people of color as a whole had only 16 cents of wealth for every dollar of white wealth (United For a Fair Economy, 2010). Globally, in 2008, the top 200 wealthiest people in the world controlled more wealth than the bottom 4 billion of the population (Moyers, 2010).

Structural violence also occurs when certain groups are not provided access to important information, such as legislative policies and programs that impact them. The *Washington Post* reported that poor and minority voters were at a disadvantage in the 2008 election due to the continued "digital divide," whereby whites' access to computers and Internet service is far greater than that of other demographic groups (Vargas, 2007). Similarly, when institutions are structured and operated in ways that certain groups do not understand or cannot participate, this is structural violence. The tremendous number of people who were prohibited from voting in the 2000 and 2004 elections due to their prison record illustrates this concept. Estimates vary on how many were excluded, but one source says at least 7,000 people were impacted in 2000 in Florida alone (Palast, 2000). Other people are excluded in different ways. For instance, the legal system in the United States uses language that many do not understand. Thus, their ability to truly comprehend the process is limited. Similarly, social services are often set up in convoluted bureaucratic ways, which result in eligible people not being able to access needed help (Mukherjee, 2007).

Hypersurveillance is another form of structural violence. It occurs when state authorities regularly pay undue attention to one group (Wong, 1998). Hypersurveillance can take the form of legal interventions such as profiling, search and seizure, arrest, and incarceration, all of which are discussed in chapter 3. Women are often subjected to harmful searches of their bodies, as are young people.

Psychological violence occurs when institutionalized and structural violence become accepted, promoted, and integrated into the collective psyche. People form harmful stereotypes about particular groups, and often those groups internalize the negative beliefs. These stereotypes of the "other" are then held to be the truth, typically generalized across groups and situations and used to justify oppression (Alport, 1954). In the end, as Iadicola and Shupe (1999) noted, violence results in a denial of human freedom.

The Dominator Model

The work of Riane Eisler (1987) can help us understand why violence at all three levels is so prevalent and considered by many to be intractable. Eisler (1987) described two ideologies or models that influence the creation and maintenance of all our major institutions, including schools, criminal justice, religion, economics, politics, and more (Eisler, 2000). These are "systems of belief and social structures that either nurture and support—or inhibit and undermine—equitable, democratic, nonviolent, and caring relations" (p.xiv). She called these the dominator model and the partnership model. The dominator model is a model of interaction based on power *over*, not power *with*. It values competition over cooperation and domination over partnership.

> The assumption that human life is based on conflicts of interest, wars, and the opposition of people to each other and to nature exists as a model, a framework, a paradigm that supplies meaning and orientation to the world. An alternative paradigm sees cooperation, caring, nurturing, and loving as equally viable ways of organizing relationships of humans to each other and to nature. (Fellman, 1998, p. 5)

Fellman (1998) called the two models the adversary paradigm and the mutuality paradigm. "According to the adversary paradigm, people are dangerous, potential competitors, inevitable combatants. In the mutuality paradigm, people are potential friends who can be trusted to respect feelings and vulnerabilities and who can be known partly though knowing oneself" (p. 27).

The dominator model teaches us that "There isn't enough of anything, neither enough 'goods'—whether jobs or jungles—nor enough 'goodness' because human beings are, well, pretty bad. These ideas have been drilled into us for centuries" (Moore-Lappe, 2006, p. 6). In all, violence is endemic to our culture, but we often find it difficult to see it and understand it in all its forms. Structural violence, Galtung (1984) argued, is built into the institutions in which "good" people operate. In fact, many times it is supposedly "for our own good" (Miller, 2002). The dominator model is dualistic, prompting us to see the world in binaries: good/bad, black/white, worthy/ unworthy.

> To a great extent, many of the problems we are experiencing result from our failure to recognize ourselves as holistic, interconnected beings who need to cultivate our abilities to embrace the world with unconditional love and care. Our lives have been organized on the assumption of separation: a separation of ourselves from each other, a separation of our destiny with our environment, and a separation of our bodies and minds from our hearts and spirits. (Lin, 2006, p. 6)

Militarism

The dominator model is essentially a militaristic model. Militaristic values include those of hierarchy, centralization of authority, discipline, and obedience (Merryfinch, 1981). Militarization is a process by which a person or group depends on the militaristic ideas for its sense of well-being. "The more militarization transforms an individual or a society, the more that individual or society comes to imagine military needs and militaristic presumptions to be not only valuable but also normal" (Enloe, 2000, p. 3). Lutz (2002) argued that militarization involves a shift in general societal beliefs and values to legitimate the use of force, the organization of large standing armies, and the higher taxes used to pay for them. The militarization of society is achieved through the naturalization of militarism. Militarism is an ideology as well as a set of institutional arrangements and everyday practices that centers on the continual mobilization of society to prepare for, support, and fight wars and to see violence as an appropriate, if not the only, response to conflict. Militarism blurs the boundaries between what can be defined as military and what can be viewed as part of civilian life. Militarism demands that an entire society become permeated with and built according to military values and priorities (Adelman, 2003)

Militarism privileges traditional notions of masculinity, favoring qualities like aggression, power over others, and control over nonviolence, shared power, and cooperation. "Central to militarized masculinity are the putative absence of women and men's distance from or rejection of anything or anybody deemed feminine" (Adelman, 2003, p. 17).

Marullo (1993) identified other American values that play an integral part in promoting militarism. These include pragmatism, efficiency, rationality, a faith in technology, capitalism and free markets, and ethnocentrism and American exceptionalism. In his books *The Powers That Be* (1999) and

Engaging the Powers (1992), theologian Walter Wink talks about domination systems being ones in which a few people control systems and institutions to their own advantage. In domination systems, you have to train people to think in ways that support the system, so they fit the system. Domination systems require people to suppress their true selves and to make moralistic judgments about others (Rosenberg, n.d.). As Rosenberg (n.d.) noted, "When you are in a position of authority you are justified in being a bully. You don't call yourself a bully—you call yourself an authority. In domination systems authorities are given legal power to bully through the system of deserve, in which punishment, rewards and other forms of coercion get you to do things."

In essence, a dominator-modeled or militaristic society is one that tends to equate peace with being boring and violence as exciting. Creativity is often considered a frivolous pursuit, something for artists and for art class, not a tool for all of us to use to develop a better world. The dominator model encourages us to accept violence as normal and as inevitable—simply just the way things are.

Domination is normalized in numerous ways. We are taught—through schools and all kinds of institutions—to see this way as normal, as right. Indeed, we come to expect a dominator model and are often uncomfortable when we encounter a different way. "Adversary training may begin with gold stars and go on to grades, prizes, trophies, salaries, and promotions, elections, and wars. Feelings of self-worth are tied to winning something at the price of another's loss" (Fellman, 1998, p. 47).

McDonaldization and Domination

Sociologist George Ritzer (1996) described this process, calling it "McDonaldization." McDonaldization is characterized by four principles: efficiency, calculability, predictability, and control. Efficiency refers to "choosing the optimal means to a given end" (p. 36). While efficiency sounds desirable, sometimes it comes at the expense of quality. Also, in a system focused on efficiency, the ends come to justify the means. Predictability means knowing what to expect and assuming it will be virtually the same every time. Calculability refers to an emphasis on quantifiable results. Perhaps the most important element of McDonaldization is control. Control can occur through direct intervention or through ideological means.

Ritzer noted that the result of McDonaldization is that human creativity and potential is stifled, as people become disenchanted and disengaged. People are less apt, and begin to lack the skills, to challenge the status quo, or to suggest new and exciting ways of being. Ritzer maintained that McDonaldization is "a quantum leap" toward the process of rationalization that sociologist Max Weber articulated. Ritzer noted that the principles on which the fast food giant operates have spread to other institutions, including the workplace, education, health care and more. Others have extended his work to discuss sports (Finley & Finley, 2006).

Media, Domination, and Militarism

Media plays a large role in teaching us that domination and militarism are normal and right. In the United States, for instance, 75 percent of programs on television between 7 and 9 p.m., the time most children are watching, show the hero either killing someone or beating them up. So by the time the average child is 15 years old, he or she has observed 30,000 beatings and murders—just by the "good guys" (Rosenberg, n.d.). The message is that violence is the best way to win, to defeat "evil." "In short, the dominator model is so deeply ingrained that it is taken for granted as simply the way things are, and the only possible way they *can* be" (Finley, 2004a).

U.S. Public High Schools and the Dominator Model

Eisler and others have written extensively about how the dominator model applies to schools. Eisler pointed out that our society generally uses a dominator model in three levels or layers: our content, our methods, and our structures. Structure refers to our environments. Methods or processes refer to the ways we operate. Content is what is taught or the information disseminated (Eisler, 2000). To illustrate how the dominator model operates at all three levels, I will first provide examples from the educational system in the United States. I will then show how the dominator model applies to other institutions.

Typical schools are structured by a dominator model. Varney (2000) noted that it is "in the interest of militarists and those who seek to gain advantage from war in any number of direct or peripheral ways, to socialize children into militarism, to make it seem logical, necessary, 'natural' and even fun" (p. 385).

Typical schools are structured on a dominator model. Most schools utilize a hierarchical authority structure, where administrators direct policy from the central office. Building-level administrators then pass these policies along to teachers, who implement them with little or no input from students, who sit at the bottom of the hierarchy. Like the military, each person higher in command has more authority over the previous level (Finley, 2004a).

School buildings today are dominator-structured, making them not just militaristic but prison-like as well. "The increased use of metal detectors, security guards, locked doors, ID cards and other punitive measures all reflect the militaristic ideology of domination and control, and, in essence, lack of trust. This is to the huge detriment of students" (Finley, 2004b). Crews and Tipton (2001) identified some of the features schools have in common with prisons, noting the uniforms and clothing standards, surveillance cameras, and influx of school police officers, among other characteristics. They maintained that this type of hypercontrolled environment stifles individuality and creativity and can impair intellectual development. But, "like the military, creativity and individualism are not rewarded in many schools, so measures that may reduce them are not considered problematic" (Finley, 2004b, p. 5).

The methods we use to teach are also militaristic. Eisler (2000) stated that,

> Many of our teaching methods also stem from much more authoritarian, inequitable, male-dominated, and violent times. Like childrearing methods based on mottoes such as 'spare the rod and spoil the child,' these teaching methods were designed to prepare people to accept their place in rigid hierarchies of domination and unquestioningly obey orders from above, whether from their teachers in school, supervisors at work, or rulers in government. (p. 12)

These same teaching or discipline methods "rely heavily on negative motivations, such as fear, guilt, and shame" (Eisler, 2000, p. 12). They emphasize obedience and conformity, not freedom and creativity. Teaching methods commonly used in schools tend to be boring. Paulo Freire (1983) called these passive methods "banking education," which he described as "the art of depositing, in which the students are the depositories and the teacher is the depositor" (p. 284). Students are to sit quietly, obediently waiting for the teachers to deliver them "the truth," not ask them their thoughts or engage in critical analysis (Finley, 2004b, p. 6). Students essentially have no voice in the process (M. Klein, 2007). According to Jackson (1983), "The habits of obedience and docility engendered in the classroom have a high payoff in other settings. So far as their power structure is concerned, classrooms are not too dissimilar from factories or offices, those ubiquitous organizations in which so much of our adult life is spent" (p. 56).

Like the military, many of our teaching practices emphasize rationality, allowing little opportunity to explore emotions. Carlton (2001) explained, "The function of competition ... [is] to assign each individual his place in the social system" (p. 37).

Disciplinary terms and practices such as "Zero Tolerance" are dominator-modeled as well. The notion of zero tolerance actually originated with the military (Skiba & Peterson, 1999). DiGuilio (1999) explained why this model is problematic:

> Indeed, any nonviolent intervention program or curriculum may be doomed to failure in schools in which abusive behavior is sanctioned by administrators, including strip searches, verbal abuse, paddling, and other forms of corporal punishment. Although the crime-and-punishment paradigm is the norm in our legal system outside-of-school (witness capital punishment as the ultimate corporal punishment), inside schools, programs that purport to teach prosocial behavior cannot work when delivered in an environment laden with fear and permissive insults to human dignity. (p. 195)

According to Casella (2001),

> Some reasons for the persistence of systemic violence can be found in national rhetoric that sanctions forms of discriminatory punishment and policing. These policies create in our society a general feeling that teenagers are no good, out of control, and morally void. They bolster punishment in favor of pedagogy, control in favor of understanding. (p. 35)

Even conflict resolution programs, which have gained popularity in recent years, tend to focus exclusively at the individual level. Instead of addressing the dominator structures that can promote violent behavior, conflict resolution generally teaches students to manage their issues within the very same conditions, hence they maintain the status quo (Pont-Brown & Krumboltz, 1999).

In regard to content or curricula, Eisler (2000) explained, "all schools teach values, whether they do so explicitly or implicitly, by inclusion or omission" (p. 30). McCarthy (2002) commented on the lack of peace coverage in schools. "At commencement, graduates are told to go into the world as peacemakers. Yet in most schools, peace is so unimportant that no place is found for it in the curriculum" (p. 6). Eisler (2000) explained that this "hidden curriculum" is detrimental, as "including certain kinds of information in the curriculum—and not including other kinds of information—effectively teaches children what is, and what is not, valuable" (p. 39).

Commonly used textbooks are also militaristic, in particular in U.S. history. In a 2002 review of 17 U.S. history texts at the elementary, middle, and high school levels, I found an average of 89.1 pages devoted to war or military engagements. Fewer than 5 pages were devoted to peace, pacifism, nonviolence and related topics. "Textbooks notoriously exclude minority contributions, or when they are included they are relegated to the "boxes" that few students read" (Finley, 2004a). Eisler (2000) stated that "in reading, science, mathematics, and social studies textbooks, even where more diversity was incorporated, it has often been in a fragmented, superficial fashion, as mere add-on to the 'important' material dealing with white Anglo-Saxon males" (p. 42). Holtzman (2000) noted that dominator-modeled curricula help those in power normalize militarism, "not through force but rather through the way that values get taught in religious, educational, and media institutions—through socialization" (p. 26).

Colleges and Universities and the Dominator Model

As noted, the dominator model is not exclusive to secondary education. College classrooms too tend to be dominator-structured. The large lecture hall, so common on large campuses (and even smaller campuses today) creates a structure in which the professor or instructor is the "sage on the stage" and the students are sitting in nice, even rows that make it difficult to create any type of collaborative environment (Sperber, 2001). The use of passive, competitive instructional methods is, if anything, more common at this level (Finley, 2004a). Because of this, findings from a 2002 survey indicated that students were generally not engaged in their coursework (Sax, Keup, Gilmartin, Stolzenberg, & Harper, 2002). Peace education programs do exist at the college level, but many times professors face great challenges in getting them started and sustaining them (Maran, 1997). Even these programs or courses often teach only *about* peace, neglecting to ensure that creative, peaceful methods are being used.

Teacher education programs are also heavily reliant on dominator models. Future educators are taught that the most important thing is to control their students. My experience was that we were never to be students' "friends." I even recall being lectured to about the evils of lecturing to students!

Krishnamurti (1981) feared that the educational system made people thoughtless and mechanical, and that it did little to counteract the violence in the world. He argued that blindly following authority is not true intelligence and that education that pushes this is denying the spirit of inquiry. Ultimately, peace education intends to stimulate the heart and the mind. To do so, it must nurture our creativity. Krishnamurti (1981) said,

> Merely to cultivate the intellect, which is develop capacity or knowledge, does not result in intelligence. There is a distinction between intellect and

intelligence. Intellect is thought functioning independently of emotion, whereas, intelligence is the capacity to feel as well as to reason; and until we approach life with intelligence, instead of intellect alone, or with emotion alone, no political or education system in the world can save us from the toils of chaos and destruction. (p. 51)

Sport and the Dominator Model

After the school day is done, and during summer, sports and other extra-curricular activities can also be dominator modeled. According to Shields and Bredemeier (1996), the connection between sports and militarism is well established. Fogarty (2000) explained, "Sports play a central role in reinforcing militarism in several ways" (p. 96). First, students interested in sport participation almost invariably compete for positions; once they are part of a team they typically must still compete, now for playing time. The competitive focus of some sports, like football, is "a model of conflict and warfare. The 'home team' provides a metaphor for the combatants of 'our side' as they do battle with those of 'the enemy'" (Fogarty, 2000, p. 96). As chapter 6 describes, this is by no means the only way to do sports. Creative individuals and groups are able to use sport for social change and as a means of peacebuilding.

Social Services and the Dominator Model

Even social service agencies, whose mission it is to assist those in need in a given community, may be dominator-modeled. Dellasega (2005) documented these toxic cultures, demonstrating that relational aggression is common even in domestic violence services. Having worked in a domestic violence agency coordinating their violence prevention programs, my experience was that the agency was more dominator- than partnership-modeled. Most centers I know of use a hierarchical authority structure, adopting far more from the bureaucratic workplace than from peace educators or from peacemaking principles. Decisions are made by those on the top and directed down. The lowest tier—those who actually provide the services—have very little, if any, voice in how the organization operates. Even the material we discussed—our content—was dominator-modeled. Batterers are "terrorists," for instance (Finley, 2010). My experience in this type of bureaucratic environment is that many people feel stifled, resulting in diminished ability to appropriately and humanely serve the victims seeking assistance.

Corporations and the Dominator Model

Corporations tend to be dominator-modeled. "Adversarialism appears in institutions like business and politics, when in order to win profits and office, it is necessary to undermine respect for and trust in someone or something else. Desires for justice, safety, and non-exploitation are sacrificed for 'victory'" (Fellman, 1998, p. 28). As Rieck (n.d.) explained, some creative directors and managers "claim to want creativity from their staff, but the environment they create is often full of stress, fear, and confusion" (para. 1). Military operations are the most commonly used method for obtaining the fossil fuels needed for the U.S. economy. Increasingly, those operations are conducted in conjunction with multinational corporations (MNCs) like Halliburton. Military might has also paved the way for U.S. corporate and economic interests in Latin America and Africa (Klein, N., 2007). As the 2003 documentary *The Corporation* explained, the corporate world has generally operated as plunderers, taking whatever they could from the earth and other people with little regard for the long-term consequences. Based on the book (which was actually published after the film's release, in 2004) *The Corporation: The Pathological Pursuit of Power* by Joel Bakan, the film makes the argument that "Corporations are required by law to elevate their own interests above those of others, making them prone to prey upon and exploit others without regard for legal rules or moral limits" (About the book, n.d.). Further, "Despite its flawed character, governments have freed the corporation from legal constraints through deregulation, and granted it ever greater power over society through privatization."

Criminal Justice and the Dominator Model

Criminal justice is perhaps the most militarized institution today. As chapters 2 and 3 document, the lines between law enforcement and the military are increasingly blurred, with soldiers now carrying out traditional police roles (for instance, in Iraq) and police officers armed, trained, and tasked with enforcing military action (Hill & Beger, 2009). Officers are often trained as though they are entering combat, rather than taught that they can and should be peace officers (DuBois, 1997; Kaufman, 1997). The United States leads the world in incarceration rates and our use of militaristic-style punishments, like boot camps, yet still has some of the highest violent-crime rates. Our retributive system demonizes and labels offenders (Reiman, 2000; Tifft & Sullivan, 2001). Politicians are hesitant to offer creative solutions to crime and crime control, as they never want to be viewed as "soft on crime." The result is often more of the same. Yet as chapters

2 and 3 show, there are indeed other more peaceful ways to understand crime and to respond to it.

Families and the Dominator Model

Families also create structures and select specific methods of teaching children important "curricula." As Deutsch (1993) explained, families and schools are the two most important institutions that teach children about love and hate. They too may do so using a dominator model. For instance, when families use corporal punishment, they teach children that violence is an acceptable means of handling a problem (Miller, 2002). Rigid gender roles and expectations reinforce domination and hierarchy, both within the family and outside of it (Eisler, 1993). "Families are the primary transmitters of values. It is in families that new members of society—children—receive their primary education about what it means to be a human being. It is in families that people develop the core belief systems that consciously or unconsciously affect how they engage in all facets of their lives—from the personal to the political" (Center for Partnership Studies, n.d.). As Eisler (2000) noted,

> People who, in their families and schools, are taught to rely on external control and fear of punishment . . . rather than on empathy and self-regulation, tend to require a social structure that uses fear or force to control the violent impulses we all sometimes experience. This in turn reinforces rigid rankings of domination, helping to replicate hurtful dominator patterns of relations in all spheres of life. (p. 232)

At the same time, families can also be the primary site for partnership or mutuality (Fellman, 1998). It is through visioning and conversation about how best to negotiate family life that some are able to do so in peaceful ways. Chapter 7 takes this up in more detail.

Media and the Dominator Model

Media, as one of the primary socialization agents in the United States, is also dominator-modeled. The format of today's journalism, for instance, is essentially combative. This was most evident to me when viewing a small segment of *ESPN*'s "Pardon the Interruption." The two hosts shouted at and argued with each other repeatedly, demonstrating that this style of commenting was not by accident but was instead structured. *ESPN* is hardly alone, however. Nor is the combative style of journalism exclusive to journalists on either side of the conservative/liberal pendulum. While perhaps Fox News' Bill O'Reilly has the worst reputation for yelling at and interrupting his guests and making fun of anyone who disagrees with his views, Keith Olbermann of MSNBC, a much more liberal source, uses similar tactics. In addition to the dominator structure and methods of modern televised news, the content they cover is also largely dominator-modeled. Media today overrepresents the amount of violent crime, for instance, resulting in a fearful populace, not necessarily one that is empowered and engaged (Hilliard, 2001). Paige (2009) argued, "Language reflects and reinforces lethality, contributing a sense of naturalness and inescapability" (p. 30). Warmaking or militaristic metaphors are common in the English language. Examples include "making a killing in the stock market," or being "stab[bed] in the back," or the dubbing of movie stars as "bombshells." Lou Dobbs's constant reference to the "war on the middle class" is another example (Friedrich & Gomes de Matos, 2009). A quick search through a movie guide reveals the popularity of violent titles like *Kill Bill* (2003), *The Matador* (2005), and *A Time to Kill* (1996). "An interesting challenge could be to try to find an equivalent number of titles displaying peace-fostering terms" (Friedrich & Gomes de Matos, 2009, p. 221).

Impact of the Dominator Model

The dominator or militaristic model is itself structurally violent. It limits our freedom and our creativity such that we do not always see better, more peaceful ways of existing. It leads to microlevel barriers or "mental traps," which stop people from making much needed change, both in regard to education as well as other social issues. Jones, Haenfler, and Johnson (2007) described what they called "the cycle of cynicism" in their book *The Better World Handbook*. The cycle begins when people find out about a problem and want to do something to help. Many times, people do not see viable options for how they can help, so they do nothing. The result is that they feel sad, angry, and powerless. They conclude that nothing can be done about the particular issue. They begin to shut down and want to tune out, to learn less about problems. In essence, they become apathetic. Additionally, Jones et al. (2007) identified ten "thought traps" or mental blocks that prevent people from getting involved to make social change. Trap #1 is when people argue, "That's just the way the world is" (p. 4). Trap #2 is when people argue that the problem is not theirs, and hence they do not need to be involved in solving it. Trap #3 occurs when people tell themselves that one person cannot make a difference, and Trap #4 is when people maintain that one person cannot make enough of a difference. Many times people do not know where to start, and they feel overwhelmed, which is Trap #5. Those who fall prey to Trap #6 argue they don't have the time or energy to get involved. Trap #7 equates doing something with being a saint—people often feel they have to be Mother Teresa, Mahatma Gandhi, or Martin Luther King Jr. to make a difference. Trap #8 occurs when people argue that they don't get involved because they do not know enough about the issue. In Trap #9, people say they simply don't know where or how to begin. Finally, Trap #10 is when people argue, "I'm not an activist" (p. 11).

Concluding Thoughts

The important message is this: It does not have to be this way! The following chapter highlights another model—a partnership or peacemaking model—which is built on mutuality, not adversarialism. This model, too, can influence our institutions at the structural, process, and content levels. It is a model that will allow us to overcome these mental traps and to see ourselves as agents of social change. It is a model for peacemaking—in schools and in other institutions.

1

Peacemaking, Positive Peace, and a Partnership Model

Smiling face, outstretched hand
Through disputes, small and grand
We will lay down our guns, we are one.

We Are One
—Emma's Revolution

In the Introduction, I presented a basic overview of what violence is, the three types of violence, and how it has become normalized in our major societal institutions via a dominator or militaristic model. In this chapter, I aim to show a different model that can help us see our commonalities, to stretch out that hand, and to create more peaceful, loving societies.

In spring 2008, I signed up to be a "career week" presenter at my daughter's pre-Kindergarten class. Since at the time I was doing multiple jobs on a contract basis as well as teaching a course at the university level, I struggled with what to say I actually *did* for a career. But, tying together the pieces

Building a Peaceful Society, pages 1–15
Copyright © 2011 by Information Age Publishing
All rights of reproduction in any form reserved.

of my various work, I decided I would tell the class I was a peace educator. And to talk about what that means, I thought I'd have a conversation about peace and then read Todd Parr's *The Peace Book*. So, I sat down with the 19 students and began by asking them, "What do you think peace is?" Per usual in a Pre-K class, lots of hands shot up. The first boy I called on said he thought it was like a butterfly because they are beautiful and gentle, which was a cute and interesting answer. The next two responses threw me for a loop, though. The second child I called on said it was "an orange" and the third said "paper." Huh? I was befuddled. Then it dawned on me—they did not conceptualize peace in the way I was meaning, but rather as a piece of something, hence a piece or slice of orange or a piece of paper.

This experience highlighted to me that, often times, we rarely engage in the basic discussion of what we mean when we talk about peace. Studies have repeatedly demonstrated that children develop a concept of war before they develop an understanding of peace. Further, children typically see war as exciting and adventurous, while peace is described as boring and silent (Alvik, 1968; Avery, Johnson, Johnson, & Mitchell, 1999; Cooper, 1965; Covell, Rose-Krasnor & Fletchter, 1994; Cretu 1988; Engel, 1984; Hakvoort, 1996; Hall 1993; Lurenco, 1999; Oppenheimer, Bar-Tal, & Raviv, 1999; Vriens, 1999; Ziller, Moriarty, & Phillips, 1999). My experience with colleagues at a domestic violence agency highlighted the fact that many adults have also never pondered precisely what peace means either. How can we expect people to work toward something—a more peaceful world—that they have never even thought about, I wondered?

Defining Peace

First, it is essential to explain what peace is. Peace scholars generally differentiate between positive and negative peace. The distinction is credited to Norwegian sociologist Johann Galtung (1984). According to Galtung (1984, 1996), negative peace is the absence of overt violent conflict. Positive peace is far more than this. It is the absence of overt violent conflict coupled with conditions of social justice. Reardon (1995) defined positive peace as "a set of social, political, and economic conditions dependent on the realization of rights and authentic democracy" (p. 7). According to O'Kane (1991), positive peace is

> A pattern of cooperation and integration between major human groups...
> [It] is about people interacting in cooperative ways; it is about social organizations of diverse peoples who willingly choose to cooperate for the benefit of all humankind; it calls for a system in which there are no winners and

losers—all are winners; it is a state so highly valued that institutions are built around it to protect and promote it. (p. 92)

Lin et al. (2008) explained that "peace is an ongoing process, attainable, and renewable" (p. xv).

Essentially, "Peace is concerned with different forms of violence and operates at many different levels of human existence" (Harris & Morrison, 2003, p. 13). There are many strategies for attaining peace. The dominant approach in the world today is peace through strength. This approach emerged from the Roman Empire and their dictum *si vis parem, para bellum* (if you desire peace, prepare for war). In modern times, this means countries acquire heavy arms so as to deter attacks from their enemies. It is the method used mostly frequently in the United States, and is more consistent with a dominator model than with true peacemaking. In peace through justice, there is concern about eliminating poverty, disease, starvation, and human misery. Pacifism, or peace through transformation, is the total absence of violence, although it is not the absence of confrontation or conflict. Even when attacked, pacifists like Quakers, Mahatma Gandhi, and Dr. Martin Luther King Jr. did not strike back. Institution-building is peace through politics. It involves the building of international institutions that resolve conflicts through peaceful methods. An example of this is UNESCO's declaration of 2000 as the Year and 2001–2010 as the Decade for a Culture of Peace and Nonviolence for the Children of the World. Among other things, it includes the notions that power is active nonviolence, that people must be mobilized toward common understanding, not toward defeat of an enemy, that democratic processes must replace hierarchical ones, and that a free flow of information is essential. The UN proposed that a culture of peace would be built on better understanding of and attention to the root causes of violence (Institute for Economics & Peace, 2010a, 2010b). Inherent in the UN's declaration is the recognition of the important role of citizen's groups and NGOs as institutions for peace-building. Peace through sustainability emphasizes the environment. It focuses on the fact that, without attention to the interrelatedness of all living creatures, peace is not possible. The last approach, peace education, "refers to teaching about peace—what it is, why it doesn't exist, and how to achieve it . . . it is both a philosophy and it inclusive of skills and processes" (Harris & Morrison, 2003, p. 25). Although it is challenging to develop peace education in a violent culture, it is only our sustained efforts to do so that can indeed transform the culture to one of peace (Baxi, 1997; Harris, 2007). And, as this book is intended to show, our creative vision, collaboration, and action will result in a better planet for all living things. Below, I share one model for how we can use our creativity to inspire just such action.

The Partnership Model

Eisler (2000) suggested that we do not have to follow a dominator model; instead, a partnership model is possible. This model would involve cooperation, shared power, and the institutionalization of mutual honor, respect, and peaceful means of conflict resolution. Partnership-based societies are built on four cornerstones: childhood relations; gender relations; economic relations; and stories, beliefs, and spirituality.

Developing healthy, peaceful children is a critical commitment. It involves ensuring that children do not suffer from abuse in the home, that they have care and nurturing as they grow, and that they are able to receive quality education throughout their development.

"How a society constructs the roles and relations of the two halves of humanity—women and men—is central to the construction of every social institution, from the family and religion to politics and economics as well as to the society's guiding systems of values. It is even central to a nation's general quality of life" (Eisler, n.d.a). Studies have shown that the status of a society's women may be a better predictor of its quality of life than traditional economic measures.

A partnership culture recognizes that current economic systems do not adequately support all humans. "We need to create economic indicators, policies, and practices that give visibility and value to the most important human work; that of caring for people, beginning in childhood, and caring for natural environment. We need a caring economics" (Eisler, n.d.a).

"We humans live by stories. Unfortunately many of the stories we inherited from earlier times teach that dominating or being dominated are the only alternatives" (Eisler, n.d.a). A partnership-based society is based on a different consciousness and on stories that emphasize interconnectedness, cooperation, empathy, and the other core partnership values.

A Partnership Model of Education

Peace education can help to address the problems of the dominator model and, eventually, replace it. Eisler (2000) described a partnership model of education that is exactly what is needed in schools and elsewhere. Again, we will first examine what this model might look like in schools, then in other areas and institutions. Importantly, a partnership model would require reconsidering the content we teach, the methods we use, and, more difficult, the structures we create, both in school and beyond. Peace education is a natural fit with partnership education, although not all peace education programs are truly partnership modeled. Programs that only pay attention to curricula, for instance, and not methods and structure may teach *about* peace, but not *for* peace.

Maria Montessori was one of the first peace educators who followed a partnership model. She saw the purpose of education as creating the suitable environment for each child to enjoy harmonious interactions that nourish and love. Thus, Montessori paid attention not just to the content that was taught, but to the methods of teaching and to the structure or environment in which that education occurred. DiGiulio (1999) explained that this type of education is more holistic. Flowers and Shiman (1997) asserted that under a partnership model, peace and human rights would be the fundamental organizing principle behind our systems of education, and all teachers (as well as prospective teachers) "would come to see themselves as human rights educators and advocates" (p. 162).

The first step in creating a partnership-modeled program is to envision what that would look like. Our creativity must be tapped individually, but also collectively. Greene (1995) explained that the mind can be nurtured to think not just about what *is*, but what *can* and *ought to be*. Lin (2006) envisioned such a system. The pedagogy for a school based on love would include reflectiveness, tranquility and silence, learning humility and simplicity, sensitivity, direct contact with nature, direct contact with people around the world, and creativity and imagination (Lin, 2006). "Education in the 21st century should be education for love, with love and through love" (Lin, 2006, p. 26). Similarly, Noddings (2004, 2005, 2006, 2007) argued for schools based on caring. For her, caring is more than empathy; it is moving away from the self toward being receptive to others. These concepts can clearly be extended beyond the traditional school walls (Yablon, 2007). As Nussbaum (2003) explained, "The relationship between compassion and social institutions is and should be a two-way street: compassionate individuals construct institutions that embody what they imagine; and institutions, in turn, influence the development of compassion in individuals" (p. 405).

Peace education can and should be partnership education. Before we can further address the creative ways to initiate and implement partnership-based peace education in places outside of schools, it is imperative to examine the various types of peace education.

What Is Peace Education?

According to Harris and Morrison (2003),

> Peace education involves students and educators in a commitment to create a more just and peaceful world order. This type of education (adaptable to all ages and all sorts of settings) provides citizens with information about current policies, sharpens their ability to analyze current states of affairs, encourages commitment to various spheres of individual and endeavor—politics, public affairs, trade union activities, social and cultural life—and strives to promote the free will necessary to make personal choices about public policy. (p. 4)

Peace education is a way to question structural violence—the dominator model—and to create an alternate system (Harris & Morrison, 2003). According to Harris and Morrison (2003), there are 10 main goals of peace education: (a) to appreciate the richness of the concept of peace; (b) to address fears; (c) to provide information about security; (d) to understand war behavior; (e) to develop intercultural understanding, (f) to provide a "futures" orientation; (g) to teach peace as a process; (h) to promote positive peace, or peace accompanied by social justice; (i) to stimulate a respect for all life; and (j) to manage conflicts nonviolently (p. 32).

Peace education takes many forms, some more focused on negative peace and others more inclusive. Peacemaking, or conflict resolution education, involves the learning and utilization of conflict resolution strategies (Smith, 1996). The narrowest programs focus on student-to-student conflicts, often utilizing peer mediation. In peer mediation, trained students help their peers resolve conflicts. Reardon (1997) explained that, when education focuses on peacemaking, it is emphasizing negative peace and on "*what should not be* than to the positive possibilities *of what could be*. So it is that peace education and peace studies (as the field is known in universities) have been a bit of a 'downer' for all but those students who are 'positive thinkers' by nature, drawn to social action fields, or simply curious about the study of the 'impossible'" (p. 21, emphasis in original). More extensive programs are for the entire school community, including teachers, counselors, administrators, students, and even custodial staff (Forcey & Harris, 1999). Such programs not only teach amazing content, but also send a powerful message: that peace matters (Thrash, 2008). In sum,

> The pursuit of peace and justice is not embodied in any particular curricular or extracurricular program. Instead, every realm of school life is involved in teaching young people about war and violence, conflict and peace. Be-

havior management patterns and the core academic curriculum, by virtue of being most of what happens in school are the most pervasive organizers of student learning about conflict, and also the most difficult to change. (Bickmore, 1999, p. 249)

Human rights education is one form of peace education that is intended to address injustices related to political oppression, prejudice, and abuses of our civil, political, social, and economic rights. Most human rights education programs take as their basis the Universal Declaration of Human Rights (Harris & Morrison, 2003). As such, it goes beyond attention to ending violent conflict and encourages the eradication of other social ills. A growing body of research highlights the importance of teaching human rights, not just in schools but in other institutions, like policing and corrections (Baxi, 1997; DuBois, 1997; Flowers & Shiman, 1997; Gierycz, 1997; Kaufman, 1997; Maran, 1997; Meintjes, 1997). International education aims to help students better understand the ways states provide for their citizens, both in terms of security as well as other essential needs. Teachers try to elicit among their students the feeling that we are all global citizens. International education often focuses on globalization and its impact on humanity (Nash, 1999). Similarly, development education provides students "with insights into the various aspects of structural violence, focusing on social institutions with their hierarchies and propensities for dominance and oppression ... the goal is to build peaceful communities by promoting an active democratic citizenry interested in an equitable sharing of the world's resources" (Harris & Morrison, 2003, pp. 74–75).

Many peace education programs draw on the work of women's studies scholars. They incorporate the gendered concepts of the three C's—care, compassion, and connectedness (Forcey & Harris, 1999). Peace educators, "like women's studies educators, engage their students in a multidisciplinary search for answers to the many problems of violence that are so rampant in the world. They favor a Socratic approach to learning, one embodying a consciousness of worldviews, a global vision, and a sensitivity to issues of gender race, and class" (Forcey & Harris, 1999, p. 7).

Environmental education, traditionally not a main emphasis for peace educators, has received far more attention in recent years. It stresses the need for ecological security. Lin (2006) explained that environmental education is in essence frugality education. It must start with students learning to reduce waste, as well as to reduce the number of possessions (Lin, 2006).

Peace educators hope to get humans to think of the Earth less as a resource for profit and more as a home that needs to be carefully maintained. Peacebuilding in its broadest sense is based upon a commitment to nonviolence in relation to both the human and natural world. Environmental educators attempt to develop an ecological world outlook that is both holistic and bio-centric, emphasizing the interconnectedness of all beings. (Harris & Morrison, 2003, p. 25)

Community-based environmental education is a form of peace education in that it enables students to participate in the planning, implementing, and evaluating of educational activities aimed at resolving local environmental concerns they themselves have identified. Most often used in a school setting, this type of environmental education can easily be incorporated into afterschool programs, social services, university coursework, and corporate programs (Wals, 1999).

Winfield (1999) argued for community-based service as a tool that awakens the power of nonviolence. An example is Syracuse, New York's Adopt-a-Park program in which the students of Frazer School, located in a poor urban neighborhood, took action with the adults of the community to clean up the park and streets. Community-based theater has shown to be an effective peace-education strategy with homeless youth (Bryant, Hanis, & Stoner, 1999).

Harris and Morrison (2003) explained that peace education is both about peace and for peace. That is, students receive both information about problems related to violence, militarism, and social inequalities at the same time that they are taught, and encouraged to use, nonviolent skills for social change. What is taught is not nearly as important as how it is taught (Harris & Morrison, 2003). In these ways, peace education reshapes dominator content and dominator methods to be partnership content and partnership methods.

Peace education holds such promise for challenging violence and militarism. Yet too often, when peace education is offered, it is implemented only in schools or institutions of higher education. And even then it tends to be included in only certain disciplinary areas, generally social studies, but rarely business, economics, or health. While surely a comprehensive, partnership-based program can have a tremendous impact, it is illogical to believe that peace education in schools alone is enough to revamp all the dominator-modeled institutions. As was noted earlier, schools are clearly not the only institutions in which people are "educated." Thus, all of these institutions must be encouraged to incorporate peace education or peace-making principles.

The Partnership Model Outside of Schools

As the authors of the Global Peace Index noted,

> Humanity is currently facing some of the greatest challenges that it has ex-
> perienced in its history. These challenges are global and mutltifaceted, en-
> compassing economic management, environmental sustainability, as well as
> a wide variety of social ills. Compounding these challenges is the inability
> of our institutions to adequately address their causes and to then create
> the remedies. This can be seen in the breakdown of the Copenhagen Cli-
> mate Change talks, burgeoning government and private sector debt, lack of
> regulation of the speculative aspects of the financial system or indeed our
> inability to articulate good capitalist models that aren't totally based on con-
> sumption. Yet such imminent and urgent challenges do provide a unique
> opportunity for us to reconsider and redefine our institutions, relationships,
> and values so that we can create a viable future in which humanity can meet
> its shared challenges and continue to prosper. (Institute for Economics and
> Peace, 2010b, p. 3)

A better understanding of peace via "education" provided through
numerous institutions can help prevent future violent conflicts as well as
maximize the opportunities for sustainable living. Although true positive
peace may not happen quickly, it should be seen as a work in progress. The
authors of the GPI noted that a 25 percent increase in peacefulness is quite
doable, which would result in numerous benefits, including approximately
$7.07 trillion in redirected or additional economic value.

One example of another way to envision a peaceful society is offered
by the Happy Planet Index. It is the first index to combine well-being and
environmental impact to show the relative efficiency with which nations
use the planet's resources to create long and happy lives for citizens (About
the Happy Planet Index, 2009). The researchers that compile the index
maintain it is an essential step in creating a new vision of "progress" that is
more sustainable and more peace-oriented. Costa Rica received the highest
happiness ranking in 2009, based on high reported life satisfaction and life
expectancy rates and low ecological footprint. Wealthy, more developed nations generally ranked in the middle. It is this type of creativity that prompts
people to think differently and to challenge the status quo.

Another example of partnership-based education outside of schools is
in Eisler's (n.d.b) proposed Caring Family Policy Agenda. Based on the core
values of caring, compassion, justice, and nonviolence, it includes three essential components: a Children's Bill of Rights, caring family values, and a
family-friendly economy. Similarly, Eisler (n.d.b) outlined how a partner-

ship approach can help us create sustainable environmental policies and programs, economic and business relations, and political arrangements that will build peace.

As the above examples show, to re-create our society to be partnership-modeled, we must tap into our individual and collective creativity.

Defining Creativity

Historically, creativity was thought of as the domain of artistic people. More recently, researchers have begun to look at creativity in the sciences, architecture and engineering, sports, and other fields. Further, creativity can be viewed as more than just an end product. This ends-focused understanding is typical of Western cultures. By contrast, Eastern cultures see creativity as a process that can provide personal fulfillment or enlightenment (Westwood & Low, 2003). As Westwood and Low (2003) explained, creativity is about individual cognitive processes, but it also has a social dimension. "Creativity takes place within, is constituted and influenced by, and has consequences for, a social context" (Westwood & Low, 2003, p. 3). Creativity is not just an individual characteristic but one that is also institutionalized (Greene, 1995).

Creativity is often considered the sole domain of young people (Urban, 1991). Most scholars of early childhood define creativity as the capacity to "bring something new into existence, or the ability to relate ideas or materials that were previously unrelated" (Feinburg & Mindess, 1994, p. 188). They often describe it as "innocent openness to experience, a charming originality, or a delight in the novel" (Feldman & Benjamin, 2006, p. 323). Well-Strand & Tjeldvoll (2003) argued that, rooted in creativity is the concept of creative inquiry, a kind of experience that involves "provision of and a control over qualities that are intimately associated with the mastery of both the method of inquiry and the subject matter children had to learn" (Dewey, 1902).

Personality studies have demonstrated that creative people tend to be nonconforming, independent, intrinsically motivated, open to new experiences, and risk seeking (Dellas & Gaier, 1970; Eysenck, 1997). Large-scale studies and meta-analyses have found that intelligence, tolerance of ambiguity, self-confidence, and cognitive flexibility also tend to be found in creative people (Feist, 1998). Individuals who pursue tasks for intrinsic rather than extrinsic purposes show enhanced creativity (Amabile, 1985, 1996; Amabile, Hennessey, & Grossman, 1986; Eisenberger & Cameron, 1996; Hennessey & Amabile, 1998). A distant-future focus, compared with a near-future focus, has been shown to lead to more creative negotiation outcomes

(Okhuysen, Galinsky, & Uptigrove, 2003) and to enhanced creative insight (Förster, Friedman, & Liberman, 2004). Focusing on potential gains rather than losses increases the accessibility of unconventional ideas and thus enhances fluency in generating creative ideas (Friedman & Förster, 2001; Lam & Chiu, 2002). Maslow (1970) was perhaps the first to recognize that the creative individual is a fulfilled one and one who has personal agency. Additionally, Maslow, and others have recognized that creativity is not the sole domain of unique individuals like Einstein but instead is open to everyday life and problem-solving (Amabile, 1996; Craft, 2003; Dacey, 1989; Feldman et al., 1994; Runco & Richards, 1997). Craft (2003) described "lifewide" creativity, meaning creativity that is useful for a breadth of tasks. This is distinct from "extraordinary creativity," which involves the production of new knowledge in an area of interest, as established by experts in that field. Finally, creativity seems to flourish when people are in positive or neutral affective states rather than negative affective states (Amabile, Barsade, Mueller, & Staw, 2005; Fong, 2006; Fredrickson, 2001), a finding that further belies the stereotype of the "starving artist."

Jackson and Shaw (2005) compiled a list of the most common ideas academics associate with creativity. There were originality, being imaginative, exploring for the purpose of discovery, doing/producing new things (invention), doing/producing things no one has ever done before (innovation), doing/producing things that have been done before but differently (adaptation, transference), and communication. As noted, there has been little focus to date on creativity and higher education (Kleiman, 2008). Yet some evidence suggests it is indeed valued. When Sternberg and Gordeeva (1996) asked 252 research psychologists what made a psychology article influential, the items that were rated as most important centered around creativity and novelty: making an obvious contribution to psychological knowledge, adding something *new* and substantial; presenting a useful *new* theory; generating *new* research; and providing *new* and exciting ideas.

Why Creativity is Necessary for Peace

I believe that it is creativity that will allow us to overcome the structural, institutional, and individual barriers that have been outlined in this book and to instead create partnership-based systems of peace education, both in and out of school. Creativity allows us to see how we have and continue to contribute to social problems in the world, why it is our responsibility to do something about them, and the difference we can make. Creativity allows us opportunities to envision a better world—the first step in making changes toward that better world (Jones et al., 2007). "Dreams and visions help to provide motivation for tasks that must be done. Peace education can help stimulate positive visions of human behavior. Dreaming and creating visions are part of everyday life. When people imagine, they express a cherished wish for how they would like to live and how they would like the world to be" (Harris & Morrison, 2003, p. 38). Creativity helps us shift our "frame of orientation," as Fromm (1973) called it, to one that is peace-oriented and life-serving.

When we use our creativity to reach people, we are viewed as more authentic. This authenticity helps people shift their value systems toward peace and justice. This is not just speculation. Youth-oriented conflict resolution (YOCR), for instance, has been found to lead to both cognitive and self-esteem increases (Van Slyck & Stern, 1999). College students have experienced a change in value orientation after taking peace education courses (Harris, 1999). There is no reason to believe such results are exclusive to formal classroom settings.

When we engage in creative peace education, we feel good. We feel powerful, as if we have the capacity to change the world. When we use our creativity, we realize that one person can indeed make a difference, and that one person can inspire others to do so as well (Jones et al., 2007). We begin to see that every one of our actions, even our *inaction*, is a form of activism toward *something*. We can "teach to transgress," as bell hooks (1994) called it, or challenge the status quo, when we step out of our normal, mundane, and repressive boxes and engage in creative peace education. When we are creative, we see that we can be more intentional about creating a more peaceful planet, and that even the little things we do make a difference. Appendix A provides a list of some of my favorite resources for creative ideas, while Appendix B lists some of my own creative ideas that can be used in a variety of settings.

Creativity helps us shift from a dominator understanding of power as something to be obtained and used over others to a partnership model, which sees power not as a dirty word but as our capacity to work together to get things done (Moore-Lappe, 2006). Moore-Lappe (2006) noted that power can help build the capacities of all involved and can be a creative, life-generating force.

Creativity helps us see unique ways to incorporate peace education into existing courses or programs, or to move forward with proposals for new programs. For example, the Brazilian educator and São Paulo Minister of Education, Paulo Freire (1974), created a progressive model of education and creativity, which he labeled The Pedagogy of the Oppressed. It developed as part of a literacy program for people living in the slum areas of

São Paulo. Freire's pedagogy is "intended to make the oppressed people creative and throw away their chains of poverty and oppression" (pp. 367–368). Freire's model can be integrated into most any context. The Center for Global Nonkilling (www.nonkilling.org) offers wonderful working papers and e-books on how a nonkilling, or partnership, perspective can be integrated into all academic areas and into a variety of institutions such as the arts, engineering, and economics. "Peace education enhances the purpose of education, which is to reveal and tap into those energies that make possible the full human enjoyment of a meaningful and productive existence" (Harris & Morrison, 2003, p. 5).

It is through creativity that we can reach learners of all sorts. By this, I mean all age ranges, in all settings, and of all learning types. Howard Gardner's work on multiple intelligences created the framework for understanding that not all people learn in the same way. Gardner, a professor of Education at Harvard University, published his ideas in 1983. He argued that humans do not just have one form of intelligence, but rather seven different ones. These are linguistic intelligence, or word smarts; logical-mathematical intelligence, or the ability to analyze problems logically; musical intelligence; bodily-kinesthetic intelligence; spatial intelligence; interpersonal intelligence; and intrapersonal intelligence. More recently, Gardner and others have argued that there are *more* than seven intelligences. In 1999, Gardner (1999b) concluded that there is a naturalist intelligence, a sort of ability to understand and appreciate nature. Lin (2006) referred to this as ecological intelligence, or the " innate ability of all species to live in harmony with their environment and to adjust to changes and be sustained and survive . . . the ability to see life as an interconnected web" (p. 55). Others have argued for a spiritual intelligence, an existential intelligence, and a moral intelligence (Goleman, 1995; Ikeda, 2001; Zohar & Marshall, 2000), although Gardner has not concluded they meet enough of the criteria he used to determine the intelligences. Daniel Goleman has expanded Gardner's work by looking at what he calls emotional intelligence, what Nussbaum (2003) called "the intelligence of emotions." Goleman (1995) explained that only about 20 percent of the factors that determine life success can be attributed to IQ, while the remaining 80 percent are determined by other factors related to our ability to connect with one another. Lin (2006) advocated a new form of intelligence, a peace intelligence. "Peace intelligence is a form of intelligence that is associated with deep love for all lives, a deep compassion for all existences, a courage and a conviction for unconditional forgiveness and reconciliation" (p. 68).

In his 1999 book *Intelligence Reframed: Multiple Intelligences for the 21st Century,* Gardner explained, "I want my children to understand the world, but not just because the world is fascinating and the human mind is curious. I want them to understand it so that they will be positioned to make it a better place" (p. 181). Thus, not only are programs devised around the multiple intelligences more creative and more appropriately suited to diverse learners, they are also well suited to teach peace. Creativity allows us to create wonderful interactive games and simulations, which are a great way to handle controversial topics in a way that encourages broad participation.

Creative Play Helps Us Learn

The dominator model often makes us believe "fun" and "challenging" are mutually exclusive. They are not. In fact, play is a powerful way to learn, not just for young people, but for anyone. Play deprivation can lead to depression and hostility in children. A study by Jaak Panksepp, involving rats deprived of play, found that the frontal lobe was impacted—the part of the brain that involves self-control. "Play is to early childhood what gas is to a car. It is the very fuel of every intellectual activity that our children engage in" (Hirsh-Pasek & Golinkoff, 2003, p. 214). Vygotsky (1978) argued that children are at the highest level of their development when they are playing. He felt play served three functions: (a) it created the child's zone of proximal development, or the time in which a child, with the help of a peer or adult, can do a little more than normal; (b) it helps separate thought and action; (c) it facilitates self-regulation. Play helps children develop scripts for how to act in society (Hirsh-Pasek & Golinkoff, 2003). "In the 21st century, creative problem solvers, independent thinkers, and people with expert social acumen will inevitably surpass those who have simply learned to be efficient at getting the right answers" (Hirsh-Pasek & Golinkoff, 2003, p. 214).

Some types of play can help solve convergent problems, which is connected to performance on standardized tests. Divergent problems have multiple solutions, which require greater amounts of creativity because there is no right answer (Hirsh-Pasek & Golinkoff, 2003). In the workplace, play can bring excitement and a sense of newness to a job, and it can help us master difficult tasks. As Brown (2009) explained, "In the long run, work does not work without play" (p. 127). Understanding how people play can also be one of the best ways to find the most innovative and creative employees (Brown, 2009). In her latest book *Plenitude* (2010), sociologist Juliet Schor argued for a new perspective on work, life, and nature, which is characterized by a commitment to enjoyment.

Concluding Thoughts

The remainder of this book is devoted to exploring the dominator model as it has influenced many of our major institutions, and then to highlighting exciting possibilities and offering creative ideas for shifting to a partnership society. As I noted in the Preface, the institutions I have focused on were selected based on my background and expertise. I hope that what is presented stimulates thinking and inspires action to integrate peacemaking in other arenas as well.

2

Crime, Criminal Justice, and Peacemaking

The Role of Peace Education

They put up my picture with silence
'Cuz my identity by itself causes violence

**%$# the Police
—NWA

Breakin' rocks in the hot sun,
I fought the law and the law won.
I needed money 'cause I had none,
I fought the law and the law won.

I Fought the Law
—The Bobby Fuller Four

The goal of this chapter is twofold: to demonstrate how policing is dominator-modeled and militaristic, and second, to provide ideas for peacemaking and examples of promising changes in the philosophy, structure, pro-

Building a Peaceful Society, pages 17–36
Copyright © 2011 by Information Age Publishing

cess, and content of law enforcement. To that end, I first provide a brief overview of the philosophical underpinnings of traditional criminal justice and a short illustration of how policing is militaristic in its structure, processes, and content. This is by no means an exhaustive account, as those are available elsewhere. Instead, it is intended to highlight, as do the above song lyrics by 1980's rappers NWA, how an adversarial or dominator model tends to prevail today in law enforcement. This system contributes to the marginalization of "the other"—those whose "identity alone causes violence." And, as the lyrics from *I Fought the Law* show, this system does very little to address why someone may commit a criminal offense.

I then provide an overview of an alternative philosophy, that of peacemaking criminology, and promising transformations in police structure and practices. This creative way of looking at crime, criminals, and criminal justice is an important development, not just to the field of criminology, but to the broader society. As Crone (2011) noted, to solve social problems like crime, we must redefine how we see them.

In 1994, David C. Couper, who at the time had more that 30 years experience in policing, wrote in the *FBI Law Enforcement Bulletin* about the "seven seeds" he envisioned for the future of policing. Among the seven, he noted the need for a changed leadership structure, calling policing perhaps "the last organization in America to maintain the authoritarian organizational structure" (para. 3). Another "seed" Couper identified was creativity. He asserted "policing chills creativity in so many ways . . . from our leadership styles to our ongoing romance with the status quo" (para. 9). Couper explained that the problems facing police today "require not more of the same, but new and creative ways and methods of policing" (para. 9). It is high time Couper's seeds begin to grow. I hope this chapter helps them to do so.

Domination: The Function of the Law?

In a dominator-structured society, the function of law is to legitimate existing arrangements that privilege some over others. Criminal justice, then, is designed to preserve and restore the existing order (Tifft, 2000, 2002; Tifft & Sullivan, 2001). Traditionally, legal definitions of crime see it as an act intended to do harm, which is then codified into state's criminal law. Those with more social power are often able to commit acts that threaten human health, well-being, and even lives, but those actions are often not defined as criminal. Thus, they are not subject to the same types of social controls as are those in other social classes, despite the fact that "our safety, security, well-being, health, freedoms, and potentialities are far more seriously damaged by the institutional behavior and decisions of those in positions of decision making in state and capitalist organizations" (Tifft, 2002, p. 245). In this sense, then, criminal justice at its origin—lawmaking—protects the status quo. As we saw in the Introduction, this is itself a form of structural violence in that the status quo is a system built on power over and exploitation of some at the expense of others.

Preserving the Existing Order

To preserve the existing order, those with power disseminate an image of criminal offenders as individual perpetrators who make poor choices or who suffer from some individual pathology. It is not to their advantage to emphasize the structural roots of crime. The crime "problem" is presented as one perpetrated largely by poor and minorities (Michalowski, 1985; Quinney, 2001; Reiman, 2001; Sheldon, 2001). Media, upon which 95 percent of citizens rely for their information about crime and criminal justice, tells us that we should be worried most about "ghetto crimes" and fear those who we are told are responsible—largely young African American males. As Kappeler, Blumberg, and Potter (2000) explained, both media and government can be viewed as "mythmakers." These myths are continually created and re-created. They "can become so compounded that they shape our thoughts about and reactions to almost any issue related to criminal justice (p. 2). Further, "the organization of views through crime myths contributes to the categorizing of social actors into artificial distinctions between law-abiding citizens, criminals, crime fighters, and victims. Casting certain segments of society into the category of 'criminal' offers others a reassuring self-concept" (Kappeler et al., 2000, p. 3). We are not "them"—the bad guys—thus we must be OK. "The central discourse is that of tertiary prevention and after-the-fact moral, public condemnation of criminal act and actor. Subsequent public wisdom is that those who commit these crimes deserve their punishments" (Tifft, 2002, p. 245). As Mumia Abu Jamal noted in a 1998 correspondence, "Americans live in a cavern of fear, a psychic, numbing force manufactured by the so-called entertainment industry, reified by the psychological industry, and buttressed by the coercion industry (ie., the courts, police, prisons, and the like)" (in Rodriguez, 2007, p. 21). We are told over and over again that more and broader powers for police will enhance our safety and curtail crime, despite their being no evidence to that effect (Kappeler et al., 2000; Robinson, 2000). The constant barrage of nasty images and brutal crime often stifles our ability to truly assess the causes of crime, its impact, and ways we can humanely intervene.

We can easily be blinded to the social harms perpetrated by those who seek to maintain these structural arrangements, as these receive far less media attention and may not be considered illegal. As Tifft (2002) noted, few people, including criminologists, look at crime in this way:

> For to focus directly on these arrangements raises a question about the acceptability and justness of these arrangements and distributions. If these arrangements are to be maintained, and the current distributions secured and believed to be right and just, then some sort of process that morally condemns actions that violate these arrangements must be initiated to secure these specific arrangements—no matter their degree of justness, no matter if they are structurally violent, and no matter if these power arrangements lead to great suffering, human indignity, and death. (p. 5)

It is sadly very easy to identify examples of social harms that were considered legal, from atrocities perpetrated in Hitler's Nazi Germany to U.S. slavery and internment of Japanese Americans (Brimmer, 1994). There is a long list of modern crimes of the state as well, including invasions, state-sanctioned torture, and capital punishment (Tifft, 2002). Additionally, some have maintained that 20th century modes of production and distribution should be considered criminal, as they create poverty, hunger, and death from preventable disease and injury (Elias, 1986).

Policing and the Dominator Model

It is not surprising, given the way crime has historically been defined and articulated, that policing—the front line in responding to the crime problem—is dominator-modeled. Fear leads to support for a system that is retributive in nature, with both police and the public often seeing each other as enemies, not as allies. Indeed, numerous scholars have demonstrated how modern policing in the United States is militaristic. Many have noted that the "war on crime" mentality coalesced with the loss of an ideological enemy at the end of the cold war (Christie, 1994; Nadelman, 1993). From President Lyndon B. Johnson's initial use of the "war on crime" metaphor in 1966 to President Nixon's expansion to focus largely on drugs as "public enemy number one," the war metaphor has become synonymous with crime reduction. Presidents Reagan, Bush I, Clinton, and Bush II all continued and even expanded the militarized response to crime (Kraska, 1999). "Metaphors play a powerful role in the construction of reality; they shape discursive practices, clarify values and understanding, and guide problem-solving practices. Filtering the crime and justice problems through militaristic metaphors, thus, will likely result in thoughts and actions which correspond with the war/military paradigm" (Kraska, 1999, p. 209). Recall that militarism is "a set of beliefs and values that stress the use of force and domination as appropriate means to solve problems and gain political power, while glorifying the means to accomplish this—military power, hardware, and technology" (Kraska, 1994, p. 3). The militaristic or crime-fighting model of policing is characterized by the use of fear and the use of force. This philosophy assumes that there is a continuing war against crime, where only superior firepower will win this war. It is a model based on fear. Not only are citizens to be fearful of crime but officers are as well. Despite the fact that law enforcement is not one of the most deadly jobs, officers are taught to distrust any citizen with whom they might have an encounter. The "us versus them" mentality is dangerous, as it destroys what could and should be good working relationships with law enforcement. If citizens distrust police, they are not likely to cooperate as witnesses or informants. As Parenti (1999) noted, "aggressive group tactics, automatic weapons, and infrared scopes all displace and preclude the social skills, forbearance, and individual discretion essential to accountable and effective civilian policing" (p. 133). This model of policing has also influenced police efforts at prevention programming, which are discussed in chapter 4.

"The military model is as pervasive as the medical model in efforts to colonize the control of crime and other forms of deviance" (Ericson & Carriere, 1994, p. 105). The result is that, "in today's socio-political environment . . . the line between waging actual war against external enemies and metaphorical wars waged against internal enemies is becoming increasingly blurred" (Kraska, 1999, p. 206). Although some have proclaimed that policing has entered a new era in which community-based approaches are central, data supports that a militaristic paradigm still prevails. This is perhaps best exemplified by the expansion of police paramilitary units (PPUs). PPUs or SWAT teams are modeled on military special operations groups.

Paramilitary Units and SWAT Teams

Kraska and his colleagues have extensively documented the militarization of U.S. police forces in general and in particular the expansion of PPUs. Kraska conducted field research as well as two national surveys covering police agencies serving populations of 25,000 persons or more. Results showed a dramatic expansion of PPUs in the later 1980s and 1990s. In 1982, approximately 55 percent of police agencies serving populations of 50,000 or more had PPUs; by 1995, some 90 percent did. Of agencies serving 25,000 to 50,000 persons, Kraska documented a 157 percent increase in PPUs from 1982 to 1995. Kraska also studied call-outs, or activity in which these units were deployed. He found approximately 30,000 call-outs in 1995, a tenfold increase from 1980. Additionally, Kraska noted a significant change in the reasons PPUs were deployed. Early on, they were most often called out to hostage situations or barricaded suspects. In the mid-to-late 1990s, PPUs and SWAT forces were frequently called out to situations that were traditionally handled by regular police personnel, including aggressive patrol work in high-crime locations and no-knock raids on the residences of persons suspected of drug crime. About 80 percent of call-outs in the 5 years immediately prior to the study were for this type of drug raid.

PPUs increasingly patrol the streets, often dressed in full battle gear and carrying automatic weapons. In particular, PPUs are being "deployed" to police crime "hot spots," or high-crime areas. This is allegedly a proactive strategy to prevent crime that is said to be consistent with a community policing initiative but is far from it (Kraska, 1999). Parenti (1999) described Fresno's Violent Crime Suppression Unit (VCSU), which was fully equipped with combat boots, fatigues, and the same submachine guns used by the Navy Seals. Fresno's unit is just one of more than 30,000 SWAT teams across the nation. SWAT teams even go after parole and probation violators (Parenti, 1999).

There is some indirect evidence that other parts of police work are increasingly militarized. Departments are increasingly purchasing military weapons, like AR-15s and M-16s, for their officers, even in small, rural communities (Parenti, 1999). The military has become more involved in collaborative activities and in conducting training for officers. The military works with Border Patrol officers, a collaboration that originally involved providing loans and equipment in the 1980s but now includes the provision of training, advisors, and ground troops. "This collaboration has often entailed serious cultural adjustments, in that law enforcement agencies (LEAs) are supposed to think in terms of legal procedures and due-process rights, while military agencies think in terms of overwhelming and destroying an adversary. Thus, the training (in small-unit tactics, interview and interrogation techniques, the use of pyrotechnics and booby traps, etc.) provided by the military to American LEAs is oriented toward the elimination of an enemy threat and inherently engenders a much more militaristic orientation in civilian police bodies" (Parenti, 1999, p. 120). Arizona's recently enacted Senate Bill 1070, which authorizes police to stop anyone and demand to see their citizenship or residency papers, will undoubtedly continue this troubling trend.

Parenti (1999) documented Fresno's "Operation Goldstar," which conducted sweeps of young people. "Assembled at staging points and done up in the usual SWAT regalia of combat boots, helmets, jumpsuits and body armor, and armed with H & K MO-5s, dogs, and battering rams, the Goldstar force sweeps Fresno city and beyond, typically netting between 75 and 100 prisoners a night." Another new unit is the Multi-Agency Gang Enforcement Consortium (MAGEC), now the dominant police program in the Latino, black, and Laotian communities of Fresno. MAGEC uses loitering statutes to stop, interview, and search on pretty much anyone in these public spaces. As Parenti (1999) commented, "This sort of 'intelligence gathering' does not merely 'discover' delinquents, but rather by its very nature *produces* criminal identities, and thus justifies ever more layers of aggressive, invasive, and brutal policing" (p. 121). In essence, police are treating entire communities as the enemy. "The aggressive nature of SWAT operations leads to greater use of violence by both police and their surprised targets" (Parenti, 1999, p. 127).

Hot Spot and Zero Tolerance Policing

Hot Spot, Zero Tolerance Policing, and other militaristic police tactics are very popular and widely used. Hot spot policing directs personnel and resources to so-called high-crime areas. Officers are generally sent to enforce what has been called zero tolerance or quality-of-life policing. The idea is that officers must crack down on minor infractions because, left unattended, they will spawn additional and more damaging crime. Police are often encouraged to stop people for whatever reason possible; problems like minor traffic violations—broken signals and rearview mirror obstructions. Then those stops are used as justification for searches that can be incredibly invasive. Police are advised to control panhandlers, addicts, rowdy teenagers, and loiterers. In New York City, a lot of attention was paid to the "squeegee operators" who offered to clean windshields at street corners and at highway entrances (Parenti, 1999). These practices were adapted from the "broken windows" thesis authored by criminologists James Q. Wilson and George Kelling in 1982. Wilson and Kelling proposed that neighborhood disorder and crime were inextricably linked. As of 2007, 63 percent of police precincts reporting to the Police Executive Research Forum had implemented hot spot policing, by far the most widely adopted response (Katel, 2008).

William Bratton was architect of New York City's zero tolerance revolution. Bratton began his career as a Military Police Officer (MP), serving in Vietnam (Parenti, 1999). He began New York City's zero tolerance plan before he was police chief, focusing on the subway system, where fare evasion was common. One of his first moves was obtaining paramilitary firepower, a symbolic gesture to show police were armed and ready. Police stationed in transit areas began to view themselves as important, as part of the action. Bratton also restructured the culture of the transit police to be far more bureaucratic. His work caught the eye of newly elected mayor Rudolph Giu- liani, who named Bratton the city's 38th police chief. Once in the central office, Bratton and his point-man Jack Maple, who once described taking down suspects as "better than sex," set about spreading the zero tolerance approach to the city at large. Precinct captains were required to report for meetings at the command center. Parenti (1999) described these meetings as "sanctimonius, paramilitary, hyper-macho ritual" (p. 76). Citizens were enlisted to cooperate, as the NYPD solicited media support, and School Chancellor Ramon Cortines sent a letter to parents and guardians about the operation. The Guiliani/Bratton approach was quickly adopted (at least in part) by other cities, including Boston, Philadelphia, New Orleans, Indianapolis, Minneapolis, and Baltimore (Parenti, 1999).

Zero tolerance is problematic from a philosophical perspective. It tells offenders that they are not accepted, not even tolerated in society. Officers find these militaristic practices "culturally intoxicating," according to Kraska, as "the elite self-perception and status granted these police units stems from the high status military special operations groups have in military culture" (in Parenti, 1999, p. 133). One of the practical problems with zero tolerance po- licing is that officers often abuse their power. Harassment claims skyrocketed when New York instituted zero tolerance policing, which was incorrectly iden- tified as the reason for a decrease in violent crime. Between 1994 and 1999, brutality complaints increased 62 percent, and the city paid out more than $100 million in damages. Police sweeps netting the arrest of huge numbers of black men were not uncommon. A rash of police killings, largely of unarmed African American men, exacerbated existing racial tensions (Parenti, 1999).

This militarization is increasingly presented as though it is the most logical and effective way to keep us safe. We are told we must trade some individual rights and freedoms for this safety, especially in a world in which the global threat of terrorism is ever-present.

> Communal security often appears to call for a new type of policing, one involving greater use of collective force, heavier weapons, full ballistic gear, aggressive patrol work, and no-knock warrants. However, such new develop- ments endanger individual rights when they begin to erode the traditional police orientation of "protect and serve" with the military orientation of "overwhelm and defeat." (Campbell & Campbell, 2010, p. 342)

Global Militarization of Police

Although my focus is on the United States, this tendency to militarize po- lice forces is a global trend. Zero tolerance policing has been exported to numerous countries, notably the UK and Mexico. For instance, the U.S. military has trained almost 2,000 Colombian National Police and about 100 Panamanian National Police since 2003, teaching them light infantry tactics. Clearly, infantry tactics are military skills, not police skills, and will likely not be useful in preventing crime or in building crime-free communities. Instead, military training emphasizes domination and suppression (Campbell & Campbell, 2010). The war on drugs in the United States and elsewhere has led to countless human rights violations. In addition to the more obvious effects of mass incarceration and torture and cruel and inhumane treatment, Human Rights Watch has noted that in some countries, police target harm-reduction efforts specifically, seeing them as easy opportunities to harass, entrap, and extort clients. The pressure to make arrests encourages officers to seek out easy targets.

Can Community Policing Reduce Militarization?

Some have pointed to the trend of community policing as a sign that the militarization phase is over. Community policing involves law enforcement collaborating with community residents to prevent crime. Although it does indeed hold great promise as a more just and humane method of law enforcement, studies have shown that community policing has not dramatically altered police departmental structure, which continues to be highly specialized, having vertical authority structures and detailed rule systems (Chappell & Lanza-Kaduce, 2010; Kraska & Cubellis, 1997). The current emphasis on homeland security likely exaggerated the militarism (Chappell & Lanza-Kaduce, 2010; Kraska, 2007). Similarly, the current emphasis on policing illegal immigration has exacerbated the co-mingling of military and police. Notably, President Obama has sent additional National Guard troops to police the Arizona-Mexico border, a move that might have received more attention were it not for that state's controversial passage of Senate Bill 1070, which authorized police to demand "papers" from any person they encounter.

Police Training

Given that community policing is intended to involve police and citizens working in collaboration to address social issues that lead to crime and to enhance the quality of life, it seems as though a militaristic structure and mentality is antithetical. To accommodate community policing, officers must be trained differently. Traditionally, police have trained through a militaristic model that fosters an "us versus them" mentality (Albuquerque & Paes-Machado, 2004). Emphasis is on physical ability, performing under stress, and the mastery of defensive tactics, weapons, and the use of force, as in the military. Police academies often feature some of the same rituals as does military boot camp, such as an emphasis on chain of command as well as group punishments and discipline. The goal of this type of socialization is to strip individuals of their personal characteristics and remake them as devoted and unquestioning team members (Albuquerque & Paes-Machado, 2004). Rarely does academy training offer rookies any theoretical models for explaining criminal behavior. The result of this is the default position that forms the basis of the U.S. criminal justice system, and that is based on a classical/neoclassical theoretical view that criminals make rational, informed choices about whether and how to commit their crimes. Given that offenders are presumed to weigh the costs of crime against the perceived benefits, the logical response seems to be to amp up the costs. This will, theoretically, deter both offenders (specific deterrence) and the general public (general deterrence). Of course, the problem is that this is not the only explanation for crime. If offenders are motivated by other, more structural or environmental factors, then this type of punitive response will not be effective.

Officers can learn additional militarized tactics by reviewing magazines like *Tactical Edge,* a publication of the National Tactical officers Association, which discusses managing SWAT teams along with new and high-powered types of ammunition, among other information. Also available is the widely read magazine *SWAT* (Campbell & Campbell, 2010).

New curricula used in police training do show some promise, but may do little when they are infused into a militaristic structure. They differ from traditional police training models, which emphasize the technical and mechanical aspects of police, such as driving skills, marksmanship, and defensive tactics, in that they focus on problem solving and community engagement strategies (Campbell & Campbell, 2010; Peak & Glensor, 2004). This is an important shift if law enforcement is to truly adapt a community policing model, which requires them to understand and appreciate diversity and be skilled in community relations (Campbell & Campbell, 2010). Unfortunately, research shows that without a change in police structure, new training may only alter officer's attitudes and behaviors in the short-term (Haarr, 2001). Even in programs that ostensibly train officers in democratic and problem-solving ideals, there seems to be a "hidden curriculum." That is, the environment in which the training occurs is still militaristic, and throughout the academy, officers tend to share "war stories" that contradict any messages about peace and harmony (Buerger, 1998; Campbell & Campbell, 2010; White, 2006). Ford (2003) found that 83 percent of the war stories told in the academy supported the traditional militaristic police subculture. Recruits are still indoctrinated into the vertical command hierarchy and are inundated with messages about loyalty, solidarity, and reliance on fellow officers.

In addition to the academy, new recruits are also trained on the job, largely by Field Training Officers (FTOS). The rationale is that it is impossible to completely learn how to police from a classroom, and that field training can help new recruits learn through observation, imitation, and reinforcement (Sun, 2003). This field training is especially important in showing new officers how they can exercise their discretion. Although originally FTO programs varied tremendously, they became more standardized in the 1980s and 1990s and are seen as a way to indoctrinate rookies into departmental culture. FTOs are both officers and trainers, responsible for their normal patrol duties as well as providing training for the recruits they are assigned. Ideally, then, they are role models not just for rookies but for their colleagues as well. Research suggests that FTOs are perhaps the most influential factor for rookies (Sun, 2003). The cumulative effect is that officers come to see themselves as soldiers. Former New York City Police Officer Jim Fyfe explained, "The more a police officer thinks of himself as a soldier, the more likely he views the citizen as the enemy" (in Redden, 2000, p. 35).

Militarized Policing and Schools

Militarized policing has spread to educational systems. SWAT teams have raided schools in search of drugs, and zero tolerance is the norm, both in philosophy and in practice. In 2003, police in Goose Creek, South Carolina, conducted a schoolwide commando-style raid on Stratford High School. They lined students face down on the floor at gunpoint while officers searched their lockers and persons for drugs. Some were handcuffed. Police dogs sniffed students, lockers, and backpacks. The incident made national news and was captured on videotape by the school's security cameras. It's difficult to see why such tactics were necessary. Police found no illegal drugs, and the school was described in media reports as having one of the best academic reputations in the state (Shein, 2009). *Newsweek* published data in June 2010 documenting the school-to-prison pipeline in New York, where zero tolerance policies have led to increasing numbers of arrests in schools (Dokoupil, 2010). Schools in New York City have "holding pens" and conduct "corridor sweeps," reminiscent of prison practices (Beger, 2002).

In sum, our general understanding of crime and the efforts needed to address it is skewed toward domination and control. Until we begin to look at these issues from a different perspective, little will likely change. However,with a creative outlook on crime, criminals, and law enforcement, we can begin to envision more just, responsive, and humane ways to prevent crime and violence.

Countering the Dominator Model: Peacemaking Criminology

Peacemaking criminology arose as a counter to this dominator system and the adversarial lens in which crime is understood and criminal justice is configured. Peacemaking criminology is a philosophical lens grounded in humanism, compassion, and love (Quinney, 2001). It seeks ways to change social and economic structures so that suffering is alleviated, as suffering is viewed as the primary cause of crime (Pepinsky & Quinney, 1991). For a peacemaking criminology to emerge, individuals must develop inner peace and must also actively re-create structures and develop processes that promote peace. Essentially, personal transformation is interconnected with societal transformation (Quinney, 1991). Barak (2005) explained that the establishment of positive peace and the development of peacemaking criminology comes from "the awareness, consciousness, and compassionate sense of the interconnectedness of all things, including people, animals, plants, clouds, and stones." This view sees crime control efforts that coercively punish or control others as perpetuating violence. Instead of "escalating the violence in our already violent society by responding to violence and conflict with state violence and conflict in the form of penal sanctions such as death and prison, we need to de-escalate violence by responding to it through forms of conciliation, mediation, and dispute settlement" (Lanier & Henry, 2004, p. 329). John Fuller (1998) has maintained that the peacemaking points of view perspective has the potential to provide lasting solutions to the problems that lead individuals to commit crime because "The war on crime perspective, with its emphasis on punishment and retribution ensures that offenders will strive only to commit their crimes in a more efficient manner so as not to get caught. The peacemaking perspective on the other hand, seeks to address the conditions of society that foster crime and to address the problems of [both] the individual offender [and the victim]" (p. 88). Although an important change in perspective, Barak (2005) cautioned that peacemaking criminology, like warmaking criminology, still reinforces dualistic thinking. Thus we are reminded that process, not just product, matters if we are to truly advance positive peace. If we tap our collective creativity, we can begin to view crime and crime-related issues more fluidly.

A peacemaking criminology renounces zero tolerance policing and zero tolerance approaches in communities and schools. Many groups have already done this, including the American Bar Association. Other groups like the National Association of School Psychologists and the American Academy of Child and Adolescent Psychiatry have at least spoken out about the problems inherent in any policy and approach that tells people they are not to be tolerated. Instead of "quality of life policing," which is essentially code for police domination, law enforcement should work toward ensuring all people enjoy the highest quality of life by treating them humanely and working to prevent crime in communities.

Changing How We Talk About Crime and Criminal Justice

It is important to change the language we use to discuss crime and criminal justice, as language shapes the way we think about, understand, and respond to the problem. One way to handle this is to rename the institutions we charge with making and enforcing laws to be peace-oriented. Costa Rica has done this, renaming its justice ministry the Ministry of Justice and Peace on September 14, 2009. Costa Rica also abolished its army in 1948 (Shutts, 2009). This makes Costa Rica the first of its kind in Latin America and the third in the world (Nepal and the Solomon Islands are the other two, although movements are underway for Departments of Peace in 32 countries including the United States). Originally, the ministry was not intended to have any role in crime prevention, only supervising research on crime and overseeing the nation's penitentiaries, but a 1998 executive decree created the National Directorate for the Prevention of Crime. This was replaced by the newly formed Directorate for the Promotion of Peace and the Peaceful Coexistence of Citizens. What a great name! This is a critical acknowledgement that peace is the goal. The Ministry now conducts peace promotion and violence prevention activities, emphasizing conflict resolution (Shutts, 2009). The Dalai Lama immediately endorsed the move:

> Peace is not something which exists independently of us, any more than war does. Those who are responsible for creating and keeping the peace are members of our own human family, the society that we as individuals participate in and help to create. Peace in the world thus depends on there being peace in the hearts of individuals. Peace based merely on political considerations or prompted by other compulsions will only be temporary and superficial.

In 1997, Costa Rica passed a law requiring that peace education be offered in every school. The law created a place for peaceful conflict resolution in the legal system, which also endorses mediation whenever possible. In 2004, the National Directorate of Alternative Conflict Resolution was created, and 2 years later the National Commission for the Prevention of Violence and Promotion of Social Peace was established. The newly overhauled Ministry of Justice and Peace will work with both.

The Peace Alliance, with numerous co-sponsors, has pushed for a U.S. Department of Peace. A bill before Congress would establish the Department, which would be led by a Secretary of Peace, who would advise the President on peace-building needs, strategies, and tactics. It would create a Peace Academy, which would be a sister to the military academies and would provide training on peace-building to military recruits and members, and would advise other branches of government. The bill also provides funding to expand existing domestic peace-building programs in communities, including mediation training for police, firefighters, and emergency personnel; alternative dispute resolution techniques; and school-based programs. As of August 2009, the bill has 232 co-sponsors in the House of Representatives and 9 in the Senate.

Gaskew (2009) conducted fieldwork in a Muslim-American community in central Florida and found high levels of alienation, mistrust, anger, and fear toward law enforcement as a result of policies enacted after the September 11th terrorist attacks. This has diminished the likelihood that Muslim-Americans will cooperate with police in crime control efforts. Gaskew argued for police training on the basic tenets of Islam and its culture and customs. Further, he recommended that police agencies must seek opportunities to engage the Muslim-American communities in dialogue and work toward building relationships based on respect, dignity, and social justice. One source for possible training on peacemaking is the UN-mandated University for Peace. In another example of bringing people together, one that was widely criticized, President Barack Obama held what is now called the "Beer Summit" as a way to mend fences. Harvard Professor Henry Louis Gates Jr. had been arrested by Cambridge, Massachusetts, police after he locked himself out of his home. Someone called the police, initially believing it to be a robbery, and despite Gates' protestations that he was the homeowner, he was arrested. The officers maintained that Gates was belligerent and rude to them. Gates, a black man, countered that the white officers were demonstrating a historical and current problem—racial profiling. Obama invited Gates to enjoy a beer and discussion of the issue with Cambridge Police Sgt. James Crowley in the White House Rose Garden on July 30, 2009 (Lozada, 2010). Although many assert this was a publicity stunt by the president, as a symbol of how two opposing groups can be brought together to discuss a concern with civility and poise, the event was a success. It demonstrated that committed persons can be creative in seeking ways to understand one another and to craft more peaceful responses.

True Community Policing

Of critical importance is that police need to listen to their communities. Citizens must have spaces in which they can articulate to police what they see as the major problems and how they'd like them resolved. Further, local communities should help teach officers about specific social issues they are grappling with. Campbell and Campbell (2010) recommend that police academies consider increasing their emphasis on the many horizontal relationships officers can and must have to be effective at community policing. This might include bringing in community members with whom the agency will or has collaborated. Having worked with several domestic violence agencies that sought to help officers better understand that social problem, I know academies are often resistant to bringing in others to train their officers. Yet this could indeed be tremendously helpful, as officers would learn more from the citizen/witness/victim side of the crime equation. Further, they would be more knowledgeable about local resources to which they can refer victims and even offenders. It would likely enhance their community relationships as well and could serve as a springboard for police involvement in prevention efforts. Additionally, local colleges can be utilized to help provide police training beyond the traditional model.

Teaching Peace to Police

I believe the trend toward requiring officers to hold a college degree is a good one as well. Rookies who have a liberal arts background will see crime, criminals, and the community differently than will those who have never been introduced to criminology, sociology, psychology, and other relevant disciplines. Those who have been introduced to peacemaking criminology, for instance, may be more willing to innovate in their work and to encourage innovation at a broader level. Peace educators can do more to include these disciplines in their scope as well. Although sociology and psychology may be included in interdisciplinary peace education programs, criminology and criminal justice is not typically part of it. Nor do all criminology and criminal justice professors even introduce their students to peacemaking views. Sanzen (1991, p. 242) claimed that macrolevel changes through individual changes can happen through the teaching of other values. Instead of teaching values of control and repression, values of peace, harmony, and human dignity should be taught.

Alternative Styles of Policing

Police organizations are starting to note that their traditional tactics may be too heavy-handed to be effective with the vast majority of the offenders they see. Officers have a great deal of discretion, yet they have traditionally used it to make arrests and engage the system formally. On the other hand, police can engage in mediation. Officers can work like third parties dealing with two actors to find a middle ground that is acceptable to both sides and does not necessarily include the formal criminal justice system. Mediation also might include attempts to convince certain targets to take voluntary actions rather than resort to involvement in the system (Buerger, Petrosino, & Petrosino, 1999; Davis, 2009).

Restorative Justice

Innovators are using restorative justice in an effort to use discretion in ways that do not engage the formal criminal justice system. Restorative justice is a method that involves offenders, victims, and community members coming together to reach consensus about how the community can repair the harm effected by criminal activity, and offenders can be positively reintegrated into society (Nicholl, 1999). Citizens and officers become invested in seeing crime prevention and response as a responsibility they share (Nicholl, 1999). Restorative justice can both deter more serious offenses and engage the community in the prevention of crime. Restorative justice preaches the sort of "rational, problem-solving response to social conflict that is highly resilient to the demands of the different policing philosophies, and promotes more of the human, face to face contact with victims and offenders that so many officers intuitively recognise as essential to rebuilding social capital and community confidence" (Pollard, 2000).

Restorative justice is based on dialogue and inclusiveness. Affected parties must be brought together in a safe and open environment in which they can communicate their needs. The focus of these meetings, or conferences, as they are often called, is on the harm done by the offender. A skilled facilitator guides the respectful dialogue, and the offender must take responsibility for his or her actions. Victims' needs are also central. The community works to identify ways in which the offender can be held responsible and the victim can be assisted in his or her healing. Community members brainstorm ways to provide needed services to both victims and offenders. Everyone involved is encouraged to creatively explore possible solutions (White, 2003).

Restorative justice can help shift the police culture to one of community problem-solving, and helps build bridges between law enforcement and social service agencies, schools, and community organizations. Pollard (2000) noted that restorative justice was rapidly adopted by Thames Valley officers in the UK, who see it as a useful counter to the adversarial, us-versus-them approach. Research has found their "restorative cautioning" approach to be significantly more effective at reducing rates of re-offense (Joseph Rountree Foundation, n.d.).

In addition to dealing with traditional street offenses of a variety of types, restorative justice and other forms of mediation have proven to be useful in addressing citizen complaints against police. Walker, Archbold, and Herbst (2002) note that these tactics create situations whereby police officers engage in dialogue in which citizens have as much power as they do. They note numerous other benefits to citizens, including better understanding of police work, more satisfaction with the process, and a feeling of empowerment. Mediation, as well, can benefit officers, who are given the opportunity to learn from their mistakes, better understand the citizens with whom they work, and create potentially important collaborations. In traditional complaint procedures, complainants never meet face-to-face with officers and thus neither party has the opportunity to see the other as human (Walker, 2001). Although some disagree, many scholars maintain that mediation techniques are effective at healing race and ethnic problems between citizens and police (Walker et al., 2002).

The U.S. Department of Justice has provided a guidebook for departments seeking to implement restorative justice as a method of community-oriented policing. Departments are cautioned to consider how the goals and processes of restorative justice can be hindered when they are implemented in a militaristic structure and are advised to consider the changes needed for it to be effective. Restorative justice requires more than tinkering with existing practices and systems. It should bring transformations in thinking and understanding about crime, communities, and the role of policing" (Nicholl, 1999, p. 9) .The implementation must be sensitive to the community's needs and culture (Nicholl, 1999).

Restorative justice's focus on harms can alter the way officers respond to crime, as well as how those involved in the dialogue think about crime, who commits it, and their motivations. "This is important to deal with crime effectively as well as prevent future crime. Thus, restorative justice is a response to crime that includes prevention. Helping victims recover, reintegrating offenders into the community, and promoting care in the community will enhance public safety. Crime is no longer seen as an unresolved issue, and people learn from the dialogue. This learning promotes positive change" (Nicholl, 1999, p. 13). In essence, restorative justice offers a shift from a dominator-focused process to one that is partnership-based. It is consistent with scholars' and activists' call to re-imagine crime as something that is socially harmful (McElrea, 1998). In contrast to traditional definitions of crime, a social harms definition of crime sees it as more than just a violation of the state's agenda. Instead, this view includes social conditions, social arrangements and the interference with person's fulfillment of fundamental human needs and potential (Gil, 1996, 1999; Tifft & Sullivan, 2001).

Restorative justice has increasingly been used in schools as well. The International Institute for Restorative Practices hosts a program called SaferSanerSchools, which utilizes restorative practices that they describe as "changing relationships by engaging people: doing things WITH them, rather than TO them or FOR them—providing both high control and high support at the same time" (Mirsky, 2003, p. 1). This approach empowers students to take action to prevent violence and other offenses, and it ensures that offenders take responsibility for their actions. Restorative practices and restorative justice programs have been shown to reduce school-based disciplinary problems. Programs in Broomfield and Boulder, Colorado, for instance, resulted in 100 percent agreement between victims, offenders, and peers on how to repair the harm (Ierley & Ivker, 2002). Restorative Justice Online (www.restorativejustice.org) is a clearinghouse of great ideas and articles on how to implement RJ in schools and in other settings.

Partnership-Based Policing

A true model of police as community protectors and helpers would be more consistent with the principles of positive peace. It changes the equation such that "control is at best irrelevant and at worst counterproductive." Community policing and problem-solving models are partnership-based in that they require officers to participate in the community. While the police officer is the central figure under the traditional model, in a partnership model the officer is one of many important stakeholders (Buerger et al., 1999, p. 127). Citizens can and have been trained to serve a peacemaking function in their community. Moore-Lappe (2006) noted that in Cincinnati, Ohio, 1,000 trained volunteers watch over 24 neighborhoods through the Citizens on Patrol program, an example of what she calls "living democracy."

True community policing seems to work. For instance, Omaha, Nebraska, police chief Alex Hayes has noted that community collaboration helped dramatically reduce response time when an incident occurred. The initiative, called Omaha 360, involves partnerships with parents, families, community groups, businesses; outreach to faith-based groups; education; job training; business development; truancy, drop-out, and gang prevention programs; and recovery programs for those being released from incarceration. More than 100 organizations are involved in the collaboration (Glissman, 2010).

Noted Buddhist monk and scholar Thich Nhat Hanh has presented numerous times to police agencies about ways individual officers can adopt a peacemaking philosophy. He trains officers to practice mindfulness while they are at work. "Mindfulness is the kind of energy that helps you be fully present, to live life in the here and now" (Hanh, 2005, p. 9). Mindful breathing and mindful walking help us to see the positives in people, an essential component of changing police officers' mentality. Further, he described a practice used in Plum Village, where he lives, called the Second Body System. Each person has a Second Body, or someone he or she takes care of besides themselves. Officers' Second Body is generally their partner. The officer can be trained to see this person as a supporter as well as in need of support, just like the rest of the community. Officers can also be trained to communicate well, both within their departments and outside of them. Further, officers can be trained to avoid mistaking the respect given to their position as a means of identifying their self worth. Thich Nhat Hanh (2005) noted that power is bestowed on officers so they can serve, and to prevent someone from hurting another is a way of not only serving the society but also of serving that particular individual.

I find it admirable that police departments across the United States have refused to enforce certain laws they feel are not a good use of their resources. For instance, some departments have announced they would not enforce provisions of the U.S. Patriot Act, and several police agencies have said they will not enforce SB 1070 in Arizona. Although their reasons are not always the same as mine would be, I think it shows that police can consider what is truly advantageous to the community. These actions should be encouraged and strengthened.

Concluding Thoughts

Although the general public may occasionally be aware of problems with policing, as in the case of high-profile examples of abuse and corruption, rarely is the militarism identified. Yet, as is clear here, policing is literally the front line of a dominator response to structural violence. Failing to acknowledge the ways that laws and policing are set up to benefit a few and to maintain the status quo, while being presented as though these tactics are the only way to keep the populace safe results in our collective inability to lobby for a different model of policing. As peace educators, we must become aware of the institutional violence of our traditional law enforcement structures, strategies, and content. Only then can we build on the creative ideas like peacemaking criminology, true community policing, and restorative justice presented here.

The following chapter focuses on the next phases of criminal justice: the courts and corrections. Although these phases too tend to be dominator-modeled, some creative thinking about alternatives has led to some innovative practices that can be fuel for inspiration.

3

Crime, Criminal Justice, and Peacemaking

Courts and Corrections

His own confession was a prosecutor's prize,
Made up of fear, of rage, of outright lies

I'm Not the Man
—10,000 Maniacs

As we saw in the last chapter, a retributive system of justice is punitive in nature. We have tended to take it for granted that a dominator-modeled system is the only thing that will work. This chapter examines how the courts and correctional systems in the United States are dominator-modeled and how this is detrimental to human betterment and to the goal of positive peace. As the lyrics from *I'm Not the Man* highlight, the adversarial system focuses on winning at all costs. In this chapter, I again offer a brief but not exhaustive review of courts and corrections in the United States as a means

Building a Peaceful Society, pages 37–53
Copyright © 2011 by Information Age Publishing
All rights of reproduction in any form reserved.

37

of problematizing the institution. This is followed by a survey of interesting and provocative ideas and actions intended to create a more just, humane, and peaceful judicial and correctional system. Our creative energy can help create a partnership-based system of courts and corrections that no longer sees people's lives as something to be won or lost but instead focuses on human betterment. As chapter 1 noted, our creative efforts to integrate authentic caring—in this case, for both victims and offenders—will pay off in the form of a more humane society.

The focus of our current criminal justice system is on using punishment as a means to deter future crime and to provide the punishment that offenders supposedly deserve, the "just desserts." Determining who is guilty and punishing them is held up as a job essential to the society's continued well-being, with these people essentially serving as moral guardians of sorts (Rynne, 2008). As Garland (1990) noted, punishment is increasingly bureaucratized. Retributive justice is guided by notions of blame, guilt, individual responsibility, and punishment for past harms. It emanates from the same theoretical perspectives discussed in the previous chapter, which pronounce crime to be the result of individual choice.

Emotions and Retributive Justice

As early as the work of Emile Durkheim, scholars have noted that punishing lawbreakers serves a critical symbolic and emotional function (Beckett, 1997; Beckett & Sasson, 2000; Dowler, 2003; Durkheim, 1933; Vidmar, 2001). Vidmar (2001) proposed a six-stage social psychological model of retributive justice. According to this model, a perceived rule or norm violation leads to negative emotional reactions, which in turn lead to a desire for punishment on the part of the victim as well as the general public. As Vidmar argued, anger plays an important role. "The arousal of the emotion of anger, therefore, is a key component to retributive responses" (Vidmar, 2001, p. 41). According to Karstedt (2002), "emotions pervade penal law and the criminal justice system" (p. 300). Pratt (2000) asserted that "emotive punishments" have reemerged in recent years. Karstedt (2002) argued that the public discourse surrounding crime and punishment in late modern societies has become increasingly emotionalized. This trend has been driven, in part, by politicians and the media, the same mythmakers discussed in the previous chapter. When people fear crime—and the groups whom they perceive are responsible for it—they may support dominator-style methods of trial and punishment. Research has generally found a positive association between fear of crime and support for punitive measures (Dowler, 2003; Pratt, 2000; Sherman, 2003), including the death penalty

(Arthur, 1998; Barkan & Cohn, 1994; Combs & Comer, 1984). Researchers have also shown that crime myths can lead to anger and outrage, which then prompts support for retributive systems. Anger has also been positively associated with support for the death penalty.

An Adversarial System

The system in which we determine guilt is an adversarial one. It is dominator-structured and utilizes dominator methods. Judges, who dress in robes to clearly demonstrate their difference from the rest of us, preside over a setting that many defendants do not truly understand. It is intimidating in the way it is set up. Having accompanied several domestic violence victims to court for restraining order hearings, I puzzle at why the waiting area for the court is structured such that the defendant sits adjacent from the petitioner, allowing him ample space to verbally harass and intimidate her with no court intervention. Also intimidating are the procedures and language used. Rather than allowing all parties the opportunity to share their perspective, the system is exclusionary when victims are not allowed to speak.

Although judicial discretion can certainly be used inappropriately, the trend over the last 3 decades has been to decrease this discretion in favor of more punitive and robotic sentences. Many crimes now carry mandatory minimums, allowing judges very little opportunity to hear the specific nuances of the case. Zero tolerance-style approaches have landed more and more people before the overloaded courts, which operate more like an assembly line than anything else. Three strikes laws demand more and lengthier incarceration, supposedly for violent offenders but often for nonviolent offenders as well. The result of this dominator system is the mass incarceration of a tremendous asset—a large chunk of our population.

Incarceration Nation

"The United States is obsessed with imprisoning human beings" (Gallagher, 2008, p. 376). We incarcerate more people per capita than anywhere in the world (724 per 100,000). We are also number one in sheer numbers, beating out both China and Russia. Each week, almost 1,000 U.S. citizens become prison "residents." Often seen as the only way to deal with offenders, we have operated on an "if you build it they will come" philosophy. That is, as Parenti (1999) noted, under our current model, there will never be an empty prison. Prison officials often convince communities that building a prison will be lucrative, with the payoff being an increase in high-paying jobs and the building or growth of ancillary businesses. In fact, most employees of the prison industry do not live in the host communities. Studies have generally found prisons are a special case in that rather than building local businesses, they may drive them away.

Prison conditions are horrific, in many cases. Lomax (2005) noted that torture is currently and has always been part of the U.S. criminal justice system, from policing to prisons. In 1995, a federal judge found widespread abuse in California's Pelican Bay Prison, including excessive use of electronic stun guns, while in 1999 another federal judge called Texas prisons "a culture of sadistic and malicious violence" when hearing evidence that guards had allowed gang members to buy and sell inmates for sex (Finley, 2008). Particularly awful are Supermax facilities, where inmates live for 23 hours a day in a cell the size of a bathroom. Inmates may receive one 5-minute phone call every 6 months, which will be monitored. In many facilities, strip searches, including invasive body cavity searches, are routinely conducted when inmates leave their cells for any purpose. The effect has been likened to that of prisoners of war, in that the deprivation of humane, social contact leads the majority to lose their minds. As Gawande (2009) noted, "One of the paradoxes of solitary confinement is that, as starved as people become for companionship, the experience typically leaves them unfit for social interaction."

Inmates may endure abuse at the hands of other inmates as well as prison guards. Reports documented terrible instances of inhumane treatment of female prisoners, including beatings, electric shocks, mock executions, death threats, and sleep and sensory deprivation (Finley, 2008). Mentally ill inmates are especially vulnerable. In 2003, Human Rights Watch documented the large number of mentally ill inmates who had died in prisons because they were held in cruel restraint chairs. Juveniles and immigrants in detention also suffer. A lawsuit was settled in 2010 that finally ended abuse in a Mississippi juvenile detention center, where youths were locked for 23 hours a day in unsanitary cells, punished with pepper spray and Mace, and held in mechanical restraint chairs. Yet, sadly, these inhumane conditions persist in other facilities that are supposed to help juveniles rehabilitate. Immigrants held in Immigration and Naturalization Services (INS) detention facilities face abusive racial epithets in addition to mistreatment. In 2006, Human Rights Watch documented the use of dogs for cell extractions. Essentially, this involves allowing dogs to attack inmates who do not want to leave their cells for whatever reason. It is not lawful in any other country, but HRW documented use in five states (Human Rights Watch, 2006). This use of dogs in prisons to establish a sense of power and to create fear was exported to Iraq, where soldiers used dogs in some of the most infamous photos of torture at Abu Ghraib prison.

The Death Penalty

The United States is the only developed country that still uses the death penalty, despite continued questions about procedures, racial bias, cost-effectiveness, quality of legal representation, and overall morality of allowing the state to kill for us. In 2009, the United States executed 52 people, and 106 people found their new home on death row, for a total of 3,279 death row inmates. While death row is intended to be a stark environment, on at least one occasion a federal judge has ruled that conditions were cruel and inhumane. An inmate in Tennessee filed suit, describing the six-foot-by-eight foot box he lived in for 23 hours a day, where temperatures reached 80 to 85 degrees (Finley, 2008).

A Different Paradigm

A shift in mentality can indeed impact our court and corrections systems. Unnever, Cullen, and Fisher (2005) examined the effect of empathy on support for the death penalty using data from the General Social Survey. They found that empathy (measured with a seven-item scale) had a significant direct and indirect negative effect on death penalty support (Johnson, 2009). A 2006 Zogby poll found 87 percent of Americans favored rehabilitation efforts for prisoners. Of those, 70 percent favored therapeutic and rehabilitative efforts after incarceration has ended to assist offenders in re-entering the community. Most favor job training and mentoring as ways to help reduce recidivism (Zogby Poll, 2006).

Woolford and Ratner (2010) noted three "informal" conflict resolution practices that can be useful in challenging traditional retributive forms of justice: civil mediation, restorative justice, and reparation politics. Civil mediation involves a variety of mediation tactics, which are used in matters of civil law. Although these programs were initially community based, the rising cost and overwhelming caseload of the civil court system has prompted many to examine civil mediation as a way to resolve conflicts before they reach the courtroom. Restorative justice involves bringing victims, offenders, and community members together to address the harms caused by crime. It is built on the values of healing and empowerment and involves practices that are consistent with teaching for peace: open dialogue, face-to-face communication, participatory involvement, and a voice for all. Like civil mediation, restorative justice originated outside the court system but is now often included in its ancillary services. Reparations politics refers to responses after mass violence and authoritarian control. It is used when states are forced to deal with their unsavory pasts and may include trials and tribunals as well as truth commissions, compensation, restitution, apologies, and other forms of memorial. Reparations politics can occur outside of state control but often do not. All three methods share the goal of empowering local actors to participate in the resolution of conflicts. Rather than the traditional roles offered in the criminal justice system of victim, offender, or witness, these three conflict resolution strategies involve community members as stakeholders who have a vested interest in repairing harm and building more peaceful communities. All three strategies are flexible in how they can be applied and are thus adaptable to different situations. While all three may today be part of the state's services and thus may in some ways serve its interests, they still stand as different, more peace-oriented models of justice (Woolford & Ratner, 2010). "Informal reckonings plainly spark a desire for transformation within participants and catalyze some initial changes in their lives, but the challenge is that of sustaining these enabling moments in the face of structural inertia and programmed compliance" (Woolford & Ratner, 2010, p. 9).

Woolford and Ratner (2010) offer three possibilities for "entrenching" informal, transformative justice. First, these programs could be set up outside of the formal justice system, as they were originally. This would put them in a very marginal position in regard to resources, the stability of services, and the ability to effect widespread influence, yet would surely offer greater autonomy and authenticity. Second, informal justice could follow a trickle up model, which would involve demonstrating to court personnel the wisdom and effectiveness of these strategies to encourage gradual adoption and an eventual transformation of the justice system. This strategy has been criticized as being too compliant with the traditional justice framework. The third option is to create informal justice counterpublics, which Woolford and Ratner (2010) envisioned as "a communicative space out of which notions and practices can arise to effectively challenge the informal-formal justice complex" (p. 10). Counterpublics are designed "to create sustainable opportunities for disruption, empowerment, and social change—that is, a justice that allows participants to collectively address societal problems and social suffering in ways that are not prefigured or readily assimilated by the institutional guardians of juridical power" (p. 15).

Restorative Justice and the Courts

As noted in the last chapter, restorative justice is an alternative way to structure a criminal justice system, one that can be more consistent with a peacemaking perspective. Rather than looking at past harm, it is a system that looks to the future with the intent of promoting harmonious community relations. Restorative justice is informed by concepts such as repairing harm, social restoration, community harmony, and problem solving (Bazemore, 1997; Bazemore & Schiff, 2001; Zehr, 1990).

There is a range of specific models and institutional approaches to restorative justice, including Family Group Conferencing, Circle Sentencing, and Victim-Offender Mediation programs (Bazemore, 1997; Braithwaite, 1999). Restorative justice has also been used in specialized courts like drug courts (O'Hear, 2009). Some approaches are based upon moral categories such as reintegrative shaming, where the aim is to shame the offense, while offering forgiveness to the offender (Braithwaite, 1989). Others are based on strategic assessments of offenders and events, usually called a balanced restorative approach. The aim of these approaches is to design interventions that best address offender accountability and development as well as community safety (Bazemore, 1997; Bilchik, 1998). Some approaches focus almost exclusively on meeting victim needs. This typically occurs through some method of restitution or compensation by the offenders. Still others emphasize community engagement to deal with underlying problems and issues, in recognition of the fact that the specific offense is but one manifestation of a larger problem.

Some proponents of restorative justice see it as essentially a diversion from the formal criminal justice system; a way to free up the court's case load. Others advocate restorative justice that is more consistent with its ideals and as a system that could eventually replace the current retributive one (see Bazemore & Schiff, 2001). The underlying thread, though, is that justice should be directed toward repairing harm. That entails healing victims, offenders, and communities, not just punishing wrongdoers (Bazemore &Schiff, 2001; Zehr & Mika, 1998).

Restorative justice emphasizes individual agency, in that participants are required to speak up and take action for themselves. It is also cost-effective compared with detention or imprisonment. Victims are far more engaged in the process than they are in the traditional court system. Communities benefit through the opportunity to connect and collaborate. In sum,

> It is peacemaking in orientation, rather than punishment based. It is socially inclusive, rather than reliant upon experts and officials. It attempts to provide a symbolic and practical solution to actual harms, rather than a response to violation of laws (that represent, in abstract, acts against the state). Victims and community, as well as offenders, are central to resolving issues of harm, rather than peripheral to the processes of criminal justice. (White, 2001, p. 7)

Restorative justice is not without critics, however. One limitation is that, in most cases, restorative justice has been used in a very limited way. It has been designed as either a form of diversionary measure at the front end of the criminal justice system or it has been integrated as a specific form of response that is appropriate only for particular types of offenders. Furthermore, some restorative justice programs may still follow a punitive philosophy in that the goal is only to shame the offender and demand restitution, not to help create peace in a community (White, 2001).

To date, restorative justice has generally been adopted as a means of dealing with institutional pressures to cut costs or as a way for politicians to sound good. Rarely has restorative justice been introduced because of its philosophical difference from adversarial justice. It has almost never been implemented as a systemic alternative intended to replace the existing system, despite its promise for doing so. Partly due to the diversity of opinion, values, and models, under the restorative justice umbrella, some forms of restorative justice have been implemented in a way that actually reproduces the dominant forms of social control (Bazemore, 1997). For example, juvenile conferencing may be used solely for first time offenders and/or trivial offences, "as a means of diversion at the 'soft' end of the juvenile justice spectrum—and therefore as a filter that reinforces the logic and necessity of the 'hard' end of the system . . . the 'real justice' of retribution and punishment" (White, 2001, p. 7). I worked as a facilitator for a very successful RJ program for youth, but we were only allowed to include first-time, nonviolent offenders.

Important to the topic of this book, it is essential to note that

> Within restorative justice frameworks the idea of social harm is generally conceptualized in immediate, direct and individualistic terms (and as such ignores the broader social processes underpinning, and patterns of, both offending and victimization). One consequence of this is that the emphasis on repairing harm tends to be restricted to the immediate violations and immediate victim concerns, thereby ignoring communal objectives and collective needs in framing reparation processes. Thus, the heart of the matter remains that of changing the offender, albeit with their involvement, rather than transforming communities and building progressive social alliances that might change the conditions under which offending takes place. (White, 2001, p. 8)

In most cases, therefore, the emphasis is on the immediate harm, the specific situation, and the individuals concerned. Less attention is paid to the patterns of social inequality or oppression that make both victims and offenders, even the communities, more prone to the experiences of criminal harm (Bazemore, 1997).

Today, scholars and practitioners are paying more attention to how restorative justice programs can help create a more just and equal society by building communities (Walgrave & Bazemore, 1999). It is clear that systemic reform of criminal justice and societal reform to address inequalities must occur simultaneously, as they are interconnected.

It is possible to reconstruct restorative justice in a way that more directly relates to social justice principles. A restorative justice system could be structured on the concepts of solidarity, compensation, and community empowerment. "Solidarity implies that the politically and socially weak members of a group need to be included rather than excluded in the sense that tasks are to be performed for and by them, and emotional support is to be given to them. Offenders and victims need to be offered solidarity, and a voice in what affects them and support in the healing process" (White, 2001, p. 9). Compensation refers to the idea that the criminal justice system, with other general social welfare policies and programs, can play a significant role in helping to address the social disadvantages of people who offend and the social harms experienced by those who are victimized. Further, the process of repairing harm has to be reconceptualized as social rather than solely individual in nature. This involves many different types of state-provided resources as well as input from individuals and groups. It must include the development of responses that go beyond simply funding conferencing to include broader social reforms and creative initiatives. "Community empowerment is about enhancing the welfare and prospects of collectivities, of which individuals are integral members. The point of intervention is to change the material conditions and circumstances of neighborhoods and family networks, with the active involvement of local people" (White, 2001, p. 9).

Restorative Justice for Juveniles

For juveniles, a peacemaking, social justice-oriented restorative justice model can stress social inclusion, responsiveness, and communal objectives, forming communities of support, and enhancing and increasing accessibility to community resources. "Victims of crime need to be fully compensated for any crimes committed against them—but this is a social responsibility, not simply the offender's . . . Repairing social harm should not be seen as a 'micro' event, involving only the immediate affected parties. It is indicative of much broader social processes, in which both victim and offender are implicated" (White, 2001, p. 10). Thus all interested parties must be included in the restorative justice conferencing, not just in airing their grievances but in the formulation of possible solutions. Minneapolis, for example, has developed a community reentry circle in which community members help an offender reenter the community by offering support and celebrate his or her successes (Bazemore & Schiff, 2001).

Social inclusion means that the specific needs and desires of a given community must be considered. This requires a sense of what is happening at the local level and which groups or individuals can most benefit from the assistance provided by the perpetrators who must serve (White, 2001). A great example of this is in Palm Beach, Florida, where young offenders work (while they are completing their court-ordered community service hours) with adult mentors in the community to plan, implement, and manage community service projects that directly benefit local neighborhoods (Bilchik, 1998). The young offenders in the program also earn money toward restitution for victims. Examples of projects include restoration and beautification of a historical black cemetery, cleaning of the playground of a shelter for HIV-positive and AIDS-infected children, painting of the homes of elderly and disabled residents, and performance by the young people at a cultural fair designed to teach tolerance and cultural sensitivity. To be reintegrated into the community, an offender must be "nested" in prosocial, caring, and welcoming relationships. Victims also need access to such relationships. This is especially so given that victims are generally members of the same neighborhood or community (White, 2001).

For restorative justice to be effective, communities must be creative in thinking of how best to access their existing resources and in developing new ones. This can begin by mapping the community's assets, capacities, skills of residents, associations, and such. Creative thinking can allow for the alternate use of existing resources. For instance, schools and college campuses can be utilized after their traditional hours, as can be vacant or underused commercial locations. Libraries often have conference or meeting rooms that are perfectly suited for community meetings and conferencing. Public malls can be used for meeting space that is socially inclusive and safe. In Santa Monica, California, the local council revitalized an old, rundown mall, which was perceived to be unsafe and little more than a blight on the community, to allow space for public seating, trees, and banners. This made the site more visually appealing. People were encouraged to use the space for a variety of interests. It was designed to be a much-needed community space. Importantly, the redesign not only enhanced the visual appeal of the area and the civic engagement in the community, but street crime was also reduced (White, 2001).

Crime Reduction Through Civic Engagement

Another example of crime reduction through an increase in civic engagement comes from the city of Burlington, Vermont. The city is using restorative community practices to engage young people and to prevent crime through their Center for Community and Neighborhoods (CCAN). CCAN brings together government, business, and citizens in a comprehensive program to inspire and support community participation and more responsive government. CCAN sponsors neighborhood and community programs such as training for grassroots leaders, community forums, and celebrations. It also hosts a Community Justice Center in which volunteers assist offenders in engaging in reparations and community service, provide help to victims, mediate disputes, repair vandalism, and support prisoners in reentering the community. As opposed to the criminal justice system, where typically 97 percent of resources are devoted to prosecuting, sentencing, and isolating offenders, CCAN's justice program utilizes most of its resources to provide support for victims, connecting them to businesses, local leaders, and others who can provide needed resources. Additionally, the project has a public education campaign and a commission that works directly with victims to improve governmental response to their needs. In 2007 alone, Parallel Justice Project supported and assisted 1,310 victims of crime, with help from 25 local businesses who offered discounted services and donated products. In 2007 alone, 248 offenders were engaged in community service to repair damaged property and repay victims (Ahladas & Sachs-Hamilton, 2008).

In all, more than 4,000 citizens take part each year in shaping municipal plans and policies, allocating city resources, revitalizing neighborhoods, resolving conflicts, and healing the damage caused by crime. CCAN intentionally reaches out to marginalized groups, including those living in poverty, people of color, new refugees, and immigrants—the very same groups who often suffer and are excluded from traditional criminal justice and civic engagement. Additionally, CCAN supports and trains 50 Americorps VISTA organizers. Successes include new traffic policies that make streets safer in neighborhoods; the creation of Neighborhood Planning Assemblies, which review and steer city budgets for street, park, and community projects; study circles on racism, which have involved more than 300 citizens and prompted the Burlington Police Department to recruit and mentor new officers, which represent the city's diversity; the cleaning of more than 1,000 graffiti tags on public and private property by a team of more than 250 volunteers and 40 businesses and organizations; and the virtual disappearance of building vacancies. The Americorps VISTA team has created a Healthy City program to educate at-risk teens about sustainable organic farming. Teens run a 12-acre farm that sells organic produce in Burlington schools and at the local hospital. In sum,

CCAN's unshakable faith in the power of an engaged citizenry, its ability to forge strong partnerships amongst unlikely partners, and its drive to involve groups normally excluded from public dialogue allow the Center to bring a critical range of perspectives to bear to improve public outcomes. CCAN has demonstrated how truly transformative change occurs when decision making is collaborative and equitable. Perhaps most important, Burlington has developed a culture of engagement, a cohesive civic infrastructure of connected people, organizations, and programs who build community together (Ahladis & Sachs-Hamilton, 2008).

Examples from the Navajo Nation

The Navajo nation offers another example of an alternative method of trial and punishment. They no longer try people for certain offenses, instead deciding in January 2000 to revamp the Navajo Nation Criminal Code so that jail time and fines for 79 different offenses were eliminated. More importantly, the code now requires the use of peacemaking in criminal cases and mandates that courts address victims' rights. Nalyeeh, a traditional concept that refers to the process of confronting someone who hurts others and requiring them to talk about what they have done, how it hurt others, and what positive can come of it, is also built into the revamped code. Navajo Nation judges had increasingly been using the western "revolving-door approach" to crime—arrest, trial, jail, then no effort to rehabilitate, so new charges. Those who were harmed by crime—the victims—were typically left out of the process. The Navajo Nation processes close to 28,000 criminal cases each year, with the largest portion of them for assault and battery involving families, or other crimes involving families. Many of the offenses are committed while the offender is intoxicated. Since there is jail space for only 220 offenders, judges and the system were overwhelmed. This move returns the Navajo Nation to its traditional roots. "The western criminal justice system assumes that the problem is the actor, and imprisonment is primarily designed to work on convicted defendants. In contrast, traditional Navajo justice deals with people's actions. Western adjudication is a search for what happened and who did it; Navajo peacemaking is about the effects of what happened. Who got hurt? What do they feel about it? What can be done to repair the harm?" (Mirsky, 2004, p. 2).

Navajo peacemaking is essentially restorative justice. Victims, offenders, and community members are involved in sessions that are moderated by a community leader called a "peacemaker." All parties talk about what happened and how they feel about it. More than just traditional crime, these conferences also address what the Navajo Nation calls "harmful acts." A harmful act is "something that gets in the way of living your life" (Mirsky,

2004, p. 3). The idea is to identify the harmful act, talk about it, and devise a plan to deal with it. Navajo peacemaking requires families to take responsibility for their family members, not in a coercive way, but in the sense that you are to love and care for those to whom you are related. In peacemaking, the relatives of those who hurt someone else come forward to help with restitution and to watch over their relative to be sure he or she does not offend again. "In Navajo thinking, thought is the inner form of speech, and speech is the inner form of action. It's a simple enough concept—as you think, so will you speak, and as you speak, so will you do" (Mirsky, 2004, p. 3). Thus, peacemaking attempts to change offenders' thinking. It encourages offenders to start the day with prayer and to take what inspiration emerges to make a plan and take action. At the end of the day, people are to reflect on what they did so that they can do better tomorrow.

Restitution for a wrongdoing can even be symbolic. It can be a prized piece of jewelry or a horse that is valued highly. This focuses the restitution on being something of meaning, not of economic value per se. The restitution should be something that says, "I honor your worth and dignity with this thing that we Navajos prize" and "Let this be a symbol and something tangible to remind us that we have talked this hurt out and entered into good relations with each other" (Yazzie, 2000).

Navajos note the peacemaking approach to justice has been effective in reducing rates of delinquency, family violence, and driving while intoxicated. They also believe it can help prevent crime and are reaching out to schools and other community organizations to help build peacemaking initiatives there.

> This is a bold experiment, but if it works, it may offer lessons to an America that is beginning to recognize that you can't lock up a major portion of the population (usually people of color). Perhaps there are other ways to deal with crime; the answers may lie in dealing with actions, not actors, allowing people to face and solve their own problems, using peacemaking for crime prevention by getting at the nayee (monster) early on, and rewriting old scripts. We Navajos knew about all that stuff traditionally, and it is time for us to remember. (Yazzie, 2000)

New Mexico is considering revamping its prison system and is looking to the Navajo for inspiration. Given the huge cost of incarceration and the high recidivism rates, the state is also looking to better treat drug addiction (85 percent of the state's prison population had a substance abuse problem), offering more prison-based life skills and educational opportunities, and removing some of the barriers to postprison employment (Jennings, 2009).

Although structural and procedural change of the criminal justice system is desperately needed, individual change is welcome as well. For instance, both Hanh (2005) and Talbot (2000) presented strategies for police, lawyers and judges to practice inner peace.

Innovative Prisons and Programs

Given that at least some portion of the population will be incarcerated, even under a more peacemaking system, it is imperative that we examine what can be done inside those walls that is consistent with our basic goals. Fortune, Thompson, Pedlar, and Yuen (2010) described a social justice model for incarcerated women that involved the introduction of circles of support, or Stride Circles. Stride Circles "are grounded in principles of restorative justice and social justice and involve men and women from the community connecting with a woman in prison. Upon the woman's release, members of the Stride Circle provide support to the woman as she returned to the community and they assist in ways that might find her a chance of reintegrating into society and staying out of prison" (p. 20). These circles help women gain self-respect and honor, and build a sense of pride and power. The circles are built on a model of trust and shared power. Further, "the social relationships that form between Circle members encourage action in the form of giving back to community and gaining a sense of control and power over the reintegration process... Circle members collectively become active agents who have the capacity to work toward creating a more socially just society—one that is committed to reducing the oppressive conditions facing one of our most marginalized and vulnerable populations" (p. 31). Another program, started by a Girl Scout troop, helps daughters and incarcerated mothers rebuild their broken relationships. The program was documented in the film, *Troop 1500: Girl Scouts Beyond Bars.*

Alabama's correctional system, not particularly noted for its humanity, offers an example of how inmates can benefit from programs intended to bring inner peace. Donaldson Correctional facility—an overcrowded, maximum-security facility—became the first maximum-security prison in North America to hold an extended Vipassana retreat. Vipassana is an ancient meditation technique that is both emotionally and physically demanding, asking its participants to meditate in silence for 10 days (Coppola, 2007). The program was described in the documentary *The Dhamma Brothers.* Similarly, the Liberation Prison Project teaches Buddhist peace principles to inmates in prison in Spain, Mexico, Mongolia, Italy, New Zealand, the United States, and Australia.

The Alternatives to Violence Project (AVP) is an association of community-based groups and prison-based groups offering experiential workshops in personal growth and creative conflict management. It was founded by Quakers in response to prisoners at Attica who were seeking ways to reduce prison violence. It is based on the Quaker principle of seeing all others as having value. Inmates, who often find it difficult to trust anyone, come to trust the volunteer facilitators and are given opportunities to practice trusting, an important skill in creating personal and societal peace. An evaluation of an AVP program in Delaware found it to be well-received and effective. Inmates noted that it helped them build skills in a nonthreatening environment and to develop a sense of community. Upon completion of the workshops, most participants expressed a desire for altruism or giving back (Sloane, 2002). Many peace educators already use the great materials provided by AVP.

In her *Little Book of Restorative Practices for People in Prison* (2006), Barbara Toews provides guidance for inmates. Tips include getting on the healing path; embracing restorative values; creating a personal sanctuary; and walking with those who offend, with victims, and with offender's families. These practices not only help the inmate personally, but can change the culture inside prisons.

Axelrod (2006) described the Freedom Project, a program to help current and former prisoners find inner peace and to build their ability to reconcile with their communities. Co-founders Lucy Leu and Rusty Thompson and their team work in three prisons in Washington, helping train prisoners in Marshall Rosenberg's nonviolent communication techniques as well as various mindfulness practices like meditation. Freedom Project teams run support groups for prisoners returning to their communities, offering daily one-on-one meetings.

Graterford State prison in Pennsylvania has developed a program that utilizes restorative principles to help prisoners understand the effects of crime and to take responsibility for their actions. Volunteers meet with prisoners for discussion and to help them write letters to their own victims with the hope that a dialogue might ensue. In May, 2010, sixteen men graduated from a program held at Columbia Correctional Institution in Wisconsin. They had attended a 30-session course on restorative justice that was intended to help them understand how they had harmed their victims, the community, and themselves (Erickson, 2010). That same prison is also using restorative principles to allow inmates to tell their stories and to begin to heal from the pain in their lives.

Learning From Other Countries

Other countries have done more to integrate restorative and peacemaking practices into their courts and correctional systems. For example, Switzerland's Saxerriet is an "open" prison—it has no walls, and inmates (including those incarcerated for serious offenses like murder) wear their own clothing and work (for pay) under the supervision of unarmed staff members. The 40 percent recidivism rate at Saxerriet is the lowest in the country, far less than the national average of 60 percent (Harman, 2001). Halden Fengsel in Norway is being dubbed the world's most humane prison. The facility has numerous amenities, including jogging trails, a guest home for inmate's families, and a sound studio. Inmates are offered a variety of educational opportunities, including cooking courses. It is designed to look as much like the outside world as possible. Halden Fengsel was built on the notion that treating inmates humanely will increase the likelihood that they will be able to reintegrate into society upon release. Prison guards do not carry guns, despite the fact that the facility houses the worst kinds of offenders—drug dealers, murderers, and rapists. Guards regularly eat meals and play sports with inmates. Half the guards are women. The idea is to create a sense of family, as most of the offenders came from poor family environments. The prison's governor, Are Hoidal, explained, "When they arrive, many of them are in bad shape. We want to build them up, give them confidence through education and work and have them leave as better people" (Adams, 2010).

Helping others learn about prisoners, to see them as fellow humans, is important to creating a world in which no one is "the other." One program that helps do this is the Inside-Out Prison Exchange Program. Inside Out (www.insideoutcenter.org) is a partnership between institutions of higher education and prisons, whereby college students and inmates are taught, together, for a semester. It helps college students challenge the stereotypes they may have about inmates and offers a life-changing program for inmates. It focuses on collaborative dialogue about significant social issues. To date, more than 250 courses have been offered and, because of the collaboration, any cost is negligible.

Concluding Thoughts

Clearly, there are some wonderful, creative peacemaking initiatives that are taking place as alternatives to traditional courts and as ways to deal with offenders. These, coupled with partnership-based prevention programs and social services, can dramatically reduce crime rates and other social problems and can help create safe, peaceful communities. The next chapter addresses prevention programming.

4

Prevention Programs and Peacemaking

How many train wrecks do we need to see?
Where'd all the good people go?
I've been changing channels, I don't see them
on the TV shows

Good People
—Jack Johnson

Programs designed to prevent crime and violence, in schools and in communities, may also be dominator-modeled. This clearly takes away from what they are intending to achieve. This chapter reviews how prevention programming can go awry, starting with stereotypical and dehumanizing portrayals about youth that lead to the creation of "get tough," fear-based interventions. As Jack Johnson noted in the lyrics above, media rarely share stories of the "good people," instead telling viewers and listeners that it is a big, bad, scary world.

Building a Peaceful Society, pages 55–73
Copyright © 2011 by Information Age Publishing
All rights of reproduction in any form reserved.

But creative prevention work does exist. This chapter highlights innovative partnership-style programs, which have been or are being used in schools and communities to prevent violence, empower youth, and create peace.

The "Panacea Phenomenon"

Too often, interventions designed to respond to or prevent youth violence and crime are simply quick fixes. Finckenauer (1982) called the process by which policymakers, practitioners, media reporters, and others sometimes latch onto quick, short-term, and inexpensive cures to solve difficult social problems the "Panacea Phenomenon." The Panacea Phenomenon has become increasingly common since the 1980s, when fear of the "juvenile superpredator" began to sweep the country. Media depicted the new wave of juvenile delinquents as more ruthless and dangerous than ever before. As Peter Elikann (1999) noted, "it is easier and more acceptable for us to beat up on monstrous animals than on kids" (p. xi), so creating fear about the superpredator allowed adults to craft laws, policies, and even so-called intervention programs, aimed at teens, which are punitive, not peaceful.

Media and Fear of Juveniles

Media attention to major shootings like the Columbine massacre of 1999 in Colorado scared many people into believing that schools were terrifically dangerous places and that an incident like this one could occur at any time. This was yet another example of media describing somewhat isolated or rare incidents as trends, as the likelihood of being killed in a school was 1 in 2 million. The result, however, is that people overestimated the likelihood that a similar event could occur again. Misplaced fear shapes school policies and societal responses. These policies, like zero tolerance laws, metal detector searches, and school police officers, may or may not help keep the school safe. What is clear, however, is that they are costly and they increase students' fear. Education itself has been commodified. Giroux (2009) explained that the neoliberal, radical, free-market culture no longer sees young people as "at-risk." Rather, "they are the risk."

Moral Panics

Fear of school violence has become a moral panic. The term *moral panic* was coined by Stanley Cohen (1980) to describe the reaction of media, politicians, and agents of social control (like police) to youth deviance. His initial work examined a group of young people in England called the Mods and Rockers. Cohen found these groups had been labeled as threats to the community and consequently were treated as such. Jock Young's 1971 book *The Drugtakers* drew additional attention to media's role in constructing deviant identities.

Cohen (1980) identified five stages of a moral panic. The first is that someone or something is defined as a threat to society's values and interests. Second, the threat is depicted by media and repeated in easily identifiable ways. Third, public concern about the so-called problem builds, until fourth, there is some type of response from authorities or opinion makers. Finally, the panic either results in social change or recedes.

It is easy to apply Cohen's five stages to the case of school violence. The 1980s and 1990s were a decades in which adolescents were viewed as problems. Even criminologists had warned of the dangerous generation of so-called superpredators, who were far more violent than any group of juveniles to precede them. Second, despite the continued decline of youth violence in the 1990s, news reports continued to focus on these "ticking time bombs." For instance, Ann Curry introduced a child psychologist on the *Today Show* and asked about the "trend" of students shooting each other. Vincent Schiraldi, the director of the Justice Policy Institute, then reminded viewers that three times as many people were struck by lightning as were killed in school shootings that year. Other national commentators such as Katie Couric emphasized that youth today were out of control, echoing the theme that schools were a site, and students the cause, of a major social problem. The response was to implement a series of punitive and technological strategies aimed at reining in the out-of-control youth. Thus, districts invested in surveillance cameras and metal detectors and hired school police officers. At the White House conference on School Safety, President Clinton proposed spending $12 million for Project SERV (School Emergency Response to Violence). Project SERV is modeled after the FEMA response to violence. He also set aside $65 million to hire 2,000 community and school police officers and $25 million for districts to develop safety plans. The Safe and Gun Free Schools Act was passed in 1994, before most of the high-profile shootings. It requires districts receiving federal funds to establish specific penalties for students found with weapons on campus. By the later 1990s, districts had used this act to justify the implementation of zero tolerance laws for numerous offenses, some well beyond weapons. In most cases, students found violating a zero tolerance law face mandatory suspension or expulsion (Killingbeck, 2001). Although this might be appropriate in some of the most serious cases, zero tolerance laws have been found to disproportionately impact students of color who have not perpetrated any act of violence. Giroux (2009) explained that today's schools, especially those populated largely by poor and minority youth, "are largely viewed as either testing centers where young people are simply bored into passivity or submission, or they are modeled after prisons . . . in short, if you are a poor black, brown or white kid, you are not considered a student or a productive citizen, but a potential criminal."

In both secondary schools and colleges, the moral panic about extreme forms of violence often leads people to fear the wrong things. That is, while the chance of being shot in a school on a college campus is fairly low, the chance that someone's property will be stolen or they will become the victim of an abusive relationship is much greater. If media attention, and school or campus policy, focuses exclusively on the worst case scenario, they might be doing students (and staff) a tremendous disservice. By far, the most common campus crime year after year is burglary. Almost all school or campus shooters were "insiders," or persons who belonged on the grounds. Yet many school districts and some colleges responded to fear of intruders by investing in ID badges or other forms of identification for students and staff. This might not be a tremendously costly measure, but it is also may not be useful. A more useful response is for a school to develop an emergency management and communication plan and to host awareness events and trainings so students and staff can identify real threats and are equipped to respond, if necessary. Growing numbers of students have also been arrested and processed through the criminal justice system over school-related incidents. Tremendous attention is now paid to preventing weapons and violence in schools, while the most frequent disciplinary matters occurring in most schools continue to be tardiness, class absences, disrespect, and noncompliance. Social scientists have suggested that the unbalanced focus on preventing violence in schools is an exaggerated response to unrealistic fears regarding school shootings (Aronson, 2000; Giroux, 2009; Killingbeck, 2001; Kohn, 2004; Lindle, 2008).

Dominator Responses

The dominator paradigm makes it seem as though the only options for preventing atrocities involve "more": more police, more laws, more prisons, more repression. Social Psychologist Elliot Aronson (2000) called these responses "pump handle interventions," in that they sound good but do not address the root cause of social violence. The adoption of school security technology has the unintended effect of augmenting or even exacerbating fear (Reddy et al., 2001). Fear often drives people into rash decisions and wrongheaded policies that may exacerbate conditions and which certainly offer unintended consequences (Kohn, 2004). For example, the American Civil Liberties Union (ACLU) expressed alarm that emerging policies against bullying showed a trend moving from remedies and prevention to active anticipation and possible entrapment (Snook, 2002). "These policies appear to be common sense, pragmatic responses, but are predicated on the assumption that violence can be stamped out one individual perpetrator at a time by a generic set of punishments" (Lindle, 2008, p. 33). Ayers, Dohrn, and Ayers (2001) summed it up nicely, explaining that "as schools become more militarized, they become less safe, in large part because the first casualty is the central, critical relationship between teacher and student, a relationship that is now being damaged or broken in favor of tough-sounding, impersonal, uniform, procedures" (p. xii).

Researchers have also documented consistent overrepresentations of low income and minority students among those expelled and suspended from school under zero tolerance policies. Under the tough antiviolence policies imposed in most school districts in the wake of the Columbine; Pearl, Mississippi; and Paducah, Kentucky episodes, African American and Latino students have borne the brunt of suspensions, expulsions, criminal prosecutions, and other punishments over school-related threats of violence. This is despite the fact that the perpetrators of the vast majority of multiple-victim school shootings have been white middle-class students (Giroux, 2009).

More Misplaced Fear

At the same time that we have gone completely berserk in our paranoia about school violence, we have also gone batty trying to prevent student drug use. One of the most widely touted, yet again, ineffective, ways to allegedly deter student drug use is to conduct school-based drug testing. The most controversial practice some schools have employed is to strip-search students accused or even suspected of having illegal drugs. Although there are numerous disturbing examples of school-based strip searches, perhaps the most upsetting involved a teenager who was suspected of "crotching" drugs—meaning he was thought to have stuffed drugs into the crotch of his pants to hide them while at school. This allegation was made by a teacher's aide, who thought the young man's genitals appeared larger than normal. The aide then coupled that observation with rumors she had heard that the student was involved in drug use and maybe sales. She passed that nugget of information around, and the school determined they should search the boy. Given that he was a minor, his mother was called. She requested that school official's wait until she could arrive before they searched her son, but they did it anyway. He was first patted down, then made to strip to his underwear and patted down again. He even had to hold out his underwear so a school official could see nothing was in there but what was supposed to be. No drugs were found, but when the young man and his mother sought legal recourse for what they believed was an unconstitutional search, the court deemed it reasonable and justifiable (Finley & Finley, 2004). Thankfully, the Supreme Court recently declared a strip search of a student to be unconstitutional, although it is unclear whether that decision will extend to strip searches conducted for other contraband or under different circumstances.

School-Based Drug Testing

Drug testing is another intervention that will supposedly deter young people from using drugs. Most often used with athletes (although after a 2002 Supreme Court decision, drug testing is now considered constitutional for all students involved in extracurricular activities), the idea is that the threat of failing a test and hence not being able to participate will give students a way to say "no" to drug pushers. The Bush administration even pushed for broader use of drug testing, offering grants to schools to establish random testing for their entire student bodies. An estimated 18 percent of the nation's school districts use some form of school-based drug testing (Finley, 2006). Mike Males (2004) commented on the faulty assumptions on which drug testing is based:

> Nothing enrages Office of National Drug Control Policy zealots—especially its current director, John Walters—like a teenager who smokes marijuana and doesn't suffer. Unfortunately for Walters, teens who smoke pot moderately and don't flunk out, disown parents, become heroin junkies, and overdose behind dumpsters comprise the vast majority of youthful drug users. Of the 100 million Americans who first tried marijuana as adolescents, 97 million-plus never gatewayed into dope fiends—or even regular pot smokers. Since most teenage marijuana users aren't hurting themselves, ONDCP's obsession is finding ways for government to harm them—by arrest, school expulsion, college loan bans, needless addiction treatment, ads branding them baby killers and terrorist accomplices...and now, mandatory drug testing.

The largest study of the effectiveness of student drug testing, published in 2003, included 76,000 students across the nation and compared those in schools with testing with those that did not have it (Kern, et al., 2006). Rates of student drug use were essentially the same, regardless of whether the school tested students. As Males (1999) noted, "the teenage drug crisis is a myth. It was concocted and maintained for political convenience" (p. 106). Further, the reality is that adults use more drugs, and more dangerous amounts of them, than do young people. Likewise, it is adults who perpetrate the majority of acts of interpersonal violence, and when it comes to institutional and structural violence, this is the sole domain of adults. Teens are easy scapegoats who often lack any voice (Males, 1999).

Fear This

Drug Abuse Resistance Education (D.A.R.E.) is one widely popular fear-based program. Its popularity, however, cannot be traced to its effectiveness. That is because numerous research studies have not found that students who completed the D.A.R.E. program are less interested or less likely to use drugs. On the contrary, some studies have even found D.A.R.E. graduates were more likely to engage in illicit drug use (Cox, 2008). The D.A.R.E. program is currently cited as ineffective by the U.S. Department of Education (DOE), the U.S. Surgeon General, the U.S. General Accountability Office, and is banned from receiving federal funding by the DOE (Shalala, 2001).

Experts say D.A.R.E's failure to deter drug use can be traced to numerous factors, including the programs length and the fact that once it ends, students may receive no other drug education. However, the primary reason D.A.R.E has failed, according to many experts, is that it is fear-based. Students are repeatedly reminded to be scared of drugs and drug "pushers," and are taught to vigorously resist peers who try to coerce them to use drugs. The problem is that students see through this message. They often know people who use drugs recreationally and are not the societal dropouts the program depicts. Thus, the program promotes harmful stereotypes. They also know the program exaggerates the consequences of some types of drug use, and thus begin distrusting all drug information that is presented. Further, youth are savvy enough to see the contradictions when they are told drugs are bad but high-powered stimulants like Ritalin are doled out at the school nurse's office. As my husband and I wrote in a previous book, "Teens see the hypocrisy of adults (especially those in authority positions who advocate harsh punishments for small-time drug offenders when they themselves were once small-time drug offenders lucky enough to avoid sanction (Presidents Clinton and Bush II, for example)" (Finley & Finley, 2004, p. 13). Faced with growing criticism, D.A.R.E. officials announced the program was being revamped in 2001. The new program uses a social norms approach, focusing on altering students' perception of how many students use drugs. This is in contrast to the previous "Just say No" approach.

Young people do indeed experience peer pressure, but not generally in the form of the aggressive "pusher" to whom they must loudly and firmly "just say no." As one class of high school students once told me, if they had a "stash" they might share it, but they have no interest in demanding that someone take their stuff. Rather, peer pressure is much subtler, and D.A.R.E. fails to prepare students to understand and resist those subtler messages. Students are most likely to try drugs, and continue using them, as a way to fit in. When they believe their peers are using drugs, or when they see them doing so, young people may feel as though joining in will help them be accepted. Further, D.A.R.E. does not address the risk factors that make young people more likely to use drugs. These are social issues like poverty, lack of parental involvement, and a failing education system. D.A.R.E. is focused solely at the individual level, rather than connecting to the broader sociological issues that are relevant.

In sum, these so-called prevention efforts negatively impact the school climate. "A negative school climate shows students the expectations the faculty have for them. If all that students see is that administrators feel they are drugged out losers or gun-wielding misfits, students may simply meet that expectation" (Finley & Finley, 2004, p. 208). Elliot Aronson (2000) explained, "A school that ignores the values of empathy, tolerance and compassion—or worse still, pays lip service to these values while doing nothing concrete and effective to promote these values—creates an atmosphere that is not only unpleasant for the 'losers,' but one that short changes the 'winners' as well" (p. 70). Research has shown that the best deterrent to school violence is a supportive teacher (Diguilio, 2001).

Painting an image of out-of-control youthful offenders helps divert attention away from some of society's bigger problems. Mike Males has repeatedly noted the "bigoted vendetta against youth" that is waged by news media and other institutions. Stories cover endless teen crises, sending the message that teens are out of control, and thus we need to crack down, and do it hard (Males, 2006).

Scared Straight

Like traditional models of policing and punishment, prevention programs are often dominator-modeled. Like the criminal justice system and the courts, they are based on fear and domination (Noguera, 1996). Many are initiated by law enforcement. Many times, law-enforcement-based prevention programming takes a "scared straight" approach. Young people hear horrific stories of crime, violence, and the awful life in jail from inmates or ex-felons, with the idea that listening to how bad their lives were will deter youth from involvement in crime. This approach is popular despite research that shows that not only is scared straight ineffective, it may actually be detrimental to kids' health (Shalala, 2001).

Scared Straight originated in New Jersey in the 1970s, when inmates serving life sentences began a program intended to scare at-risk or delinquent youth as a means of deterring them from future involvement in crime. It featured aggressive, detailed presentations by inmates to juveniles while they visited the prison. Inmates told about the most horrific elements of life in prison, including stories of murder and rape that may or may not have been true (Finckenauer, 1982). The idea caught on after a 1979 television documentary showed that 94 percent of the delinquents who attended Scared Straight remained law-abiding 3 years later (Finckenauer, 1982). Media and politicians sang the praises of this "get tough" style of prevention, and the program was soon replicated in more than 30 locations across the United States. Petrosino, Turpin-Petrosino, and Buehler (2003) explained why these programs are so popular: "they fit with common notions by some on how to prevent or reduce crime (by "getting tough"), they are very inexpensive (a Maryland program was estimated to cost less than U.S. $1 per participant), and they provide one way for incarcerated offenders to contribute productively to society by preventing youngsters from following down the same path" (p. 43).

More extensive research, however, including randomized trials over a 25-year span and involving almost 1,000 participants, has not found that Scared Straight programs alone prevent crime. In fact, experimental research has found that these programs may actually increase the likelihood that participants will commit another delinquent offense (Petrosino et al., 2003). In 2000, Petrosino, Turpin-Petrosino, and Finckenauer reported on a systematic review of Scared Straight and similar interventions. They found that Scared Straight and like interventions generally *increased* crime between 1 percent and 28 percent when compared with a no-treatment control group. Other reviews have addressed deterrence-based prevention programs and have not found them to be successful, either (Lipsey 1992; Lundman 1993; Sherman et al., 1997). In fact, the University of Maryland's well-publicized review of more than 500 crime prevention evaluations listed Scared Straight as one program that does not work (Sherman et al., 1997).

Despite the evidence, fear-based prevention programs remain popular. For example, a program in Carson City, Nevada, brings juvenile delinquents on a tour of an adult Nevada state prison (Scripps, 1999). One youngster claimed that the part of the tour that made the most impact on him was "all the inmates calling us for sex and fighting for our belongings" (Scripps, 1999). In 2001, a group of guards—apparently without the knowledge of administrators—strip-searched Washington, DC, students during their tours of a local jail under the guise that they were using "a sound strategy to turn around the lives of wayward kids." They cited the prior "success" of Scared Straight (Blum & Woodlee, 2001). In fact, Scared Straight and similar fear-based approaches have been exported to other countries, including Australia, the United Kingdom, Germany, and Norway (Petrosino et al., 2003).

Addressing Youth Gangs

Experts say there are some 21,500 gangs in the United States, with more than 731,000 members (Triplett, 2004). Just as gangs engage in turf wars, federal, state, and local entities charged with reducing gang violence and preventing gang involvement often battle over turf as well (Triplett, 2004). Law enforcement battle for resources and credit in a war on gangs. The focus is generally on identifying, arresting, and prosecuting members, with the hopes that this will deter future involvement and membership. Many times, "gang databases" include any young people of color.

Criminological interventions, when they cause harm, are not only toxic to the participants but also they result in an increased misery to ordinary citizens, which comes from the "extra" criminal victimization created as compared with just doing nothing at all (Petrosino et al., 2003). That is, the approach we are currently using is not only ineffective, but damaging to our society.

One of the most important things we must change in order to reduce or eliminate youth violence (and structural violence, too) is to stop demonizing young people. As Males (1996) explained, we have made a whole generation of youth our scapegoats for too many social ills. Instead of seeing young people as dangerous or silly, we can see them as powerful and unique change-makers (Baumgardner & Richards, 2005).

A Philosophical Shift to Peacemaking

Peacemaking criminology, which was presented in chapter 3, can be utilized to create prevention programs that are humane and effective. Many have asserted that support for a real minimum wage and a full employment bill, coupled with nationalized health care and ending the prohibition on drugs, would help reduce both teen and adult criminality.

A philosophical shift toward a more peacemaking perspective can perhaps be seen in the movement toward a public health approach to youth-violence prevention. The Centers for Disease Control (CDC) has been a leader in seeing violence as predictable—as patterned and interrelated—and thus as preventable. CDC's Division of Violence Prevention (DVP) collects and analyzes data to develop strategies and programs. DVP uses a multidisciplinary approach to identify the factors associated with violence and to create, disseminate, and support prevention initiatives. Thus it integrates psychology to examine individual factors with sociological views to see trends and the impact of violence on society at-large. DVP's focus is primary prevention; that is, preventing violence before it occurs. The primary emphasis focuses on reducing the factors that put people at risk while increasing the factors that protect people from becoming perpetrators of violence (Hammond, Haegerich, & Saul, 2009). Caution must be taken, however, to ensure that the public health approach does not reinforce the same paranoia and stereotypes of dangerous, out of control youth, but instead utilizes all community resources to create more livable communities.

The Center for Disease Control (CDC) and the *American Psychologist* have published reports on "best practices" for Youth Violence Prevention (YVP) Programs. Critical components of school-based YVP programs identified in the reports include interactive student participation; the fostering of relationships between students, staff, and families; rewards for positive behaviors; and total school involvement. Prevention programs designed specifically for elementary school children should also include largely group activities; active participation in story-based or narrative learning; opportunities to practice negotiation skills with peers and authority figures; and humor and playfulness.

Prevention programs should encourage youth involvement and provide youth a voice. As Hernandez (1998) explained, "Violence is not something you stop by preaching. Violence disappears as children experience success and discipline and begin believing in their own possibilities" (p. 128). Jack Calhoun, former Executive Director of the National Crime Prevention Council, identified five key factors he believed can help youth to be resilient through difficult times. These include (a) a locus of control: " youth do not feel like pawns in the hands of fate. Young people must develop goals and recognize that their success or failure is in their own hands;" (b) a skill: those who feel confident about their abilities also tend to feel more secure; (c) an adult who is always present and supportive; (d) optimism: "whether defined in a secular way ("I have hope for the future.") or theologically ("I am held in His hand."), youth must feel that the future is bright"; and (e) altruism: helping others allows youth to see that we are all interconnected and have something of value to contribute to others (Prevention Institute, 2006, p. 9).

Innovative Programs

The Prevention Institute (2006) has identified several large community coalitions that have shown great promise in creating a coordinated, multifaceted approach to violence prevention. Blueprint for a Safer Philadelphia involved a coalition of over 100 elected officials and community organizations and experts. It also included several focus groups of residents for input. Leadership and initial funding came from a State Representative, Dwight Evans, who was inspired by public health efforts in Boston and the book *Murder is no Accident*. Evans brought in Dr. Deborah Prothrow-Stith, the book's author, to help the community begin to see violence as a public health issue. The public health approach helped the community to focus on systematic efforts and to see that violence is preventable. Campaigns and activities are broad in scope, focusing on the most violent neighborhoods, domestic and dating violence, sexual violence, and child abuse and neglect. Philadelphia area universities, including Drexel University, Temple University, and the University of Pennsylvania, are involved in the process and are helping ensure the programs are evaluated. Mee Productions, a community media firm focused on social marketing to youth of color and their families, has helped to design the outreach. The city's largest radio stations are involved in disseminating information about events and strategies. This broad community/government partnership is helpful in ensuring that plans are implemented, a broad array of resources and commitments are ensured, and the program is sustainable for the long term. Importantly, it sees youth as a community asset that must be nurtured. Alameda County, California, which includes the high-crime city of Oakland, has developed a similar program.

The National Crime Prevention Council has also helped six city governments (Boston, Fort Worth, Denver, New York, Hartford, and San Diego) create unified plans to reduce violence. Each city used a range of law enforcement and community-based programs to dramatically reduce crime. All programs involved collaborative partnerships and the use of targeted policy strategies, and each city not also addressed crime but other quality of life concerns as well. The goal was to get at the root causes of crime by bringing together formal and informal leaders to identify the main problems, assess community assets and resources, form coalitions and partnerships, and establish priorities.

The CDC recently created a new national initiative called Urban Networks to Increase Thriving Youth (UNITY). UNITY's aim is to maximize existing government and community resources for the long-term sustainability of youth-violence prevention. The idea is for cities to share information and effective strategies that bring together young people, violence prevention advocates, and leaders in order to shape urban youth violence-prevention strategies they can then take back to their cities. UNITY will provide tools, training, and technical assistance to help cities be more effective in preventing youth violence. Initially, UNITY will focus largely on the 45 largest cities in the country, but will make its tools and information available more broadly. Success in these cities will then serve as a model that can be used elsewhere. UNITY's lead partners are Prevention Institute, Harvard School of Public Health, and the UCLA Southern California Injury Prevention Research Center.

Barrios Unidos (BU) in Santa Cruz, California, has developed a program that seeks to assist struggling youth and promote unity among families and neighbors through community building efforts. It has been in operation for 25 years. BU builds community and social cohesion by restoring cultural traditions and by actively working to create interracial alliances and coalitions. Community self-reliance, economic development, and nonviolent action for social change are three important elements. BU, in collaboration with the Santa Cruz County Office of Education, helped develop an alternative high school called Cesar E. Chavez School for Social Change. BU also runs a silk-screening business that provides jobs for youth from local communities. BU has been noted for its gang prevention work, but prefers to emphasize that it is focused on all youth.

Noguera (1996) provided several examples of effective youth-violence prevention programs. One of these is for schools and communities to bridge the gap that normally separates them. He cited the example of a school in Oakland, California, a community suffering from many social problems including high rates of juvenile violence. Frustrated that the traditional strategies were not working, educators got creative. The school began to offer additional meals, clothing, and recreational activities so that young people could feel a sense of security and stability. Community groups began to use the school at night and on weekends. These changes transformed the school culture and was a starting point for community change toward peace.

In the Miami area, Seed 305 is a 12-week program for youth who want to take on leadership roles in their communities. Using the Freireian concept of popular education, weekly sessions focus on understanding societal issues like poverty, racism, sexism, homophobia, and much more. It helps young people find their voice and motivates them to take action. Heal the Streets is an Oakland, California, youth-led violence-prevention effort. They host community meetings called "Solution Salons" in which youth unite with community members and policymakers to brainstorm violence-prevention efforts. Ten youth ages 15 to 17 have received 10-month fellowships with Heal the Streets. During the fellowship, teens receive leadership training and are tasked with first identifying and then addressing the root causes of violence in the community (Flynn, 2010).

Arts-Based Programs

Arts-based programs can be a tremendous way to organize youth for self-expression, healing, and leadership toward a more peaceful world. One example is City at Peace, an intensive, year-long afterschool leadership program in Santa Barbara, California, combining training in nonviolent conflict resolution and cross-cultural understanding with original theater. City at Peace utilizes the performing arts to bring together young people from diverse backgrounds to explore the issues affecting them and discover nonviolent resolutions to their conflicts. By creating and performing musical theater pieces, drawn from their lives, these teens not only change their own behavior but educate their families, their peers, and their community. This gives them a powerful voice of hope for the future. City at Peace is free to all youth ages 13 to 19.

Urban Improv (UI) is a school-based program that has operated in the Boston Public Schools for 14 years. UI utilizes structured theater improvisation to assist youth with making difficult decisions, controlling their impulses, and resolving nonviolently. An evaluation of UI found increased prosocial behaviors. UI helped prevent new aggression and decreased hyperactivity among participants.

Branch Out is an arts-based program created by Molly Foote, which focuses on developing interpersonal empathy and open communications among participants. It has been used primarily in the northwest portion of the United States and can be integrated into whole-class curricula as well as large and small group programs. Creative activities help students learn personal empowerment, social skills, career awareness, diversity appreciation, and community building. Counselors facilitate discussion during and after the activities and can add role playing or other creative activity to enhance students' understanding.

Another example is Elijah's Kite, a children's opera that addresses bullying. One evaluation of 104 fourth- and fifth-grade students showed significant increases in knowledge about bullying and reductions in self-reported victimization among those who viewed the opera. The Richmond Youth Peace Project (RYPP) is a violence-prevention initiative that utilizes youth as leaders and educators, rather than simply recipients. The RYPP is focused on artistic and creative modes of expression as a way of giving voice to the youth, who use spoken-word poetry, drumming, dance, rap, and speech to describe the conditions of their lives and to envision a more peaceful future (Scharf & Bagat, 2007).

Innovative Gang Prevention

There are many exemplary gang-prevention programs that utilize partnership or peacemaking structures and methods. The Tariq Khamisa Foundation (TKF; see www.tfk.org.) is a school-based program designed to teach young people about the realities of gangs, violence, and revenge. It empowers kids by teaching them peace. Azim Khamisa founded TKF after his 20-year-old son Tariq was killed in 1995 by a 14-year-old gang member. Curricula emphasizes that violence hurts everyone and actions have consequences. It also stresses that young people can make good, nonviolent choices and can work toward understanding social ills and forgiveness instead of revenge. The program is built on the foundation that everyone deserves to be loved.

Gang Peace (http://web.mit.edu/groove/www/chapter/gangpeace. html) is a Boston-based program that Rodney Dailey has operated since 1989. Dailey has worked with some of the most troubled youth and focuses on showing these young people their worth and redirecting them to education and career-oriented activities. Gang Peace has been credited with helping reduce the city's gang violence. His group has set up summer job programs, support groups, a small recording studio for neighborhood rap groups, a mentoring program, and summer concerts. Gang Peace also offers 32 hours of college courses through a computer hookup with Atlantic Union College in Boston. Nearly 600 local youths ranging from 8 to 23 years of age participate in Gang Peace programs. Gang members are not pressured to leave gangs but are encouraged to develop skills and self-esteem. "Gang Peace recognizes that young men will affiliate with each other, but that those affiliations can be turned toward positive purposes," said Ted Landsmark, who runs the city's Safe Neighborhoods program, which has given two small grants to Mr. Dailey's group. "They have worked to get gang members to recognize that some of the skills used in negative ways to deal drugs or other contraband can be used just as effectively within a legitimate business context" ("Offering Boston's gangs", 1992).

G.R.E.A.T

The Gang Resistance Education and Training (G.R.E.A.T) program is a school-based program designed to prevent youth violence and delinquency, in particular, membership in gangs. Similar to D.A.R.E, trained law enforcement officers provide instruction in public school classrooms. They also work with community youth organizations like the Boys & Girls Clubs of America and the National Association of Police Athletic Leagues. Not only does this help educate young people, but these collaborations build important community relationships. Since it was created 1991, G.R.E.A.T. has certified over 10,000 law enforcement officers as instructors. More than 5 million students have graduated from the G.R.E.A.T. program.

The G.R.E.A.T. programs include a 13-session middle school curriculum, an elementary school curriculum, a summer program, and training for families. Unlike D.A.R.E., lessons focus on providing life skills to students to help them avoid using delinquent behavior and violence to solve problems. The G.R.E.A.T. program offers a continuum of components for students and their families. Specifically, the elementary program, which is six 30–45 minute lessons, focuses on building positive bonds between students and law enforcement. Lessons cover bullying; discussing the role of offenders, victims, and bystanders; how to communicate; how to cool down when you feel angry; appreciating our differences; and how to identify adults who can help when needed. It is typically implemented in fourth or fifth grades. The middle school program is designed for sixth or seventh graders and focuses more specifically on gang prevention. Students learn facts and fiction about gangs and violence and what they can do to help. They also discuss verbal and nonverbal communication, empathy, resisting peer pressure, and other social skills. The summer program is flexible but is really intended to help reduce the boredom that leads many youth to trouble when they are out of school. Programs might take field trips and participate in other outdoor activities or games in addition to receiving information about gangs, violence, and positive conflict resolution. There are six sessions in the family program, which is designed to help parents and guardians identify warning signs of youth crime and violence and resist participation in gangs or other deviant or criminal behavior.

All instructors are sworn law enforcement officers who receive additional training on the G.R.E.A.T. curriculum at one of four regional training centers.

The G.R.E.A.T. program (www.great-online.org) was developed in 1991 by the U.S. Bureau of Alcohol, Tobacco, Firearms and Explosives (ATF) and the Phoenix Police Department (PPD). It was originally an eight-lesson middle school curriculum, but in early 1992, the Federal Law Enforcement Training Center (FLETC) joined the ATF and PPD to expand the program. The first G.R.E.A.T. officer training was held in 1992, and by 1998, the La Crosse, Wisconsin, Police Department; the Orange County, Florida Sheriff's Office; the Philadelphia, Pennsylvania Police Department; and the Portland, Oregon Police Bureau were providing assistance.

A 5-year longitudinal evaluation of the program was launched in 1995. Results showed that students who completed the training had lower levels of victimization, more negative views about gangs, and more favorable attitudes about police. Researchers also found a reduction in risk-seeking behaviors and increased association with peers involved in prosocial activities.

The program underwent an extensive program and curriculum review in 1999–2000. The review led to the addition of lessons, from 8 to 13, and included more active learning. In 2001, the new curriculum was piloted in 14 cities nationwide and implemented nationally beginning in 2003.

Community Gang Prevention

Hernandez (1998) offered eight steps to a gang-free community. I believe these steps, described below, are consistent with a peacemaking perspective.

1. The community affirms all its children, even the ones with troubles.
2. Involve the community so that everyone knows as much as possible about what is going on with its young people, including the statistics on gangs, juvenile delinquency, reading levels, mental illness, poverty, etc. "Once a community accustoms itself to hearing these statistics regularly, then it becomes aware of its children in the same manner that it is aware of the record of its local sports franchise . . . keeping track of our 'bad children' makes them visible and real to us as children. And gathering this information as a community forces us to think of ourselves as people with a common cause—a family, a clan, a village, or one big company—as a group of people who must put their heads together and figure out what to do with all its children" (p. 143).
3. Creating and supporting transformative schools—these schools affirm the good work of bad kids when it occurs and allow them opportunity to succeed. They have small student-to-teacher ratios, ties to the community for internships, weekly community support groups, support efforts for parents, field trips to colleges, specialists to work with learning disabilities.
4. View parents as partners, not patients.
5. Support transitions between institutions, including to different educational levels and support for those on probation.
6. Identify those with disabilities or in need of special help.
7. Help children have something to care about and take pride in— sports, arts, recreational activities.
8. Promote recovery from addictions.

Addressing School Violence

Scholars have noted that extreme acts of school violence have been perpetrated almost exclusively by young men. Some have called it a masculinity crisis (Katz & Jhally, 2000; Seaton, 2000; Watts & Erevelle, 2004). This perspective argues that communities have failed young men, who are too often socialized to be aggressive and controlling (Seaton, 2000; Watts & Erevelle, 2004). Families, educators, and communities frequently allow boys to behave more forcefully, interpreting physical interactions among males as normal (Kivel, 1999; Solomon, 2006; Watts & Erevelle, 2004).

Violence prevention efforts both in and out schools should address gender roles and expectations. Peace education can be a great vehicle to do so, as it shows young men that they are not being accused or attacked but solicited as part of a solution to ending violence. In addition, teachers can be powerful influences on lowering the potential for violence if they are perceived as personally connected and caring about students (Astor, Vargas, Pitner, & Meyer, 1999; Watts & Erevelle, 2004). The more impersonal the school culture, the more likely the risk and occurrence of school violence (Aronson, 2001).

Student voice can be a powerful way to reduce school-based violence (Quaglia, 2000). Schools that recognize collective student achievement and whole-school betterment, as opposed to competitive rewards, build student pride (Bey & Turner, 1995; DiGiulio, 1999, 2001; Johnson & Johnson, 2005; Lintott, 2004). School support mechanisms should extend beyond school walls and also beyond the expertise of school personnel to tap into community resources (Batavick, 1997; Bowen & Bowen, 1999; Deutsch, 1993). "The answer to issues of school security and safety lies in the development of community. Community development is not a policy end, but a political process. Community development is not solely a school process; it requires development of social capital among neighborhoods and throughout the ecological system surrounding students to end the fear of violence and abuse in school" (Lindle, 2008, p. 39).

Some Cool Resources for Youth

There are some great Web-based resources to empower young people. My favorite is Do Something (www.dosomething.org), a wealth of information about peace, justice, human rights, the environment, and more. Do Something urges teenagers to learn more so that they can be active participants in the world. It empowers youth to take action in a fun and interactive way. It provides a host of ideas for action that range from something as simple as sending an e-mail, to dedicating your time and energy into larger projects of your choice. Young people can even create their own Do Something Club in their schools or communities. Groups complete a simple online application. This organization allows students the flexibility to fix the problems that they see in and outside of a school environment with their own creativity. Do Something even gives grant money to student projects. Do Something.org offers students a way to fulfill Mahatma Gandhi's famous quote, "Be the change that you want to see in the world."

Youth Noise (www.youthnoise.com) also offers young people a wealth of information about a variety of topics, from animal rights to war and peace. One tab on the Web site is focused on PlayCity, an online community for those using sports to promote social change. The site features blogs and discussion boards for teens to communicate with one another, and links for scholarships and awards. Similarly, the Free Child Project (www.freechild.org) and What Kids Can Do provide information, communication tools, scholarship opportunities, and more.

Concluding Thoughts

As was noted throughout this chapter, communities must be equipped to provide needed resources and services to residents, both young and old, in order to prevent violence. However, too often those services are inadequate. One reason is that many are not focused on partnership-based peacemaking. They are often dominator-modeled and suffer the same lack of creativity I have identified in other chapters. But the efforts to assess best practices and to use our creativity to craft unique prevention programs is beginning to pay off, as the examples at the end of the chapter demonstrate.

The next chapter addresses how nonprofits, nongovernmental organizations, and social services can be dominator-modeled and offers some promising ways to shift to more partnership structures, methods, and content.

5

Nonprofits/NGOs, Social Services, and Peace Education

Everybody looks so ill at ease
so distrustful, so displeased.
Running down the table,
I see a borderline.

Borderlines
—Joni Mitchell

$\mathbf{A}$s the story that opened the Preface to this book shows, my experience has been that nonprofits and social services do not generally see their work as part of a movement for peace. Their failure to see this connection results in organizations and services that often reproduce the militarism and domination we have examined in criminal justice and prevention programs. These bureaucratic social services often create, as Joni Mitchell noted, "a borderline" between the helpers and the helped. A partnership model for social services and NGOs would instead be inclusive and would utilize all creative voices to assist those in need.

Building a Peaceful Society, pages 75–91
Copyright © 2011 by Information Age Publishing

This chapter begins by examining some of the concerns about nonprofits, nongovernmental organizations (NGOs), and social services. It then provides some suggestions and unique examples that are more aligned with peacemaking principles and practices. It is through our creative visioning that we will begin to see this work as peace education. Instead of replicating the domination that occurs daily in the lives of people seeking help from social services, nonprofits, and NGOs, we can work collectively to serve and unite.

Scope of Nonprofit Industry

An estimated 2 million nonprofits or NGOs operate in the United States alone. Most were formed in the last 30 years. By 2004, the combined annual expenditures of all the not-for-profit organizations that were required to file Form 990 with the U.S. Internal Revenue Service had grown to nearly $1 trillion, about half what the federal government spends each year for everything except defense. The nonprofit sector is a significant employer, offering jobs to approximately 12 million people in 2001. Roughly 85 percent of this work is in health care, largely at hospitals and nursing homes or in social services like child care, job training, and education. If volunteer time were added, nonprofits would represent over 10 percent of all U.S. employment. It is likely that these statistics underreport the size of America's nonprofit sector, because they often don't include large religious organizations, which have a distinct tax status, nor do they include state universities and colleges, which are technically government entities but now often register as nonprofits. The rapid growth of NGOs is true outside of the United States as well. Although virtually none existed before the fall of communism, today there are at least 65,000 NGOs in Russia. Approximately 240 NGOs are created in Kenya each year (Goodhand, 2006).

Can There Be Too Many?

One concern is that, in some places, there is a glut of NGOs. Instead of helping, these NGOs may compete with one another and perhaps undermine efforts by the state to assist the people. Collier (2010) noted, "Even before the earthquake, NGOs provided most of Haiti's health care and education, yet they have been accountable neither to users nor funders . . . without oversight or competition from the public sector, the NGOs become inconsistent in performance. NGO workers are largely dedicated and serious, but individual dedication does not guarantee organizational quality, and the groups vary in ability and cost-effectiveness." Goodhand (2006) and Anderson (1999), among others, have noted that NGOs—charged with helping reduce conflict—often exacerbate it.

The title *nongovernmental organization* was first used by the United Nations. It was intended to describe groups that were distanced from official governmental entities that did things governments could not or would not do. This is not exactly the case today. In many ways, NGOs have come to do the work that governments are supposed to be doing (Alexander, 2007).

Internationally, a growing portion of government-sponsored emergency relief, aid, and development spending is done through NGOs. Between 1990 and 1994, the proportion of the EU's relief aid that was channeled through NGOs increased 20 percent, from 47 percent to 67 percent. For instance, most of the UN's World Food Programme food delivered in Albanian refugee camps has been handed out by NGOs. NGOs now distribute more funds than does the World Bank. World Vision U.S., a Christian relief fund, received $55 million in funding from the U. S government, while Medecins Sans Frontieres (MSF) gets 46 percent of its funding from government sources. Governments may be more willing to pay NGOs to deliver humanitarian aid during conflicts than to do it themselves. In essence, "the principal reason for the recent boom in NGOs is...western governments finance them" (Sins of the Secular Missionaries, 2000). In essence, this makes them privatized versions of the government.

Criticisms of Nonprofits and NGOs

The growth of nonprofits has been critiqued by both the left and the right. The left fears that nonprofits have taken on duties and responsibilities that are intended to be coordinated and conducted by the government. Conservatives have expressed concern that too many nonprofits "gravitate through the years to agendas not only that their original donors never intended but that are unrepresentative of American society. And then they are immune to reform" (Alexander, 2007). Critics on both sides express concern that NGOs can easily become self-perpetuating. For example, some nonprofits are financed largely through endowments that allow them to operate in perpetuity. They are not accountable to shareholders, customers, or voters. Once the problem for which they were founded has been solved or at least minimized, they may identify new campaigns and new funds. Critics contend that NGOs should aim for their own abolition instead (Alexander, 2007).

Nonprofits get the bulk of their money either through donations; from government subsidies; or by charging fees like tuition, hospital bills, and AAA memberships. The Foundation Center estimates that the combined assets of grant-making bodies (in current dollars) grew from $30 billion in 1975 to $227 billion in 1995 and about $525 billion in 2005 (Alexander, 2007). The Gates Foundation is the largest, with about $29 billion even before Warren Buffett's $30 billion, multiyear pledge. The Ford Foundation is in second place with around $12 billion. All U.S. foundations combined (including corporate foundations) gave away $33.6 billion in 2005, more than double in real terms what they gave only a decade earlier.

Nonprofit Industrial Complex

Other critics have likened nonprofits to the military and prison industrial complexes. The nonprofit industrial complex (NPIC) has been defined as "a set of symbiotic relationships that link political and financial technologies of state and owning class control with surveillance over public political ideology, including and especially emergent progressive and leftist social movements" (Rodriguez, 2007, p. 8). The NPIC

> manages and controls dissent by incorporating it into the state apparatus, functioning as a 'shadow state' constituted by a network of institutions that do much of what government agencies are supposed to do with tax money in the areas of education and social services. The NPIC functions as an alibi that allows government to make war, expand punishment, and proliferate market economies under the veil of partnership between the public and private sectors. (D. Smith, 2007, p. 9)

The "shadow state" is

> The contemporary rise of the voluntary sector that is involved in direct social services previously provided by wholly public New Deal/Great Society agencies. Legislatures and executive branches transformed bureaucracies basically into policing bodies, whose role became to oversee service provision rather than to provide it themselves. This abandonment provoked a response among organizations that advocated on behalf of certain categories of state clients: the elderly, mothers, children, and so forth. It also encouraged the formation of new groups that, lacking an advocacy past, were designed solely to get contracts and the jobs that came with them. To do business with the state, the organizations had to be formally incorporated, so they became non-profits. Thus, for different reasons, non-profits stepped up to fill a service void. (Gilmore, 2007, p. 45)

As Milward and Provan (1993) observed, social services are increasingly co-produced by governments, nonprofits, and firms through contracting schemes and public/private partnerships. This hollowing of the state has accelerated in recent years. Since the passage of federal welfare reform legislation in 1996, diminished funding for direct cash assistance has been replaced by the Earned Income Tax Credit and an ever-growing sector of nonprofit service providers (Allard, 2009). According to Allard (2009), "the number of employment and human service nonprofits registering with the Internal Revenue Service (IRS) has increased by almost two-thirds since 1990 and revenues for that sector now total about $80 billion" (p. 4). Allard (2009) argued that "we effectively have privatized a substantial portion of the contemporary safety net" (p. 31).

Further, nonprofits that provide direct services have become highly professionalized. They have had to conform to public rules governing public money and have found that "being fiduciary agents in some ways trumps their principal desire to comfort and assist those abandoned to their care" (Gilmore, 2007, p. 45). The nonprofit world also has its own jargon and both formal as well as informal hierarchies. The issues nonprofits are paid to address have been narrowed to program-specific categories and remedies that make staff essentially technocrats. "The shadow state, then, is real but without significant political clout, forbidden by law to advocate for systemic change, and bound by public rules and non-profit charters to stick to its mission or get out of business and suffer legal consequences if it strays along the way" (Gilmore, 2007, pp. 45–46).

Bureaucratized Services

Some nonprofit agencies resemble corporations, even factories. They are bureaucratic and hierarchical. Further, as not-for-profit agencies that are often dependent on private-sector funding, many times service providers are constrained by the parameters these funders place on them. Funding sources might be conservative in nature and are often not looking for creative innovations but rather those things that have been "documented" as "best practices."

Radical, even semiradical, activism, which calls attention to broader systems of inequality, would most certainly not be encouraged by funders (Berns, 2004). As Rodriguez (2007) explained,

> Under current circumstances, organized dissent movements and organizations in the United States are often compelled to replicate the bureaucratic structures of the small business, large corporation, and state—creating centralized national officers, gathering political (and, at times, Hollywood) celebrities and luminaries onto boards of directors, and hiring 'professional activists' whose salaries depend largely on the effectiveness of professional grant writers. (p. 33)

The bureaucratization of nonprofits and social services negatively impacts those who are intended to receive the services. In 1996, Congress passed the Personal Responsibility and Work Opportunity Reconciliation Act (PWORA), which reduced subsidies, emphasized work requirements, and aimed to promote self-sufficiency (Jurik, 2005,). Traditional welfare programs have been dismantled; nonprofits and even corporations contract to offer social services to the poor. Advocates of these modifications emphasize individual initiative and responsibility and market-based measures as mechanisms for alleviating poverty (Jurik, Cavendar, & Cowgill, 2009; Quadagno, 1999). Crook (2001) found that residential service organizations with relatively low bureaucracy; indigenous participatory leadership; and personalized, concrete, and humane program approaches offered clients more positive experiences than other agency configurations. Traditional welfare agencies have been criticized for promoting discourses and practices that reinforce the dominance of white, masculine, and middle-class society (Jurik et al., 2009; Quadagno & Fobes, 1995; Rose 1995).

Rojas asked, "Are the cops in our heads and hearts?" That is, employees of these organizations come to internalize the institutional limitations. "One of the scariest manifestations of modern capitalism is the system's ability to co-opt experiences, practices, even culture, and to then re-create and repackage them within a careerist, profit-driven (even in 'non-profits'), and competitive logic. The non-profit system . . . supports the professionalization of activism rather than a model of everyday activism" (Rojas, 2007, p. 205). The culture expects and rewards short-term success. "They are not interested in funding the much slower work of base building, which takes years and years to do. Consequently, non-profits become short-term-goal oriented, even if they did not begin that way. Many also become focused on 'smoke and mirrors' organizing, in which you do something that looks good for a photo op but has no real power behind it" (Rojas, 2007, p. 205).

Some nonprofits or social services that are intended to help victims of violence in effect reproduce that violence through their structures, methods, and content. My experience working at a domestic violence center demonstrates how this happens. In presenting my thoughts about this issue, I have heard from others that many environmental organizations operate similarly. Sadly, I suspect this is true of other types of organizations as well. Baumgardner and Richards (2005) explained that conversations with young people working in nonprofits found them to often be disillusioned at their lack of voice and the "hidden hierarchies in a workplace that promotes egalitarianism" (p. 135). My colleagues and I have seen firsthand how persons seeking assistance at social service agencies are often treated like animals. They are verbally harassed and made to wait for long periods of time just to have a 5-minute conversation with a caseworker. They are often shuffled between entities, as few services are available in a one-stop format that would be easiest for those in need.

The Case Foundation noted that nonprofit work can be notoriously difficult to measure, hence success may appear elusive. Work environments may be frustrating, as employees tend to be overworked, underpaid, and lack the best resources to achieve their goals. The method we currently use to evaluate charities, through efficiency ratios, provides no information about the effectiveness of an individual charity and leads an organization to focus exclusively on the short term (at the cost of long-term planning) and develop extreme risk-averse preferences (which leaves them unwilling to take risks that could lead to innovations)

Some critics assert the problem is too many constraints on nonprofits. Pallotta (2008) reviewed the constraints the public expects from nonprofits, including the ban on paid advertising, inability to engage in political activity, and the substandard wages for nonprofit employees. Palotta (2008) argued,

> If we want the nonprofit sector to do without the successful tactics of the business sector—say, marketing—how can we expect the nonprofit sector to aspire to greatness? How will it ever grow, get results, and reach new supporters? Why, for instance, did the American Cancer Society spend only $1 million on anti-tobacco legislation in 1998, when, during that same year, the five largest cigarette manufacturers spent more than 6,000 times that amount in advertising and promotions? (in Irvin, 2009)

Others maintain the answer is opposite of what Pallotta (2008) suggests. That is, some radical activists maintain that true change cannot occur in this type of corporate atmosphere. Rather, grassroots activism is what is needed.

> New organizing models pose some important challenges to the non-profit system. First, they challenge the notion that hierarchy and centralization are required to do mass-based political organizing. In the current non-profit system, organizations, particularly those that have a scope extending beyond the local level, tend to be based on a hierarchical governance model, with an executive director, board of directors, and on down. People often argue that collective and horizontal decision-making structures are inefficient. And to the extent that they do work, many activists insist that they work only for local organizing projects or projects that are small in scope. (Rojas, 2007, p. 203)

Rojas noted that in Latin America, very large horizontal structures have created social change. These groups often hold large asambleas populares (popular assemblies) in which they use consensus to determine agendas and tactics. She cited the Zapatistas and the MGT in Argentina. Other examples include the movement of unemployed landless workers of Brazil (MST).

> Grounded in the underlying principle of direct collective power, these practices are used to avoid power cementing in certain people placed in representative roles. People gather locally, in their community or neighborhood, on a street corner or somewhere else public and easily accessible to discuss and reflect on issues that need to be decided. What seems like a facilitator's nightmare—a large, sometimes very large, group of people without a set agenda—becomes a space to practice how we want to live collectively...These models demonstrate that everyday life is political and that everyone can participate politically. Political work is not outside the struggle for subsistence or in an organization's office or center, but in life. (Rojas, 2007, p. 203)

Peace activists recognize that their issue not only can but must be political. However, nonprofits and NGOs are often prohibited from engaging in political activity. For instance, in the field of domestic violence work in the state of Florida, employees at certified agencies cannot engage in any political involvement or lobbying. The Florida Coalition Against Domestic Violence (FCADV) reserves the right to do any political lobbying needed and can even revoke the funding of centers that defy their regulations. Although surely this makes some sense in that a unified lobbying effort may be more effective than a hodge-podge one. I believe it also creates a situation whereby advocates are encouraged to see their efforts as work that ends only when they clock out. As I have written elsewhere, "I believe that because we are told we must not engage in any form of lobbying or political activity, the effect has been to divorce our daily work from the bigger social efforts to end domestic violence. Not only does this prevent advocates from getting involved to effect change, I believe it precludes many from attaining an in-depth knowledge of other social issues" (Finley, 2010, p. 61).

Peacemaking and Partnership-Based Nonprofits and NGOs

Despite these challenges, across the globe, nonprofit organizations and NGOs are helping call attention to critical social issues, providing needed services, and helping make social change. Nonprofits and NGOs can utilize peace education principles and practices in their work, and some already do. I will first provide examples from some groups with whom I am affiliated.

A nonprofit I work with called No More Tears, which helps provide assistance to victims of domestic violence and their children while also educating to prevent abuse, has developed peace education curricula to be delivered to children, youth, and college-aged populations. The materials focus not only on identifying the signs of abuse but also on the societal roots of oppression and the patriarchy that enable it. Programs use interactive methods to bring about awareness as well as to incite action. We also host educational events in the community and on college campuses, helping to coordinate activities for domestic violence awareness month, the International Day of Peace, Human Rights Day, and women's history month. In 2011, we will be helping sponsor the first College Bride's Walk, an educational event intended to commemorate the life of Gladys Ricar, who was killed in New York in 1999 by her jealous ex-boyfriend, who shot her on her wedding day while she posed for photographs. A good friend, Josie Ashton, was outraged by the community's response to the murder, as many blamed Gladys or otherwise asserted "she had it coming." Josie, with the permission of Gladys' family, walked in her wedding dress from the home where she was killed to the chapel where she was to be married as a way to call attention to the horror of domestic violence and to this specific case. She did not stop there, though. Josie was determined to raise awareness across the country, so she set off to walk from New York to Miami, where she lived. She mostly walked alone, through the elements, staying at women's shelters and in hotels. She even had to quit her job to do it. Today, Bride's Walks are held across the United States, but none bring together college students in the way that we are planning.

As a grassroots-style nonprofit, NMT receives no state or federal funding and thus is free to use its resources in the ways victim's need. We are creative in what we do for the victims we serve, always seeking to treat them as humans first. We personally interact with them so that they are not only helped, but treated with love and kindness. Although finding adequate funds is a perpetual challenge, we use the methods that are consistent with our mission. That is, we host small, informal and fun educational events, which raise funds at the same time. Further, as an all-volunteer entity, NMT consists of people who authentically believe in the cause and who are passionate about making change. "When we focus on organizing as part of everyday life, the process becomes as important as the final product." (Rojas, 2007, p. 205). Given that there is no funder or governing body to whom we must report, NMT is also free to lobby for social change. Learn more about No More Tears at www.nmtproject.org.

Advocates of grassroots political change have analyzed how events and perceived injustices lead to changes in consciousness, individual and small group resistance, and the mobilization of resources, which can coalesce into larger-scale movements for social change (Piven & Cloward, 1977). Advocates of community organizing hope that what Gilliom (2005) calls "protests from below," that is, the involvement of individuals from disadvantaged communities in meaningful work and civic affairs, will promote increased community cohesion and collective demands for social and economic equality (Jurik et al., 2009).

Amnesty International (AI) offers another model that is tied closely to positive peace. Since 1961, AI has been monitoring human rights around the globe and advocating governmental responsibility for ensuring all persons are treated with dignity regardless of their race, ethnicity, nationality, gender, sexual orientation, or other qualities. AI has more than 2.8 million members in 150 countries. In the United States, members are people who sign up and give a small donation. All members vote on who will constitute AIUSA's board of directors and thus have a critical function in determining what are the priority human rights issues that AI should be addressing and how they should go about doing it. Current campaigns focus on ending torture and the death penalty, ensuring women's rights, protecting prisoners of conscience, protecting the rights of refugees and migrants, and reducing the global arms trade, among others. In 2009, AI began a campaign called "Demand Dignity," which addresses poverty and health care as human rights issues. AI has also developed curricula for human rights education that can be conducted not only in schools but also in other arenas and institutions. The organization's Web site, www.amnestyusa.org, also features online training related to understanding and campaigning to end poverty and other related issues. The Web site also contains some great film guides as well as AI's many wonderful reports, publications, and videos, which can be utilized by other nonprofits and social service agencies. I was recently elected to AIUSA's board for a 3-year term and am excited to have the chance to further assist in directing this important work and in further forging the connections to peace.

I am also a member-at-large on the board of the United Nations Development Fund for Women (UNIFEM)'s East Florida Chapter. UNIFEM is the only UN entity specifically charged with ensuring women's rights and the empowerment of females. UNIFEM USA has only one paid staff member, so all its regional groups are coordinated and run by volunteers who have a passion for women's rights. Groups help raise funds and memberships for UNIFEM, which then go toward providing small grants to groups doing work all over the world to assist women. Groups also sponsor educational and awareness activities, such as walks, panel discussions, film screenings, and more. More information about UNIFEM is available at www.unifem.org.

Another group I am involved with is the Peace and Justice Studies Association (PJSA), which is a nonprofit organization that was founded in 2001. It seeks to create a more just and peaceful world by promoting peace studies at all levels of education; by forging alliances between educators, scholars, students, activists, and other peace practitioners; and by creating and nurturing alternatives to structures of inequality, injustice, war, and violence through education, research, and action. PJSA hosts an annual conference, which brings together a diverse group of people to educate, share ideas, and craft coalitions. In 2010, PJSA also sponsored a youth conference. In addition, PJSA disseminates two peace resources: *The Peace Chronicle* and *Peace & Change: A Journal of Peace Research*. A listserve was added in 2009 so that members from all over the world can communicate. PJSA partners with other entities to offer opportunities to members, including global educational exchange programs. See the organization's Web site, www.peacejusticestudies.org, for more information.

Finally, I am involved with a collaborative group called the South Florida Diversity Alliance, which aims to unite the campuses, organizations, and nonprofits in Miami, Broward, and Palm Beach counties to promote diversity, inclusion, and social change. We are not a nonprofit entity, and all members volunteer their time promoting events that bring the community together. Annually, we sponsor a Diversity Summit for the community, where attendees learn more about diversity-related issues and how to get involved. We also sponsor film screenings and panel discussions about critical issues in the community.

There are many other grassroots groups that also use partnership structures, methods, and content. Also working toward ending violence against women as well as structural violence and inequalities is INCITE! Women of Color Against Violence. INCITE! is not a nonprofit but instead chooses to operate as a collaborative network. Food Not Bombs is an all-volunteer movement to help provide healthy vegetarian food to people in need. Food Not Bombs is not a charity but a grassroots community effort devoted to nonviolent social change. Groups have been started in more than 50 countries, all with no formal leaders. At the same time they serve the community, members are also activists seeking to end violent conflict and poverty and to promote peaceful coexistence. In addition to serving food to hungry people (always in public spaces without restrictions), Food Not Bombs also serves protest groups and provides food during disaster relief efforts. Learn more about Food Not Bombs at www.foodnotbombs.net.

The Coalition of Immokalee Workers and the Student Farmworkers Alliance are grassroots collaboratives that help provide a voice for the people who put the food on our tables. They have actively confronted the injustices faced by farmworkers, including human trafficking and sweatshop conditions. In 2002, they united college students and other community organizations on the Taco Bell Truth Tour, a walk across the country to the Irvine, California, headquarters of Taco Bell, where they requested a one-penny-per-pound raise for those who pick 32-pound buckets of tomatoes all day, every day. The campaign was eventually successful and set the stage for more nonviolent grassroots campaigns by the groups (learn more at www.ciw-online.org and www.sfalliance.org). CIW also helped coordinate the Modern-Day Slavery Museum, a traveling exhibit that documents the history and evolution of slavery in the fields of Florida. The museum traveled to many communities, schools, and colleges to provide an interactive education about the problems in our fields and to inspire action.

There are also some great alternative funding sources that do not require recipients to jump through eighteen hoops to obtain. Some even allow or encourage innovative, creative responses to social issues and do not prohibit political or activist work. For instance, Ben and Jerry's offers grants for innovative social change projects (www.benandjerrysfoundation.org). A recent trend has been toward online competitions, which can be an interesting way to obtain needed funds. Chase Foundation and Refresh Pepsi, for instance, allow nonprofits and even individuals to submit proposals for projects they want to do in their communities. Then people vote online for the best projects to receive funding.

Nonprofits, NGOs, and social services can utilize the many great resources available on the Web, in books, and journal articles to better align their work with peacemaking. A sample of some useful resources is listed in Appendix A. Additionally, many colleges and other organizations offer online coursework on peace-building, which is relevant to those working in a variety of service fields and positions. The U.S. Institute of Peace and the University for Peace in Costa Rica both offer this kind of training.

Peacemaking in Social Services

Even within organized social services, peacemaking is emerging as an alternative. The Massachusetts Department of Social Services and the Department of Youth Services are considering using peacemaking circles in their programming for youth and families. This move follows the lead of Roca, a youth and young adult development organization in Massachusetts that began using peacemaking circles in 1999. The Navajo people refer to the circle as "a gift from the creator to keep us in harmony" (Meyer, 2002). It is a traditional method for solving problems. The circle served as a tool to seek solutions to problems and to help restore harmony to the community.

It is an alternate form of communication and dispute resolution that is adaptable to a variety of contexts (Price & Dunnigan, 1995; Ross, 1996). The circle is based on the principles of the medicine wheel, which teaches about the interconnectedness of life (Pranis, Stuart, & Wedge, 2003). The medicine wheel teaches that when a person is committing harm to others or to themselves, they are living out of balance in some way (Yazzie, 1994). Since all of life's elements are interconnected, if one person is out of balance, then the larger community is also out of balance. A solution can only be identified by understanding the problem and seeing what needs to changed so that balance can be restored (Boyes-Watson, 2005).

The structure of the circle is egalitarian. Everyone present is part of the circle, regardless of their age, race, gender, or social status. Every place is equal because every voice is valued. The egalitarian structure of the circle demonstrates the understanding that many different perspectives on an issue exist, and all of them are required to fully understand the problem. "In the American culture, people tend to immediately focus on problems. This is an approach that emphasizes what is going wrong rather than what is going right, a deficit-based approach rather than an asset-based one. The rituals of the circle help participants perceive their strengths as individuals and as a community before beginning to address their weaknesses" (Boyes-Watson, 2005, p. 195).

The rituals of the circle help participants develop shared understandings and sustain them throughout the process and beyond. We participate in rituals every day, although most are rituals of power that reinforce hierarchies of control. They continually remind people of their place in stratified systems of inequality. For example, students automatically enter classrooms and shift their eyes to the person at the podium. In a courtroom, the judge, elevated above all, is the center of attention.

"A ritual is not a passive experience: When we perform rituals, we are "doing" the structure of society, literally enacting and re-creating our relationships with one another" (Boyes-Watson, 2005, p. 196). The circle allows people to practice a different kind of relationship—one built on inclusivity, equality, and respect. Essentially, this is a partnership-based peacemaking practice. "A circle has no table to hide behind or back of the room to which to retreat. Each person faces others as a human being, leaving titles that signify position outside, using first names only. Everyone is given an equal chance to participate and is encouraged to speak from his or her own heart and experience" (Boyes-Watson, 2005, p. 196).

The circle has four rituals: opening and closing in a good way, talking piece, guidelines, and keepers. The purpose of an opening is to show that the circle meeting is very different from ordinary meetings. An opening might be a poem, quotation, music, meditation, or minute of silence—anything that helps people maintain an open attitude toward what will occur. The same is done at the end of the circle—someone closes with a brief reading or wish. The opening sets the tone while the closing reminds participants of the importance of hope, of the progress they may have made, and the commitment they brought to the circle and thus to the community. Openings and closings help participants remain focused on their desires and their capacity to create a better future. The opening and closing also help demonstrate that the process is as important as the outcome of the meeting (Boyes-Watson, 2005).

One of the most transformative elements of the circle is the use of a talking piece during the circle. Although traditionally it was an eagle feather, it can also be a rock, stick, or any object that has meaning to the community holding the circle. Only the person holding the talking piece may speak, and an individual is free to pass the talking piece without speaking. The talking piece generally moves around the circle in a clockwise direction following the path of the sun. The use of the talking piece as guided by the values of the circle creates a profoundly different environment in which to speak and be heard, particularly for those who have been silenced in our society. The talking piece brings out the quiet voices. It creates an opportunity for dialogue without domination by one or two people. In fact, the talking piece is more about listening than it is about talking. The power of the ritual is the space it creates for listening. When a person is speaking without interruption or pressure, they feel others are actually listening. Most of the time in circle is spent listening. The talking piece helps people pay attention without needing to worry about breaking in or preparing to respond. Each person must learn patience as the talking piece slowly makes it way around the circle. The pace is slower, so people relax, concentrate on what others are saying, and have time to reflect before responding. The result of the talking piece ritual is an environment for listening that does not exist elsewhere.

At the start of every circle, time is spent discussing how participants want to treat one another in the circle. This ritual of setting guidelines is essential so that each participant can get what he or she needs in order to feel safe in the circle. People generally articulate values such as respect, trust, honesty, confidentiality, and patience. This process can take a long time as people grapple with what these values mean and whether they can agree to practice them in the circle. Guidelines often involve a genuine discussion about the meaning of these words and the concrete implications of living those values. This may be the first time people have articulated their values and what they mean to them. The ritual of guidelines requires consensus. Even before tackling the problem that has brought a family to the circle, the family is practicing coming to an agreement over guidelines. Unlike rules, which are invented and enforced by a person in a position of authority, guidelines reflect how the group collectively decides to be with one another, so the group learns a deeper lesson from the ritual of guidelines. Unlike most social contexts, in which a structure of authority enforces compliance with rules, the circle is a place of shared leadership. The lesson of the guidelines is that these values are meaningless unless each participant chooses to practice them (Boyes-Watson, 2005).

Every circle has at least one, and often two, keepers. Keepers are facilitators who understand that their role is to be responsible for "holding the space" of the circle. The responsibilities of the keeper include helping people get ready for the circle; planning the circle; arranging the physical space; preparing an opening, a closing, and a set of questions; welcoming people; and maintaining the rituals and tone during the circle. During the circle itself, the keeper poses questions and topics, passes the talking piece, clarifies issues, sometimes takes notes, and records agreements. Keepers will make many decisions during a circle, such as when to keep the talking piece circulating, when to take a break or switch to new topic, and when it is time to close a circle and plan for another (Boyes-Watson, 2005).

The keeper, however, is not responsible for the outcome of the circle. The keeper's role is distinct from the Western role of mediator. Keepers are not professionals but are people familiar with the circle process and its underlying values; young people, parents, or community members may serve as keepers of the circle. It is not the job of the keeper to bring people to agreement or find a solution. Keeping is a skill that involves maintaining an atmosphere of respect and safety. Keepers neither control the process nor are responsible for its outcome. One of the hidden lessons of the circle is the experience of shared leadership. In the aboriginal understanding, genuine leadership is situational. For every challenge, some person is uniquely situated to provide the inspiration and wisdom needed for that moment. In a family circle, it may be a young person, an aunt, or a neighbor who shares just the right memory or the right insight that helps people move beyond a particular stalemate or conflict. The circle creates an opening for the creativity and leadership in the family and community to emerge (Boyes-Watson, 2005). Because it is impossible to know beforehand who will emerge to help move the circle forward toward a solution, experienced keepers say that they "trust the circle" to handle a difficult or tense situation. Of course, it is not the circle they trust, but the capacity of people in the circle to find a way toward a constructive solution. Circles promote trust and respect, egalitarian communication, support, emotional healing, creativity, problem solving, unity, and a shared purpose (Yazzie, 1994).

Children and families thrive best when connected to a rich network of social supports, both formal and informal. Shifting our attention from poor children's deficits to sources of resiliency in their lives surfaces the crucial role of relationships that support and nurture children and families (Burger, 1994; Werner & Smith, 1992). For this reason, child welfare professionals are moving toward closer collaboration with communities. In transition from the traditional service paradigm, professionals are seeking to empower families as partners in a process that views the wider family and community as valued resources (Batavick, 1997; Boyes-Watson, 2005; Saleeby, 1992; Seita, 2000). The circles help improve families' ability to communicate among themselves as well as with a wider network of people in the community. This enhanced communication builds social capital. Social capital refers to the networks of social connection beyond the immediate family (Putnam, 2001). It includes neighbors, co-workers, parents of children's friends, church members, and members of a soccer team or bowling league. These informal relationships facilitate many forms of positive social support: people pass on information about job openings or available housing, pick up trash in the street, carry groceries upstairs for an elderly person, call the police if someone is perusing a neighbor's house, carpool for one other, admonish each other's children, and care for each other's children. The more social capital a community has, the better off are the people who live in that community (Runyan et al., 1998).

Additionally, the circles create a greater sense of trust between clients and the systems that provide much-needed social services. The circle breaks down barriers of status, organization, and hierarchy, which are often inimical to genuine communication and collaboration. Although a circle may begin around one family in crisis, the relationships in that circle are mutual. The wisdom of the circle is that everyone in the community is a valued resource. The interconnectedness that is the underlying structure of reality means that each person contributes to the well-being of the whole. Circles help liberate that potential by reducing the isolation that keeps people apart from one another in the community. Circles build community by helping establish the trust and sense of unity that is the foundation for community. Circles also challenge norms of professionalism by promoting role equality in the circle. One of the greatest barriers to genuine community collaboration is the requisite adjustment in power sharing such a partnership requires (Batavick, 1997). The circle builds trust in both directions: professionals are better able to see the strengths in the community, and the community is better able to accept assistance from professionals. The circle process can be used to meet many traditional child welfare responsibilities, such as assessing, developing a service plan, removing a child from the home for reasons of safety, or celebrating the closing of a case with the family (Boyes-Watson, 2005).

Concluding Thoughts

I believe the peacemaking circles are a very promising way to help those in need. They not only assist in achieving peace, but use peaceful methods to do so. I am proud of my involvement with several nonprofits and NGOs that are creatively integrating peacemaking into their work, whether it be their overt mission or not. The next chapter turns to an institution not often identified as peaceful but which also holds much promise.

6

Sport and Peacemaking

Who killed Davey Moore
Why and what's the reason for?
Not us says the angry crowd
whose screams filled the arena loud.
It's too bad he died that night
but we just like to see a fight

Who Killed Davey Moore
—Bob Dylan

This chapter addresses the ways sport is dominator-modeled. As the above lyrics show, even when violence occurs in the course of a sporting event, it is often chalked up to simply how the game is played. It is as if it is assumed there is no other way to enjoy physical fitness and games than to dominate others. There is another model, however, that sees sport as a form of peacemaking and social change. In this chapter, I offer some promising innovations that should inspire even more creative action.

Building a Peaceful Society, pages 93–109
Copyright © 2011 by Information Age Publishing
93

The sports industry is huge, globally and in the United States. The sports industry, which includes the teams, facilities, equipment, marketing, products, and much more, is in the top ten largest industries in the United States (Finley & Finley, 2006). Sports consume a tremendous amount of media coverage, with approximately one fifth of major network television time devoted to it (Finley & Finley, 2006). As the world becomes more globalized, so too has sports. Globalization can be defined as "the compression of the world and the intensification of consciousness of the world as a whole" (Robertson, 1992, p. 8). Sport has been impacted by these changes in a number of ways, both positive and negative. Miller, Lawrence, McKay, and Rowe (2001) called sport "the most universal aspect of popular culture" (p. 1). International sporting bodies are now among the largest global organizations. The Federation International de Football Association (FIFA) has a larger membership than the United Nations, with 208 member nations compared with 192 (Tomlinson & Young, 2006; Wertheim, 2004; Westerbeek & Smith, 2003). The International Olympic Committee (IOC) has 11 more member nations than does the UN (Giulianotti & Robertson, 2007a, 2007b). Because sport is of such global importance and scope, the Vatican established a sports department in August 2004, under the leadership of the late Pope John Paul II ("Pope sets up," 2004). Children participate in youth sports as well. Some 30,000,000 children are involved in youth sports in North America, under the direction of 4.5 million coaches and 1.5 million administrators (Canadian Center for Peace Education, n.d.).

Globalization and Its Impact on Sport

Although globalization has had some positive impact on sport, it has not been entirely favorable. Some have maintained that "the globalization of sport has been achieved at the expense of individuals, organizations, and countries with limited resources" essentially, "on the backs of the poor" (Thibault, 2009, p. 4). Wertheim (2004) maintained that the globalization of sport has widened the gap between rich and poor societies, devastated the environment, and increased dependence on outsourcing. A recent study by the Financial Action Task Force (FATF), an intergovernmental body, which was founded by the Group of Seven nations, noted that sport is particularly vulnerable to abuse by criminals. Because of the easy entry into sport and the lack of financial diligence of sporting authorities, criminals are easily able to engage in tax evasion, drugs, and human trafficking via sport (European Commission on Sport, 2009). Soccer is now a multibillion dollar industry, and the Organization for Economic Cooperation and Development (OECD) of Belfast, Ireland, found it is particularly vulnerable to money laundering, match fixing, trafficking, and drug smuggling. The

OECD cited more than 20 cases of money laundering in 25 different countries (Transparency International, 2008).

Violence and Sport

Sport today is rife with violence, ranging from self-harm to state-sponsored crime and even structural violence. The hypercompetitive atmosphere prompts far too many athletes to consume dangerous performance-enhancing substances and to engage in hazardous weight-control practices. Athletes play when they are in pain, sometimes enduring life-threatening injuries so they can continue in their sport. Others cheat by engaging in academic fraud, dirty-play and on-field rules violations. To initiate rookies, teams may haze players by forcing them to drink huge amounts of alcohol, humiliate themselves, and perform embarrassing sex acts. A number of athletes have died from out-of-control hazing. The making of sports equipment and promotional items is often done under inhumane conditions. For instance, workers may toil in sweatshops to make soccer balls they could never afford to purchase (Finley & Finley, 2006). Similarly, exploitative labor practices are often used in the construction of stadiums and sport-related facilities. An estimated 1 million migrant construction workers came to China to help construct facilities for the Beijing Olympics in 2008. They worked in harsh and unsafe conditions and were often unable to access the most rudimentary public services. When a subway tunnel under construction collapsed in March 2008, trapping six workers, the employer immediately confiscated their cell phones so that the workers could not report the accident (Human Rights Watch, 2008). An outbreak of serious diseases prompted some attention to the crowded temporary camps used as living quarters for laborers building sites in Delhi for the 2010 Commonwealth Games, yet no real action was taken (Wade, 2008).

Off the field, the culture of entitlement that is endemic in modern high-profile sports leads many to believe they are above the law. Male athletes in what are called the "power performance" sports—football, basketball—are disproportionately arrested for sexual assault and domestic violence. These athletes often see themselves as above the law. Players sometimes engage in fights with one another on the field, as well as with fans during games or matches. Fan violence or hooliganism is another major concern in sports, and there have been a number of postevent riots.

Some forms of violence in sports are more clearly linked to the state. Critics contend that when countries with horrific human rights records are selected to host international sporting events, it is a sign of acceptance for that country's policies. In order to "clean up" some host cities, governments have authorized brutal tactics. One of the earliest problems with police brutality surrounding a sporting event took place just weeks before the 1968 Olympics in Mexico City. About 500 students and workers were massacred at Tlatelolco Square. Declassified documents now show that the police were acting in an attempt to stifle protest before the Games. After the event, records are often burned so that the evidence of police repression and human rights abuses is destroyed (Goodman, 2009). Misha Glenny (2008), author of *McMafia: A Journey Through the Global Criminal Underworld,* explained that China is a police state and that, early in its preparations for the 2008 Olympics, China "ordered a 'social cleansing' to clear Beijing of beggars, hawkers and prostitutes" (Edwards, 2008, p. A02). During the Games, 36,000 plainclothes police were stationed around Olympic venues. At subway stations, officers checked 70 million passengers and 72 million bags, yet only 30 people were detained. Human Rights Watch (2008) noted that efforts to "rid Beijing of undesirables...accelerated the eviction of petitioners—citizens from the countryside who come to the capital seeking redress for grievances ranging from illegal land seizures to official corruption. In September-October the Beijing municipal government demolished a settlement in Fengtai district that housed up to 4,000 petitioners" (p. 1). Approximately 2 million people were displaced and some arrested for signing petitions requesting that the government not kick them out of their homes (Goodman, 2009). In South Africa, some 20,000 people have been removed from the Joe Slovo settlement in Cape Town, which World Cup organizers called an eyesore, to make way for stadiums and to ensure that visitors don't have to witness the depressing poverty (Zirin, 2010). The government, pressured by FIFA, has passed new legislation specifying where people may drive and park their cars, where they may and may not trade and advertise, even where they may walk their dogs. Beggars are subject to arrest during the event, as are those using foul language. Two people have been assassinated for "whistle-blowing" about suspected corruption in the construction of the Mbombela Stadium (Zirin, 2010).

Unfortunately, as Alfie Kohn as has noted, too often youth sports stress competition and winning at all costs. When these programs place inordinate emphasis on competition and winning, they become detrimental. Most youth sport coaches lack even rudimentary knowledge of the emotional, psychological, social and physical needs of children (Canadian Center for Peace Education, n.d.).

Sport and Militarism

Sport has long-been considered militaristic. President Dwight Eisenhower once noted that "Sports are perfect for preparing young men for war" (cited in Zirin, 2005, p. 129). Zirin (2007) explained that football in particular uses military metaphors and language, such as "throwing bombs" and the inclusions of F-14 bombers buzzing the stadium at a typical NFL game. Zirin also noted that "Politicians from the days of Teddy Roosevelt have successfully used the games to manipulate public sentiment" (p. 171). He cited the case of former Arizona Cardinal Pat Tillman, who became an Army Ranger and died in Afghanistan. Official sources originally reported that Tillman died "a warrior's death," but it was later revealed that Tillman died at the hands of his own team in an accident. Tillman's death was used to generate support for the war. ESPN's *SportsCenter* even broadcast a week of shows from Kuwait, cast on a set constructed to look like a bunker (Zirin, 2007). Zirin (2007) also described a meeting between Coach Mike Kryzewski, coach of the U.S. basketball team that underperformed at the 2002 world championships and 2004 Olympic Games, and USA Basketball managing director Jerry Colangelo about how the team could be more closely linked to the military.

Sport and Social Change

Yet, despite these concerns, sport can also be a powerful vehicle for social change (Zirin, 2005). Throughout history, social movements have used sports as a platform for challenging racism, violence, and other social issues.

> Although sports is often described as, and wished to be, a depoliticized zone where athletes may be free from intense social and cultural hostilities, the global mass mediation of many sports over the past four decades have transformed them into attractive targets for doing new social movements (NSM) work. Equally, because sports mega-events such as the World Cup and the Olympics bring international political rivals into close contexts, it makes sense that hostilities from the outside will become interlaced with competition on the inside. (Atkinson, 2009, p. 61)

Although it ended in tragedy, the events leading up to the 1968 Mexico City Olympics showcased the concerns of students in Mexico. Before the opening ceremonies, more than 5,000 middle-class university students gathered multiple times near Olympic venues to express their anger over the government's expenditures on the games. The students felt that the Mexican government, led by President Gustavo Ortiz, could have used the more than $140 million they spent on the Games on education, labor opportunities, and health improvements. Ortiz authorized the Mexican army to clear out the protesters 10 days before the opening ceremonies. Soldiers fired on demonstrators with machine guns. Estimates of those killed by the assault range from 32 to 300, and 2,000 students were jailed (Atkinson, 2009). Another good example of how sport can contribute to peace is the case of South Africa, where sport was one of the most important fronts in the struggle against apartheid. Since apartheid ended, sport was an essential vehicle of former President Nelson Mandela's efforts to unify the divided country and to forge a "rainbow nation (Keim, 2003). These efforts were documented with the recent release of the film *Invictus.* John Carlin, who authored the book that inspired the film, explained that the reason Mandela prevailed was that he saw the good in even the worst offenders (Carlin, 2007).

Sport can help bridge relationships across social, economic, and cultural divides within society. It can help build a sense of shared identity and fellowship among groups that might otherwise distrust one another, a central component of peace-building. In essence, sport helps to "rehumanize" opposing groups to their enemies. "By sharing sport experiences, sport participants from conflicting groups increasingly grow to feel that they are alike, rather than different. This shared "ritual identity," or sense of belonging to the same group on the basis of a shared ritual experience, helps to erase the dehumanizing effects of persistent negative characterizations of opposing groups" (Right to Play, 2000, p. 7). Sport is an important way to reach out to socially marginalized peoples because it is like a universal language. Women and girls have benefitted from global sport. In Kenya, the Together for Girls project was established by the UN High Commissioner for Refugees (with help from private industry) to encourage girls to participate in sports as a way to get them to attend and stay in school. The result was an 88 percent increase in enrollment at the preschool level and a 75 percent increase in participation in sports by girls at all levels (Ogi, 2005).

Sport programs can create opportunities for social contact that involve connections at the community level as well as links to leaders and decision makers. Sport has been used successfully to help demobilize and disarm combatants in violent conflicts and to reintegrate former soldiers. Sport has also helped those harmed by war-related trauma to heal by providing safe spaces and a sense of normalcy. In El Salvador, for example, where communities are struggling with a legacy of gang violence in the aftermath of a prolonged civil war, the Scotiabank Salud Escolar Integral program uses sport, play, and physical activity to teach life skills—especially conflict prevention and nonviolent conflict resolution—to primary and secondary school children, equipping them to make healthy choices later in their lives.

High-profile events and elite athletes can help prompt attention to social issues and promote solutions. Because of its global popularity, elite sport is ideal for communicating a message of peace to the masses. Although this most often occurs at the international level, it can be built and sustained in local communities as well. A great example is the famous "ping-pong diplomacy" between the People's Republic of China and the United States in 1971. An American national table tennis player missed his bus after a practice and was invited onto the Chinese team's bus. One of the Chinese players offered a silkscreen portrait to his American counterpart in greeting. The American later presented the Chinese player with a T-shirt containing the peace symbol and the words "Let it be." The media attention that followed this incident led to an invitation for an American government delegation to visit China. More recently, the term "cricket diplomacy" has been used to describe the improvement of relations between India and Pakistan resulting from an informal invitation from Prime Minister Singh to General Musharraf to watch an international cricket match between the two nations.

In September 2008, the presidents of Armenia and Turkey used soccer to reopen diplomatic dialogue. The two countries had severed relations and sealed their common border more than a decade earlier, but a World Cup qualifying match between their national teams prompted Armenian President Serzh Sargsyan to extend an invitation to his Turkish counterpart. It was the first-ever visit to Armenia by a Turkish head of state (Hofstetter, 2010).

Other examples of influential elite athletes include Molly Barker, a world-class triathlete and four-time Hawaii Ironman triathlete, who founded and directs Girls on the Run International (GOTRI). GOTRI is a running program for preteen girls intended to help them develop self-respect and healthy lifestyles. It is a 12-week, 24-lesson curriculum that has been implemented by volunteers across the United States and Canada.

Sport offers powerful stories of social change as well as community and social betterment. These can be integrated into virtually any peace education program. A list of literature about sport and social change is available at http://www.teachingforchange.org/publications/lists/sports. Sportswriter and author Dave Zirin has chronicled athletes who resist what has been called "the jockocracy" to speak out about injustices and to advocate social change in his books *What's My Name, Fool?* (2005) and *Welcome to the Terrordome* (2007). One noted example is Muhammad Ali, who refused to go to Vietnam when drafted because "he had no quarrel with the Vietcong" (Plimpton, 1999, para. 6).

The Hope of the Olympics

Certainly there are problems with the Olympic Games, from the politics involved with deciding who hosts to refereeing scandals and much more. But the Games can also be seen as a way to promote positive peace. One of the fundamental principles of the Olympic Movement is to contribute to building a peaceful and better world through sport. This is why the International Olympic Committee revived the ancient Greek tradition of *Ekecheiria,* or the Olympic Truce. In 1993, the United Nations restored the ancient tradition of the Olympic Truce, under which athletes from warring nations are granted safe passage to participate in Olympic Games. Since 1993, prior to every Olympics, the Olympic Truce has been reaffirmed by the United Nations General Assembly through a symbolic resolution entitled Building a Peaceful and Better World Through Sport and the Olympic Ideal. More recently, the Olympic Truce has been extended to include the Paralympic Games as well. The truce begins 7 days before the start of each Olympic/Paralympic Games and continues until 7 days after the closing ceremony, reminding the world that sport offers an opportunity to bridge even the most bitter political divides.

The Olympics have much to teach us about peace. The first lesson about peace that can be demonstrated by the Olympic Games is the importance of specifically setting aside a time and place for peace, hence the Olympic Truce. The second lesson is that all parties must be viewed as equals, at least in some sense. The third lesson is respect for one another's differences within the larger world community (Georgiadis & Syrigos, 2009).

Four main beliefs underlie the "peace through sport" movement associated with the modern Olympics:

1. Sport enhances or contributes to social peace through the cooperation between generations, social classes, genders and sciences.
2. Sports competitions contribute to the idea of respect for the homeland, the exchange of ideas between countries, international meetings, joint celebration, reconciliation between peoples and not their amalgamation.
3. There is a balance between love for one's country and love for mankind. International meetings in the context of the Olympic Movement would facilitate mutual respect of common rules, the development of a pacifist predisposition as a means of promoting social justice.
4. Ever since the early days, the concept of reconciliation through sport has been connected with education, human rights, human dignity, and man's improvement through his own efforts. (Georgiadis & Syrigos, 2009)

The torch relay, which opens the Games, is a symbolic expression of peaceful cooperation between humans, between generations, and between countries (Georgiadis & Syrigos, 2009).

Sport and Peacemaking

In 1993, Adolf Ogi was appointed the first United Nations Special Advisor to the Secretary General on Sport for Development and Peace. Since then, the UN has expanded its efforts to help achieve the United Nations' Millenium Goals through sport (http://www.un.org//themes/sport/). Over the past few years, the United Nations General Assembly has adopted a series of resolutions on Sport for Development and Peace. The importance of sport in promoting peace and also helping achieve the Millennium Development Goals is highlighted in the 2003 report of the United Nations Inter-Agency Task Force of Sport for Development and Peace. The Task Force's main finding was that "well-designed sport-based initiatives are practical and cost-effective tools to achieve objectives in development and peace." The Task Force then concluded and recommended that "sport is a powerful vehicle that should be increasingly considered by the United Nations as complementary to existing activities."

In order to call attention to sport's valuable role, the 191 UN member countries unanimously declared 2005 the International Year of Sport and Physical Education. The most recent publication invites Member States, the United Nations system (including the governing bodies of United Nations agencies), sport-related organizations, the media, civil society, and the private sector to collaborate to promote greater awareness and action to foster peace. Building on the spirit of the UN General Assembly resolutions, in 2007 the International Olympic Committee, the Association of National Olympic Committees of Africa, and the African Union issued the Brazzaville Declaration, proposing to join their efforts with those of governments, NGOs, and private partners to create a fund for sport-for-peace initiatives. These international frameworks reflect growing awareness of sport's potential to help prevent conflict and build peace.

To be effective, sport-for-peace initiatives must be carefully designed with specific conflict-prevention or peace-building goals in mind. These initiatives should be undertaken only after a rigorous assessment of the context and dynamics involved in order to minimize the risk that they will inflame the tensions they are intended to address. Widespread programmatic sport-for-peace initiatives, however, are relatively new, and there is little scientific research that documents their impact. In such cases, programmatic examples provide useful evidence of sport's impact in the area of peace building.

Partnership-Based Sport

Although many see sporting activities as only competitive in nature, there are wonderful games for children and young people that can be played co-operatively. Terry Orlick, a sports psychologist at the University of Ottawa, showed how even musical chairs could be adjusted to be more cooperative. The basic format of removing chairs could still be used, but the goal could be changed so that groups try to fit everyone in the diminishing number of seats. That way, no one is excluded. Orlick and others have devised or collected hundreds of such games for children and adults alike. "The underlying theory is simple: All games involve achieving a goal despite the presence of an obstacle, but nowhere is it written that the obstacle has to be someone else. The idea can be for each person on the field to make a specified contribution to the goal, or for all the players to reach a certain score, or for everyone to work with her partners against a time limit." In cooperative games, opponents become partners (Kohn, 1990). Kohn has argued that while sport brings huge benefits, none of those benefits are the result of its competitive nature.

> Some people point to the camaraderie that results from teamwork, but that's precisely the benefit of cooperative activity, whose very essence is that *everyone* on the field is working together for a common goal. By contrast, the distinguishing feature of team competition is that a given player works with, and is encouraged to feel warmly toward, only half of those present. Worse, a we-versus-they dynamic is set up, which George Orwell once called "war minus the shooting." (Kohn, 1990)

Competition is not character-building, Kohn argued. A person's value becomes tied to what they have done and who they have beaten, not who they truly are. Further, competition negatively impacts relationships in that we must inevitably see others as obstacles. "Competition leads people to envy winners, to dismiss losers (there's no nastier epithet in our language than "Loser!"), and to be suspicious of just about everyone. Competition makes it difficult to regard others as potential friends or collaborators; even if you're not my rival today, you could be tomorrow" (Kohn, 1990).

Kohn (1990) also explained why it is sport itself that requires examination:

> No matter how many bad feelings erupt during competition, we have a marvelous talent for blaming the individuals rather than focusing on the structure of the game itself, a structure that makes my success depend on your failure. Cheating may just represent the logical conclusion of this ar-

rangement rather than an aberration. And sportsmanship is nothing more than an artificial way to try to limit the damage of competition. If we weren't set against each other on the court or the track, we wouldn't need to keep urging people to be good sports; they might well be working *with* each other in the first place.

Peacemaking Examples

Football for Peace (F4P) is a sport-based project for Jewish and Arab children. F4P was organized by the University of Brighton, in partnership with the British Council. Since 2001, it has been running in towns and villages of the Galilee region of Israel. Galilee is an area in the northeast of the country with a population of 1.146 million, which is 17 percent of the population of Israel. Almost half of Galilee's residents are Arabs. Most are Muslims, but there is a sizable minority of Christians. It is an area that has been economically ravaged, with unemployment rates 50 percent higher than the national average. Galilee is very segregated. In rural areas, Jews and Arabs live in separate towns or villages, while in the more urban areas they live in separate enclaves. The Jewish areas are much better off in terms of socioeconomics (Sa'ar, 2004).

Sport, like everything else is Israel, is highly politicized. Professional football has been largely forged, like most other state-sponsored sports, by Jewish political parties and interests. Thus, Israeli Arabs found it difficult to participate. Further, it hurt Israel's international reputation (Ben-Porat, 1998). The Federation International de Football Association (FIFA) removed Israel from the Asian Football Confederation (AFC), placing them with the Oceania Football Confederation (OFC) and then later with the European Association for World Cup qualification purposes so as to avoid conflicts with other Arab states (Sugden & Tomlinson, 1999). A shift began in 1967 when the Israeli state began to modernize. It was continued in the later 1980s and 1990s as sport, like everything else, became more globalized. Professional football became more open to Arab players as it became good business to recruit players who, regardless of their race or ethnic/national origin, could propel the team to success and, consequently, financial reward (Ben-Porat & Ben-Porat, 2004). More Arab-Israeli players have sought the opportunities sport provides, allowing for the potential that football has an integrative function in Israel (Sorek, 2003).

Inclusion alone does not make agreement or peace, however. With more Arab players, teams, and fans, there is also more potential for racial, ethnic, or national conflicts. Since 2004, the New Israel Fund (NIF) has tallied a weekly racism incitement index to help address the chanting of racist and vicious slurs during games. The NIF has also worked with the Israeli Football Association (IFA) and the English Football Association (EFA), the latter a group that has a long history of dealing with racism in football (Sorek, 2003).

F4P, then, is a grassroots movement intended to build bridges between these two divided communities. Specifically, it aims to provide opportunities for cross-community social contact, promote mutual understanding, encourage participants to commit to and seek peaceful co-existence, and to enhance football knowledge and skills. It kicked off in 2001 when World Sport Peace Project volunteer coaches, coupled with a staff leader, research assistant, and project director to conduct a week-long coaching camp in the Arab town of Ibilin. The original goal was to partner this site with a nearby Jewish municipality, Misgav. Yet the camp coincided with the second Intifada (uprising), and a series of violent incidents discouraged Misgav from sending any children. Thus, the 2001 project included 100 Muslim-Arab and Christian-Arab 10- to 14-year-olds, as Christians and Muslims too lived separately and often harbored animosity toward each other (Sugden, 2006).

A second project took place in 2002, with eight coaches and two staff leaders. Coordinators secured the cooperation of Ibilin as well as the Jewish communities of Misgav and Tivon, so the final count included 150 Arab and Jewish children. This time, 20 girls were also included. And, in addition to Ibilin, organizers obtained the cooperation of two Jewish communities. This project improved on the last in that it was more inclusive and better utilized local volunteer coaches and community sport leaders (Sugden, 2006).

The project grew in 2003, with twelve coaches and three leaders heading three projects in six locations simultaneously. Approximately 300 children from six communities in Galilee participated, and volunteer coaches from the UK worked with Arab and Jewish volunteer coaches in preparing the program. At this time, the focus on the program was largely football-skills training. In postprogram evaluations, everyone agreed that more was needed. Young people needed to not only play together, but have opportunities to talk and to confront more of the serious and divisive issues between their communities. Research is clear that simple contact does not necessarily enhance intergroup or interethnic relations (Amir, 1998). Further, contact must promote equal status between the groups, promote common goals, require cooperation, and reward positive examples of cross-community connections (Pettigrew & Tropp, 2000).

Building on these achievements and tweaking the program to be more in line with peacemaking, the 2004 F4P project included 700 children from 16 communities across northern Israel. The UK volunteers worked with 60 local Jewish and Arab-Israeli volunteers at seven different sites. One was a girls-only team. The communities were paired, so that half of the practices took place in one town and half in the others. Arab coaches have proclaimed the project useful, and enjoyed that it gave local children the opportunity to see what conditions were like elsewhere and for different groups (Sugden, 2006).

Another great example of peace education through sport is provided by programs coordinated by young peacemakers in the Mathare slums. The Mathare and neighboring areas, home to more than half a million people from multiple ethnic groups, are some of the largest and worst slums in Africa. In 1987, the Mathare Youth Sports Association began a sports program in the area that was designed to bring together the many ethnic groups. Today, MYSA is the largest self-help youth sports and community development program in the world, with more than 21,000 boys and girls participating in over 120 leagues in 16 zones. Activities include more than sports: also included are environmental cleanup, AIDS prevention activities, drama, music, dance, photography, building of libraries and study halls, and various community service activities. Both boys and girls are included in the Executive Council, which is the top decision-making body. Researchers say that the reason the MYSA has been so successful is because it is youth run. The MYSA is a source of pride. Although the area is not completely free of violence, it has experienced less than other areas (Munro, 2009).

A similar program was established at the Kakuma refugee camp. The camp was established in 1992 and managed by the United Nations High Commissioner for Refugees (UNHCR), with assistance from the World Lutheran Federation (WLF). By 1999, more than 70,000 refugees called Kakuma their home. Some 70 percent of the refugees were from Sudan, with the rest from seven other countries (Somalia, Ethiopia, Democratic Republic of Congo, Uganda, Rwanda, Burundi, and Eritrea). The majority (more than two thirds) of the refugees were youth under the age of 25, and almost one third were unaccompanied. Each different nationality, as well as the different clans from southern Sudan, largely lived in their own areas of the camp due to numerous factors, among them being stereotypes and historical conflicts. In the early 1990s, camp managers began a sports program, and by 1998, there were 200 teams playing football, basketball, and volleyball. Yet they remained generally ethnically segregated and there were no organized leagues. Girls were virtually excluded, despite there being some 20,000 of them at Kakuma. In early 1999, at the request of the UNHCR and the WLF, and with the financial support of the Dutch government through the Netherlands National Olympic Committee/National Sports Federation (NOC/NSF), some volunteers went to Kakuma to initiate a new youth sports and community development program. They modeled it after programs initiated by the MYSA of Kenya in the slums of Mathare the previous decade. The MYSA appointed a founding member and former top striker for Mathare United FC, 26-year-old Peter Serrys, to head up the new program. Only 18 months later, more than 12,000 youth were playing on 940 basketball, football, netball, and volleyball teams. This figure included more than 1,800 girls on 184 teams. The program also included sports activities within the primary and secondary schools at Kakuma camp and in the neighboring town of Kakuma, as well as special volleyball, wheelchair basketball, table tennis, darts, and other games for youth with disabilities.

This remarkable program did not come easily, however. One challenge was to break though the fierce ethnic barriers that divided the camp. The camp was divided into eight zones that cut across ethnic and national areas. The town of Kakuma was the ninth zone. Each zone had its own ethnically diverse Sports Council and appointed representatives that were from multiple ethnic groups to the overall Supreme Sports Council. Each sport also had a technical committee, which was made up of representatives from the different ethnic groups. A second challenge was to break through the gender barriers. Many resisted allowing girls to participate, citing numerous reasons, such as allowing girls to wear the uniforms. A compromise was made such that, in some sports, girls wore shorts instead of trousers. At least 3 of the 11 members of each sport's council had to be girls, and 1 girl was required to represent each of the nine zones on the overall Supreme Sports Council. Girls also lacked confidence that they could play traditional "boys" games, like football. A team of top MYSA girl players was flown in to show them otherwise and soon joined the girls from the camp for a special tournament together. A third challenge was breaking what was called the dependency cycle, whereby refugees were reluctant to get involved in much of anything, having lived in some cases 10 years or more as a dependent refugee at the camp. Camp coordinators emphasized that the sport program was not to be done for them but by these youth and those living in Kakuma town. Almost all the program personnel were volunteers and, of the paid personnel, all except three were themselves refugees. A fourth challenge was to establish a program culture in which participants felt the need to give back to the community. Again, drawing on their experience in the Mathare slums, all sports activities were linked to new community and environmental improvement activities at Kakuma camp and in Kakuma town. This included taking care of the sporting environment as well as the creation of "green belts" in the area. This involved taking care of the garbage and building small dams, which provided water to plant trees in and around the camp. Teams received extra points in the league standings for completing these community service projects. A fifth challenge was to use the sports programs to address the social and health risks facing the refugees, including family planning and AIDS awareness. A core group of 30 supervisors and volunteers were trained as peer educators for information and awareness campaigns around these issues. Also included was the distribution of free condoms to refugees. A sixth challenges was how best to integrate those with physical and mental disabilities into the sports activities, as there was a large group of such young people who had previously been excluded. As was noted, the program included special leagues with adaptive equipment like crutches and wheelchairs. Young people with disabilities were included on the Supreme Sports Council as well.

An external review in mid-2000 concluded that a strong organizational structure had been established and that volunteers were being adequately trained. Further, it noted that the disabled youth were particularly excited about having the same opportunities as did able-bodied youth. It also noted that within 18 months, the sports program was already helping break down barriers and prejudices between nationalities, ethnic groups, genders, those with disabilities, and those without. Evaluators noted that the program helped raise the self-esteem of the refugees who were involved. The report noted that sports kept the youth busy, which helped prevent them from deviant activity. It noted a reduction in the tensions and the impact of the community service project on the camp and called it the most cost-effective program at the camp.

A final element of the Kakuma Sports Program was to follow some of the refugees home. Many of those who were involved in sports activities were from southern Sudan, and the expectation was that they would use their expertise to establish similar sport and community development programs upon their return. The MYSA agreed to help them get funding for their projects. In 2005, the first program in southern Sudan was started in the town of Rumbe, home to a large reintegration center for child soldiers.

Nonprofit organizations around the world now seek to bridge cultural divides and eliminate hatred by getting conflicting groups to play sports together. Los Angeles Lakers guard Jordan Farmar led basketball camps in Israel, which brought together Arab and Jewish children. An organization called PeacePlayers International runs similar youth basketball leagues for Protestants and Catholics in Northern Ireland, blacks and whites in South Africa, Israelis and Palestinians, and Turkish and Greek factions in Cyprus.

Peace and Sport (http://www.peace-sport.org/gb/burundi_actions.htm) is an international organization that uses sport to teach individuals in communities in which conflict has occurred how to live in peace. They promote meetings between communities and positive dialogue in an effort toward harmonious living. They have coordinated projects in Burundi, Cote d' Ivoire, and Timor Leste.

Sport 4 Peace (http://www.sport4peace.org/) seeks to improve sport opportunities for girls. It aims to promote a holistic, healthy lifestyle and to bring communities together. Programs include athletic training camps for Iraqi girls and for refugees.

Athletes United for Peace (AUP) is a nonprofit organization located in the San Francisco Bay area, which works to promote peace, education, and friendship through sport and other projects. AUP helps bring together people from various cultural or thenic groups. AUP is a member of the United Nations teams of NGOs working on sport, peace, and development. More information is available at www.athletesunitedforpeace.org.

The Interreligious Peace Sports Festival (IPSF; http://www.joinipsf.org/) brings together youth from multiple faiths and nations to enjoy sport and share their beliefs and cultures. The goal is for these young people to transcend their differences and form long-lasting bonds that help create peace.

CARE's *Sport for Social Change* (http://www.care.org/careswork/whatwedo/initiatives/sportforsocialchange.asp) initiative is a program that uses sport to minimize the effects of poverty. It helps connect people of different backgrounds and statuses to address serious and difficult issues and to inculcate confidence and motivation. It also helps build self-esteem, leadership, social skills, and critical thinking. CARE has worked with Nike and the MYSA to empower girls in Kenya through a soccer exchange program.

Ultimate Peace is a collective of elite players and coaches of Ultimate Frisbee who aim to travel to disadvantaged and conflict-driven areas giving children the opportunity to learn and enjoy the game (Worman, 2006, 2009).

Peace Players International (http://www.sportanddev.org/learnmore/sport_and_peace_building/) has sponsored a basketball program in South Africa, which brings together children from different communities. An evaluation found that most participants expressed fewer racial stereotypes and less racism compared with youth who did not participate. Participants were also more likely to support racial integration.

Other innovative sport programs like *Building Bridges Basketball Camp, Playing for Peace,* and the NFL's *One World* program all help build peace, collaboration, and unity (Thibault, 2009).

Concluding Thoughts

In sum, Zirin (2007) offered a better vision for sports, one that I think these examples highlight:

> Sports could be woven into the fabric of our existence, more cooperative, more accessible, its competitive spirit removed from the cash pump and the destructive will to win at all costs. This would require a completely different world...Sports would become part of building integrated, whole people. Fun, yes, but also respectful, balanced, and available to all both to participate in and enjoy. (p. 293)

7

Peacemaking in Other Institutions

I don't need no leader
that's gonna force feed
a concept that'll make me think I need to
fear my brother, fear my sister,
and shoot my neighbor with my big missile ... One tribe

One Tribe
—Black-Eyed Peas

Although there is still much work to be done to fully incorporate partnership-modeled peace education into all institutions, there are, as Fellman (1998) noted, many promising "seeds," both in old institutions and in new institutions. These seeds show how peace educators have used creative methods to resist domination and, as the Black-Eyed Peas discuss, help us build a "one tribe" philosophy.

Activists, educators, scholars, and others across the globe have helped positive peace-building by developing more just and democratic systems that address poverty, illiteracy, and other root causes of violence. Interna-

Building a Peaceful Society, pages 111–124
Copyright © 2011 by Information Age Publishing
111

tional peace education efforts can and have gone beyond the classroom to help ensure fair relief after natural and human disasters and to make sure that basic human needs are met; to break down barriers; and build cohesion across political, racial, ethnic, and national groups; and to strengthen civil society (Bar-Tal, 1998; Kriesberg, 1998a; Kuppermintz & Salomon, 2003; Lederach, 1998; Solnit, 2009).

Peacemaking in Conflict Areas

These same efforts have occurred in locations where violent conflicts have already broken out. Even in areas of intractable conflict (typically defined as lasting 25 years, being fought over existential goals, and being perceived as unsolvable), committed peace educators have helped mitigate the effects of violence and built structures upon which peace can be restored and sustained (Africa News, 2007; Bar-Tal, 1998, 2007; Kriesberg, 1998b).

In areas of intractable conflict, like Sri Lanka or parts of the Middle East, conflict has become a cultural norm, "dominated by societal beliefs of collective memory and ethos of conflict and by emotions of collective emotional orientations" (Bar-Tal & Rosen, 2009, p. 557). This becomes a collective history of conflict, remembered differently by different members of society and is an obstacle to any peace process (Cairns & Roe, 2003). The younger generation learns this "history" through family, mass media, and through other socialization agents and cultural products. Schools are the major agent of socialization for conflict through textbooks, instructional materials, teachers' instructions, and other rituals. To achieve peace, then, this history must essentially be rewritten. A common outlook that both parties can agree to must be forged (Gardner-Feldman, 1999; Hayner, 1999; Lederach, 1998; Norval, 1998). Beyond acknowledgement, some have called for a process of reconciliation and collective forgiveness, seeing it as the only way for scarred nations to heal (Arthur, 1999; Hayner, 1999; Lederach, 1998; Lin, 2008; Shiver, 1995; Staub, Pearlman, Gubin, & Hagengimana, 2005). Lin (2008) has advocated a global ethic of love, forgiveness, and reconciliation. "Forgiveness requires a decision to learn new aspects about ones own group, to open a new perspective on the rival group, and to develop a vision of the future that allows new positive relations with the perpetrator"(Bar-Tal & Rosen, 2009, p. 558).

Peace education can be used to promote reconciliation (Aall, Helsing, & Tidwell, 2007; Abu-Nimer, 2004; Kriesberg, 1998a). Where there is intractable conflict, peace education can help the society, including its youth, construct a new worldview that facilitates conflict resolution and the peace process (Abu-Nimer, 2004; Fountain, 1999; Iram, 2006; Salomon, 2004).

Powerful peace education utilizes all the socialization agents that once were used to disseminate a collective history of anger, distrust, and violence. Mass media can transmit information and peaceful goals, processes, and successes (Bruck & Roach, 1993; Calleja, 1994; Elhance & Ahmar, 1995; Norval, 1999). NGOs may have a role to play, helping establish cooperative relations and providing economic assistance; but it is essential that peacemaking and reconciliations be largely the efforts of the local community, which is empowered to make change (Staub et al., 2005).

As noted in chapter 7, societies with long histories of conflict and atrocities may wish to establish truth and reconciliation commissions, which help reveal the truth and establish a forum for forgiveness (Asmal, Asmal, & Roberts, 1997; Kaye, 1997; Liebenberg & Zegeye, 1998; Moller, 2008). In recent years, truth and reconciliation commissions of some sort have been established in South Africa, Chile, Argentina, El Salvador, Honduras, Uruguay, and Rwanda (Asmal et al., 1997; Liebenberg & Zegeye, 1998; Norval, 1998; Staub et al., 2005).

Peace education in areas of intractable conflict can be indirect or direct. Indirect peace education does not directly address the conflict but is concerned with peace-making in general. It is often organized thematically, focusing on topics like identity, ecological security, violence, empathy, human rights, and conflict resolution skills. Direct peace education specifically addresses all of the issues that contributed to the culture of conflict. It presents themes that will help create a culture of peace and forge a new collective memory (Bar-Tal, 2007). Direct peace education, as already mentioned, can be launched when the societal and political conditions are ripe and the educational system is ready, both administratively and pedagogically, for this major endeavor. An example of direct peace education is the Education for Peace project carried out in Bosnia and Herzegovina in the past decade, which attempted to transform the lives of the students, teachers, and the whole community by directly confronting participants with the issues that were at the heart of the conflict (Clarke-Habibi, 2005). Some of the suggested themes for peace education in areas of intractable conflict include reflective thinking, tolerance, ethno-empathy, human rights, and conflict resolution. These all encourage openness, exposure to alternative ideas, empathy for other groups, and critical thinking.

Important Qualities in Peace Education Programs

Reflective thinking involves questioning dominant assumptions. It requires one to be open-minded and to consider new alternatives (Dewey, 1933). Reflective thinking also helps one learn and see connections between ideas and practices (Marsick, Sauquet, & Yorks, 2006; Marsick & Watkins, 1990). Individuals can practice collective thinking, and it can also be practiced at the collective level when there is conflict.

Tolerance is the recognition and acceptance of all individuals. It is a willingness to allow others to share thoughts, opinions, and attitudes and to exhibit behaviors different from others (Agius & Ambrosewicz, 2003). It involves a readiness to allow for contradictions and a rejection of stereotypes and prejudices. To become more tolerant, people must learn about others, actively challenge bias, and engage in dialogue about issues of controversy (Bullard, 1996; Vogt, 1997).

"Ethno-empathy is the ability of a person or a group to experience what the other ethnic group feels and thinks" (Bar-Tal & Rosen, 2009, p. 565). Empathy operates in both the cognitive and affective domains. Cognitively, we can work toward becoming more aware of others' thoughts and perspectives, while affectively we attempt to vicariously experience what the other feels (Hoffman, 2000). In essence, empathy involves perspective-taking and kindness (Deutsch, 2000; Ferrucci, 2006; Hoffman, 2000; McCully, O'Doherty, & Smyth, 1999; Selman, 1980).

Human rights are "basic rights and freedoms that all people are entitled to regardless of nationality, sex, national or ethnic origin, race, religion, language or other status" (Human Rights, 2010, para. 1). Peace education can strengthen human rights by promoting respect and dignity for all. "Increasing the ability to analyze situations in terms of human rights can also deepen awareness of both sides' abuses of those rights, of the costs for the societies caught up in the conflict, and of their respective contributions to the continuation of the conflict. Furthermore, becoming informed about human rights supposedly develops a sense of responsibility for defending the rights of other people, and this of course includes the rival" (Bar-Tal & Rosen, 2009, p. 566).

Conflict resolution skills include negotiation, mediation, and collaborative problem-solving. As so many others have noted, conflict resolution is not the eradication of conflict, which is inevitable. Instead, it involves skills to resolve conflict peacefully. Conflict resolution skills are a mainstay of peace education (Johnson & Johnson, 2005). According to Deutsch (2005), the key concept of conflict resolution education is "to instill the attitudes, knowledge, and skills which are conducive to effective, cooperative problem solving and to discourage the attitudes and habitual responses which give rise to win-lose struggles" (p. 18).

I would suggest creativity should be added, and that these qualities should form the basis for all positive peace education. Without the willingness to use varied methods and multiple perspectives, none of the above can occur. I provide more information about the benefits of creativity in the next chapter.

Direct peace education can specifically address the source of the conflict, the reasons why it persists, and the impact of it. It can examine what peace would mean, what it would look like, how it can be obtained, and obstacles to achieving it. It can also include an examination of the roles of various institutions in the quest for peace (Avery et al., 1999; Fountain, 1999; Galtung, 1996). It should legitimate the opponents, meaning it presents them as humans with whom it is possible to build a positive relationship. The history of the conflict is presented and analyzed without bias, demanding that each side consider their own actions as well as the actions of their opponents. In addition to the content included, direct peace education should craft new affect and emotions. Collective hope, trust, and acceptance can be fostered (Bar-Tal, Halperin, & de Rivera, 2007). The groups move forward together to create new peaceful goals and strategies to attain and sustain them.

In some conflict-ridden communities, remarkable individuals have established whole schools devoted to peace. The Hope Flower School lies in the middle of the Israeli/Palestinian conflict. Started by Palestinian refugee Hussein Ibrahim Issa, it is built on Weil's (2003) concept of "the art of living in peace," which focuses on human, social, and environmental influences. The school provides an "educational experience that is geared toward peace, not a manual or set of ideals that must be followed but a process for building relationships" (Noe, 2008, p. 147). All subject areas use Freirian problem-posing techniques (Noe, 2008). In addition to what happens with the enrolled children, the school also reaches out to the community through its Center for Peace and Democracy Activities. The school sponsors parent meetings and discussion groups about important local issues. In 2005, Hope Flower School organized a PeaceTrees Bethlehem project in which they brought youth from many other nations to work with local young people on community conservation and restoration projects (Noe, 2008).

Peace Education for Former Child Soldiers

Globally, an estimated 300,000 children work under horrifying conditions. These children serve in many positions, including as sex slaves (Brett & McCallin, 1996; Machel, 2001; Singer, 2005). One of the most common positions is that of child soldier. Nearly half of the soldiers in the fighting in Liberia since 2002 have been children. In Sierra Leone, where the war ended in 2001, nearly half the Revolutionary United Front (RUF) soldiers were children. A quarter of them were girls (McKay & Mazurana, 2004). In Colombia, almost half of the members of some guerilla units are children (Coalition to Stop the Use of Child Soldiers [CSC], 2008). Burmese government forces utilized an estimated 50,000 child soldiers in the mid-2000s. Children are easy to exploit as soldiers, as they are available and cheap. Conducting peace education with children who have once committed atrocities during warfare is challenging, but committed and creative groups have found ways to teach these kids peace and at the same time, help build peace in their war-ravaged communities.

While the conflict in Sierra Leone officially ended in January 2002, the people in rural villages said they felt nowhere near peace. Many explained, "What peace? We were hungry before the war, during the war, and still now we are hungry." The country was in ruins physically, and mentally, its young people, appeared wrecked as well. Most were still armed. One 17-year-old who had fought for the RUF explained, "This gun gives me power, and I know how to get what I need. Why should I go back to the village when I have no money and no job, no education?" (Wessells, 2005, p. 366). Clearly, peace education needed to involve far more than discussion; it had to address very significant structural and institutional issues and, specifically, needed to help reintegrate these child soldiers into their communities. UNICEF coupled with other NGOs, including the Christian Children's Fund, to develop a holistic peace education program in the Northern Province, which had been home to the RUF. Communities feared the child soldiers who returned there, as they had once been their attackers. Former child soldiers were frequently stigmatized as rebels, and girls who had been raped and who had become mothers were harassed or regarded as if they were damaged goods (Kostelny, 2004). The project began with open meetings in 15 different communities to discuss the end of the war. Villagers were encouraged to share their thoughts, fears, and ideas. Villagers identified the need to build schools and health facilities, many of which had been destroyed during the war. The community then prioritized their needs and selected a project. At the same time, staff facilitated dialogue about villagers' fears of the returning child soldiers. They shared how these children had suffered and were in need as well. The goal was to build empathy and set the stage for reconciliation, which villagers desperately wanted. Villagers shared proverbs, songs, and dances related to unity and forgiveness. Youth who participated in the community's selected project received a small stipend, which helped the former soldiers be able to stay there instead of returning to the bush. When the villagers saw the former child soldiers' productivity, they began to view them as people who could contribute to the community. Further, the community betterment projects increased everyone's hopes as they saw tangible signs of improvement. Dialogue continued as the projects went on. Local healers were asked to perform cleansing rituals on the girls who had been violated so they were no longer seen as dirty (Kostelny, 2004). These rituals were important because in many sub-Saharan countries, local people view spiritual contamination as the major barrier to a child soldier's reconciliation with the community (Wessells & Monteiro, 2004). Another stage of the project includes training former child soldiers in skills such as carpentry, tailoring, and tie-dyeing. Market research had indicated these were promising jobs locally. During their training with a master artisan, who was also their mentor, these young people discussed how to handle conflict nonviolently and shared their hopes for the future and their ideas about how they fit into the community. The villagers determined that, aside from the war, conflicts often occurred over land and women, so they created conflict resolution committees to mediate disputes.

This project, which has subsequently been expanded into other provinces, enjoyed considerable success, visible in reductions of fighting and increased integration of former child soldiers into their villages. Despite dire predictions that villages would never accept back the youth who had attacked them, over 90 percent of former child soldiers have gone home and say they now have a civilian identity and hope of a positive life as civilians. Communities, too, say they see the former child soldiers not as troublemakers but as youth who have a spirit of community service (Wessells, 1997).

I recall having a very interesting conversation about peace at an international conference some years ago sponsored by the Ahimsa Center at Cal-Poly Pomona, which highlighted the many ways people approach peace education. While I was there to discuss efforts to train teachers for more traditional school-based approaches, I vividly remember one man who had worked with refugees at a camp in Sri Lanka describing his form of peace education. He said that most of the children he was teaching had suffered a major, debilitating injury or illness during war. Many had lost limbs, vision, or hearing. Additionally, the camp suffered from a lack of resources, so he had to teach with none of the traditional items associated with schooling, like pencils, paper, or books. Instead, he argued that he taught peace education by having his students make beautiful music with whatever was available to them, be it a can, a stick, or even a part of their body.

Peace Education for Military

Zoppi and Yaeger (2008) maintained that peace education can even become part of military training, although certainly some peace scholars would disagree. They explained that three things must occur for peace education to be built into military training. First, the President and the Department of Defense must take a leadership role in crafting policies that would mandate peace education training at all levels of military rank structure and for civilian personnel in support roles. Second, the new curriculum should be developed by the U.S. Army Peacekeeping and Stability Operations Institute, in collaboration with a soon-to-be-created U.S. Department of Peace and the U.S. Department of Defense. Third, inner peace training must be included, and each individual soldier should be given time, space, and encouragement to develop inner peace. Military educational systems like the National Defense War College, West Point, and the other academies and colleges can help retrain returning soldiers who have witnessed the effects of war to work for peace by finding ways they can heal and helping others to do so. Peace educators at colleges can help these military training institutes adapt their curricula, techniques, and even their structures. With the help of peace educators, these institutions can increase diversity training as well (Zoppi & Yaeger, 2008).

Peacemaking for Civic Engagement

Areas where there has been no specific war or conflict are also using positive peacemaking education for community betterment. The 49th Ward of Chicago, Illinois, is experimenting with "participatory budgeting." More than 1,600 members of the community are coming together to decide how to spend $1.3 million in taxpayer money. Known more for its political corruption and lack of transparency, Chicago may seem an unlikely site for what is really a revolutionary concept—empowering everyone to take part in structuring policy and practice in their community. Yet the long history of struggle and competition has prompted residents to seek a new, more cooperative model. The idea was borne out of the 2007 U.S. Social Forum, where Alderman Joe Moore heard about residents of Porto Alegre, Brazil, who had, since 1990, directly decided how to spend as much as 20 percent of their city's annual budget. Moore also learned that participatory budgeting had spread rapidly, with more than 1,200 cities around the world trying it. The United Nations had recognized it as a best practice of democratic governance. "At the community meetings everyone was complaining about their block," says 49th Ward resident Laurent Pernot. "But now every single committee has taken stewardship of the whole ward as their mission." In 2009, a steering committee was formed to determine a structure and timeline for the process. They then held a series of neighborhood meetings in which they brainstormed community needs and projects to address them. Eventually, six thematic committees were formed. Each thoroughly examined their specific issues and consulted with experts to determine which ideas were most viable. After many months of activities and neighborhood meetings, 36 budget proposals were presented at an artistic exhibit describing them. All community residents over the age of 16, regardless of whether they were registered voters or their citizenship status, were allowed to vote on the proposals. A total of 1,652 voters came out, "not to elect someone to decide for them, but to make their own decisions about the ward." The $1.3 million was enough to cover 14 projects. While far from perfect, the project is an embodiment of Freire's praxis and demonstrates the potential for communities (Lerner & Antieu, 2010).

Peacemaking and the Economy

Warmaking is not good for overall economic growth. As Brauer and Tepper-Marlin (2009) showed, worldwide violence, or the credible threat thereof, cost the world approximately 9 percent in gross world product (GWP). They vehemently argued that war and preparations for it help a country economically, as was often argued in the United States after World War II. In her 2007 book *The Real Wealth of Nations: Creating a Caring Economics,* Riane Eisler showed how many of our modern economic practices are the result of a dominator model. She asserted that the "real wealth of nations" lies in its people and its environment. Real Wealth Impact Statements (RWIS) should be developed as measures of global social and economic health. They could draw from existing indicators such as the UN Human Development Reports and new metrics to be developed, including those related to health, families, education, workplace, the elderly, democracy and equality, and other measures of quality of life. Within the category of health, Eisler recommended considering prenatal and child health rates, infant and maternal mortality rates, access to food, national nutritional standards, drug safety, emotional stress levels, drug and alcohol dependence, work-related stress, unwanted pregnancies and the availability of reproductive care, and the qualities of elder care. A metric related to families would include the availability of parenting education in schools, levels of family violence, types of parental discipline, teenage pregnancy rates and family planning programs, gender equality, recognition of nontraditional families, and tax credits and benefits for family caregivers. For education, critical criteria would be funding for and participation in early childhood programs; after-school and youth programs; level of access and opportunities based on race, gender, class and other criteria; teacher pay; benefits; training; and comprehensive sex education. In the workplace, Eisler's metric would consider paid vacation time, sick days and parental leave, the availability of childcare, paycheck fairness and equal pay for comparable worth, workplace recycling and environmental protection, and the rights of workers to organize. Important criteria for supporting elderly would include programs for community engagement and continuing education, local agencies, facilities and resources for aging with dignity, adequate Social Security benefits, and support for home care and other forms of care. The democracy and equality metric would consider school-based education for democracy; free media (including the Internet); proportional representation of women in national politics; levels of voter registration, participation, and reliable vote counting; entertainment and news media that do not perpetuate stereotypes, inequality, and violence; and fair credit and lending practices for equality of opportunity. In addition to these, Eisler noted the following key measures of quality of life:

- poverty and hunger levels, broken out for women and families
- crime levels, broken out for violent and nonviolent crimes
- quality of environment including toxicity levels, water quality, etc.
- enforcement of antidiscrimination laws on gender, race, ability, age, etc.
- equal valuing of "feminine" and "masculine" activities
- comparison of military spending with funding for human needs and opportunities

Eisler (n.d.b) has also authored a jobs proposal for President Obama, which would be based on the creation of a new, caring economy. She explained, "By creating and subsidizing jobs in industries like childcare, education, and eldercare, as well as subsidizing caring in homes, we support families, radically reduce poverty, effectively address crime, more fully recognize women's economic contributions, and create high capacity human capital" (p. 3). To coordinate these efforts, Eisler recommended a cabinet post or advisory council on human infrastructure development be created.

Peacemaking and Corporations

Many corporations today exploit their employees and the earth, creating a culture of domination, consumption, and waste (Leonard, 2010). These companies "will perhaps gain in the short term, but in the long run they compete less favorably than those that, in their own interests, do not take advantage of employees, respect the environment, and place themselves at the service of clients" (Ferrucci, 2006, p. 10). Yet this is not the only model. Examples of the partnership approach in the corporate world include the European Institute of Business Administrations, which is a France-based alliance of business leaders and educators that wants to initiate changes in business practices to be more in line with human rights. Google Company, home of the most widely used Internet search engine in the world, has a philosophy that "you can make money without doing evil." Although far from perfect, *Fortune* magazine named them the number one company to work for in 2007 because of their commitment to creating a corporate culture that values and provides for employees and that nurtures their creativity ("100 Best Companies," 2007). Whole Foods Market made the 2009 list at number 22 for its treatment of employees, in particular for providing them with opportunities to impact the workplace ("100 Best Companies," 2009). Whole Foods helps the community by holding "5 percent days," in which they donate 5 percent of net profits on a specific day to local charities. They also support development of human potential and eradication of poverty, hunger, and disease through their Whole Planet Foundation. A list of the most socially responsible corporations is available at *The Better World Shopping Guide,* a companion to the excellent *Better World Handbook.*

The University for Peace in San Jose, Costa Rica, offers coursework designed to assist business executives in understanding and applying peacemaking principles in the corporate world. Through their Centre for Executive Education, U-Peace offers courses in sustainable business practices, nonprofit leadership, corporate social responsibility, leadership through conflict resolution, and more. The CEO of PespsiCo, Indra Nooyi, has argued that all CEOs should have experience working in an NGO or in government so that they can interact with a variety of people and develop empathy. Cisco has a Leadership Fellows Program, which places senior managers with international NGOs. At the same international conference at Cal-Poly Pomona I mentioned earlier, I remember hearing a speaker discuss how the first step to making more peaceful corporate environments was for employees to begin conversations with customers having complaints with two simple words: "I'm sorry."

Francis Moore-Lappe (2006) recommended cooperatives as a business model of living democracy. Co-ops involve equitable sharing of resources, benefits, and responsibilities. Co-ops provide more than 100 million jobs worldwide, with membership doubling in the last 30 years. They are far more popular outside the United States. Examples include Italy's Emilia Romagna region, where a network of 5,000 cooperatives generate more than 30 percent of the economic output in one of the wealthiest areas of Europe. In 2007, Colombia's Saludcoop, a health care initiative, was the nation's second-largest employer, which served one quarter of the nation's people. Also in 2007, India was the world's largest milk producer, in large part due to its more than 100,000 dairy cooperatives. On a much smaller scale, I enjoyed working (not for pay) for a short time at a book cooperative in Boulder, Colorado called Left Hand Books, where workers were invited to share in visioning for the store, coordinating special events, and enjoying the books at the store. Although not cooperatives, there are some great examples of corporate sharing in the United States. In 2010, Panera Bread opened their first nonprofit store in which customers are invited to pay what they can for the items they purchase. The store is located in Clayton, Missouri, and if it goes well, Panera plans to open more ("Panera Bread Co. opens," 2010). Salt Lake City's One World, Everybody Eats (www.oneworldeverybodyeats.com) vegetarian restaurant runs on the same model and is dedicated to eliminating world hunger, serving unprocessed foods and reducing waste.

Peacemaking in Families

Fellman (1998) explained that families are the primary sites of mutuality in most cases. The values of caring, respect, support, and love are the basis on which functioning families are built. Families can utilize positive parenting techniques that reduce power differentials and offer nurture, guidance, compassion, and creativity (Drew, 2000; Rosenberg, 2004). Rather than "do as I say," partnership-based families practice "do what I do" (Rosenberg, 2004). Drew outlined 17 keys to peaceful parenting. These include (a) recognizing that peace begins with them; (b) understanding that they must make their home a place of peace; (c) finding ways to catch children engaged in positive behavior and immediately and specifically praising them for it; (d) spending at least 15 to 20 minutes every day being fully present and devoted to each child; (e) setting and enforcing clear standards of behavior; (f) providing children the opportunity to play and simply "be kids"; (g) holding regularly scheduled family meetings in which the children have a voice; (h) creating an established set of guidelines for a peaceful family; (i) remembering that they are the parents and deserve to be listened to; (j) having fair and reasonable consequences for negative behaviors, which are only employed when absolutely essential; (k) listening with all their hearts to their children and teaching their children to do the same to others; (l) teaching children, and modeling for them, how to handle anger nonviolently; (m) resolving conflicts peacefully and teaching their children to do so as well; (n) finding ways to help their children succeed; (o) ensuring that all their actions are guided by love, compassion, fairness and respect; (p) continually living the commitment to peaceful parenting; and (q) remembering daily that everything we do impacts our children and the world around us.

Peaceful parents model for children democratic decision making, positive forms of conflict management, and the importance of action for social justice. Peacemaking families understand that they are "works in progress" who, upon encountering additional information about some facet of positive peace, do their best to incorporate it into their lives. There are a number of great resources available to families who wish to learn more about peace and peacemaking. The Education for Peace Foundation (www.efpinternational.org) recognizes that "The family is the world in microcosm, the arena for individual and social development, and the workshop of civilization." EFP provides resources for families on developing harmonious relationships, creating a love-based, not power-based home, practicing gender equality, and managing conflict nonviolently. The Alliance for Childhood (2005) has provided a list of 10 steps for peace education at home.

1. Making room, or space, for family members to develop and practice inner peace;
2. Finding peace in nature by exploring outdoors;
3. Making time for creative play, with careful choices of toys that inspire;
4. Encouraging children's hands and hearts by allowing them to make and give things;
5. Establishing a "family foundation" to collect donatons for those in need;
6. Supporting peace education at school;
7. Engaging in community service to meet local needs;
8. Help children collaborate with others to make a difference;
9. Celebrate peace, on the International Day of Peace and beyond;
10. Share inspiring words of peace from different cultures. (Alliance for Childhood, 2005)

It has been my experience that parents often do not know what to do or how to do it, but they definitely want to create peaceful families. Further, I believe that many people still underestimate children's ability to understand complex social issues and their capacity to get involved. Personally, I am committed to helping my daughter understand positive peace and see that she has a role to play in creating it. We attend educational events together, and she has been involved in volunteerism and activism all her life.

Families can help teach and create peace by engaging in cross-cultural programs. Radomski (2008) described the Youth Exchange and Study (YES) program that promotes cross-cultural understanding between the United States and the Muslim world by bringing Muslim students to the United States for an academic year to live with an American family. Studies have found that students benefit tremendously from these programs. One study found that those who self-rated as ethnocentric prior to the program made positive gains in their understanding of other cultures after a student exchange program (Hammer, 2005). Exchange programs also benefit the host families and even the broader community. Studies by the U.S. Department of State assessed the impact of exchange programs on the communities. Researchers found that residents believed the program to have a positive impact on international friendship and peace and was useful in promoting mutual understanding and peace. For families and communities, exchange programs offer the type of extended contact that takes place among people with equal status and with institutional supports that Allport (1954) explained could help reduce prejudice.

Concluding Thoughts

In sum, these examples highlight how peacemaking can be built into any institution. If it is possible to integrate peace education into refugee camps and in areas that have experienced long-term violent conflict, it seems to me that it is possible to integrate peace education anywhere. In the final chapter, I synthesize all that has been presented to offer some general guidelines and ideas that I believe can be useful for building and sustaining peace in any setting.

8

Moving Forward

The little boy went first day of school
He got some crayons and started to draw
He put colors all over the paper
For colors was what he saw
And the teacher said . . . What you doin' young man
I'm paintin' flowers he said
She said . . . It's not the time for art young man
And anyway flowers are green and red
There's a time for everything young man
And a way it should be done
You've got to show concern for everyone else
For you're not the only one

And she said . . .
Flowers are red young man
Green leaves are green
There's no need to see flowers any other way
Than they way they always have been seen

Flowers are Red
—Harry Chapin

Readers may be wondering, why the song? What does that have to do with peacemaking? Like Harry Chapin's *Flowers are Red*, rather than capturing the natural energy, inquisitiveness, and inspiration of young people, schools are stifling. Instead of emphasizing our uniqueness, they often stress conformity. Rear ends in seats, facing front, at attention—this is what is generally expected (Postman, 1971). In essence, education as it is currently done in the United States is dominator-modeled and the dominator-model discourages creativity. A Catholic priest, Ivan Illich, wrote *Deschooling Society* (2000), an educational bestseller about education and creativity seen from the radical humanist paradigm. His central theme is that schooling in general is dysfunctional for creative individual development. Schooling tends to make people more stupid than if they had not been in school. The best learning goes on outside school, in real environments (Illich, 1970). In a Norwegian context, the same radical humanist ideas of schooling were elaborated by Nils Christie in his book *If School Did Not Exist* (Christie, 1971). There is no meaningful narrative, or "god," as Postman (1996) called it, to unify us. The result is that the entire process is lifeless. This is a form of structural violence in and of itself, and as this book has shown, the same stifling conditions are true in so many other institutions. Yet they do not have to be. Instead, if we tap into our own personal creativity, we can re-create our schools, our criminal justice system, our social services, our athletic organizations—all our major institutions—in ways that allow all people to flourish (Hayes, 2004). This, to me, is true peace education.

This chapter offers ideas and recommendations for moving toward a society in which all institutions are partnership-modeled and pace education is considered everyone's business and responsibility. To begin moving toward such a society, I believe we must first develop a vision of what it will look, feel, and be like. To that end, as noted throughout this book, I see creativity as one of the most important components, as it is our creative thinking and collaboration that will allow such a vision to emerge and to be sustained.

Where is the Creativity?

Complaints about the failure to nurture creativity did not originate with Harry Chapin's song. On the contrary, in 1949, psychologist J. P. Guilford issued an address to the American Psychological Association in which he argued that conventional conceptions of intelligence were too focused on speed, accuracy, correctness and logic, what he called "convergent thinking." Instead, Guilford argued for more divergent thinking, which he explained incorporated creativity (Cropley, 2001). Guilford was not advocating this change in schools alone, but rather in all aspects of our lives. Aside from Guilford's call, in the United States, the drive to study creativity arose from concerns about national defense and focused on technological inventiveness. As the focus shifted toward defining creativity as rebelliousness or as having the capacity to break with tradition, the research community quickly found itself without government support. Differing ideas about creativity, embedded in conflicting cultural values, led to a dearth of creativity research in America for several decades (Craft, 2003). In July 2010, *Newsweek* featured a special section on creativity, which discussed the decline in U.S. creativity scores since 1990. The most significant decrease has been among children in kindergarten through 6th grade. Although there is no precise source of the problem, "likely culprits" include the excessive amount of time American children spend watching TV and videogames and the "lack of creativity development in our schools" (Bronson & Merryman, 2010, p. 45). Other nations have made creativity development a priority. For instance, the European Union called 2009 the European Year of Creativity and Innovation, while China has sought to reform its schools, once known for their traditional, rote methods, to focus on problem-based learning (Bronson & Merryman, 2010).

Using Creativity to Solve Social Problems

Using our creativity, there are a number of ways we can solve or at least minimize social problems to create a more peaceful world. Bronson and Merryman (2010) noted,

> It's not just about sustaining our nation's economic growth. All around us are matters of national and international importance that are crying out for creative solutions, from saving the Gulf of Mexico to bringing peace to Afghanistan to delivering health care. Such solutions emerge from a healthy marketplace of ideas, sustained by a populace constantly contributing original ideas and receptive to the ideas of others. (p. 45)

Otto and Lupton (2009) recommended four strategic principles for making world peace: (a) making peace user-friendly, so that everyone and every group can see how they can contribute; (b) reposition world peace to make it fun, participatory, understandable and achievable; (c) invite and include everyone; (d) increase collaboration. Additionally, they outlined six tactical modules to implement these principles: (a) A Global Peace Treaty (GPT) is the political anchor for creating world peace in 5 years, or by 2014. The GPT would provide a set of ground rules for international practices and agreements regarding what must be done when violations occur, much like the World Trade Organization. (b) Set standards for peace safety, which will move peace from "passive" to "active." A manual developed by experts will describe peace safety at various levels. (c) Make a national plan for peace using a collaborative approach. (d) Create a series of user-friendly processes to implement the national plans, including tools for ongoing measurement. (e) Grassroots action to help people align their lives with peace. (f) Media services to "market" peace.

According to Crone (2011), one of the most important ways to address social problems is to change our social construction of reality. Given that humans are constantly creating our reality, we can also re-create it in new and more peaceful ways. Central to this process is raising consciousness. As more people become aware of the true structural causes of violence and inequality, they will be moved to take action. Organizations like Amnesty International and Human Rights Watch have been central to helping raise consciousness about many types of structural violence. Similarly, international NGOs like OXFAM constantly monitor developments worldwide, and through cooperation with research institutes and governmental and United Nations relief efforts help to address the structural issues of poverty and famine.

Another way to address social problems is to redefine them. That is, some social issues can be alleviated by a change of perspective. For instance, illicit drug use is a criminal problem because it is defined as a violation of law. But is simple use really so problematic? Many have noted that virtually all so-called illegal drugs have some positive function, for instance, medicinal marijuana or the use of Ecstasy in psychotherapy (Sullum, 2003). And despite the stereotype, many people can and do use illicit substances in small amounts for recreational purposes and are still able to function in society (Sullum 2003). Another example is the criminalization of many normal youth activities, like hanging out with friends (which in some cities violates curfew laws) or wearing sagging pants (in some cities, this is an infraction). Decriminalizing these behaviors allows us to see kids as just that—kids. And it decreases the number of young people who have negative encounters with law enforcement that can then spiral into greater criminal involvement. Instead, we can use our creativity to brainstorm the real problems, if there are any, and some more logical, less formal responses. To redefine a social problem takes a lot of work, and likely involves not only consciousness raising of the general populace but also of persons who hold the most power in society, those who largely benefit from the current systems, structures, and policies. Shifting our focus toward the identification of common values can help reduce social problems as well. Putting the shared values of equal opportunity, fairness, freedom, justice, and democracy at the center of discussions will help focus our efforts (Crone, 2011).

Further, we should consider how to create more incentives than disincentives. "If people are shown how they can benefit from giving up some of their resources to solve a social problem, they will be more willing to part with some of their resources in the form of taxes" (Crone, 2011, p. 41). Additionally, activists must show the general population as well as policymakers and people with power how urgent these social issues are and how many people are affected, using valid data. "One crucial step in creating new social policy is to study how new and existing social policies can relate to and complement each other" (p. 40). Multinational Companies (MNCs) are key actors in the creation and maintenance of structural violence. Thus, monitoring the actions of MNCs, obtaining their support, and holding them accountable for structural violence, is another way to help effect positive peace. MNCs must become less structurally violent, thus we must use our creativity to help ensure that social, cultural, and ethical concerns become a part of MNC agendas (Groff & Smoker, n.d.).

In order to survive in a business climate, companies must innovate. Creativity is an essential part of innovation, as it is the source of ideas and inspiration (Westwood & Low, 2003). Fritz (1994) explained that the most important developments in the world have come from the creative process. Craft (2003) explained that "The economy demands creativity, and a healthy economy is necessary to a wealthy society which then produces assets for general consumption; better public amenities and services" (p. 114). Economists are now seeing creativity as a form or capital, and thus as an engine of economic growth and social dynamism. Florida (2004) emphasized that a company's most important asset is not raw materials, transportation systems, or political influence; rather, it is creative capital—creative thinkers whose ideas can be turned into valuable products and services.

We can analyze how social problems interrelate, which provides for a more encompassing response. For instance, I have learned that domestic violence work is about much more than ending violence in the home. It is about gender roles. It is about poverty. It is about lack of quality education. To truly address one social issue, we must see the connections with others. This is positive peace, and it calls for creative approaches that build and sustain coordinated human activism. Moreover, it is essential that we look to other countries for models of how to, and how not to, address social problems (Caldicott, 2005).

Creativity can help us create what Boulding (1978) called "the movement for peace." He contrasted this with "the peace movement," which involved organizations that overtly and consciously exist to promote peace activities. The movement for peace involves any type of cooperative activity that indirectly supports the creation of a more peaceful world, regardless of whether that was the original intent or conscious purpose of the activity. Looking at it this way helps us see how all individuals, groups, and institutions can contribute, how their work can be seen as peace education. Smoker (1969) studied two types of worlds: one in which states were the main actors and another that was less state-centered and involved many actors—multinational corporations, nonprofits and NGOs, and other organizations. He found that, in the last 50 years, the second type of world experienced far fewer wars (Groff & Smoker, n.d.).

Examples of Creativity in Institutions—The Media

Media is critical to changing consciousness. First, media must begin to utilize a partnership, not dominator, model. It can begin by adjusting the style of televised reporting so that instead of screaming at and interrupting one another, journalists can practice civility and true listening. Creative news, ways to share information, and alternative sources can be explored. For instance, Independent Media Center (www.indymedia.org) offers a non-corporate perspective on major global issues. *Yes! Magazine* and *GOOD* are two publications that explicitly focus on sharing positive stories and equipping readers with tools to take action. More specifically addressing peace and peace-related issues is *PeaceVoice,* which features a collection of articles and commentary by peace professionals. They are available on the Web site www.peacevoice.info, and journalists across the globe are encouraged to reprint these stories in their newspapers or online sources. MediaPeace is specifically devoted to coverage of war and the anti-war movement in the United States, Europe, and the UK (www.mediapeace.org). Project Censored (www.projectcensored.org) is a great source for learning about important global news that received minimal mainstream coverage.

Great short videos are available for free or small fees that help people understand how media can make a difference. One source is http://www.humanmedia.org. The U.S. Institute of Peace also has a collection of peace videos and audio resources with teaching guides available as well (www.peacemedia.usip.org). I am also a fan of Morgan Spurlock's show *30 Days*, which aired on FX. Spurlock selected controversial social issues and brought two people with divergent views on each issue to live together for 30 days. One episode called "Straight Man in a Gay World" documented a conservative heterosexual man living with a gay man in San Francisco's Castro district for 30 days. Both learned from each other and gained new insight into the other's perspectives, beliefs, and lifestyle. At the end of the 30 days, the conservative heterosexual had a new appreciation and acceptance for homosexual men. Another episode brought a Christian man from West Virginia to live with an Islamic family in Dearborn, Michigan. He had to follow Muslim worship traditions as well as immerse himself in the community, which was still suffering the negative repercussions of the September 11th terrorist attacks and the assumption that all Muslims are terrorists. Again, the Christian man grew tremendously in his understanding of Islam, the people who practice it, and their culture.

Dan Gillmor, author of *We the Media* (2004), envisions a world in which all people have a voice in media. WorldChanging (www.worldchanging.org) and World Pulse (www.worldpulse.com) are two of my favorites. Others are provided in Appendix A. The University for Peace offers a master's degree in Media, Peace, and Conflict Studies to help make that dream a reality.

Examples of Creative Methods

In crafting creative education for positive peace in all areas and institutions, we can borrow from the successful tactics of direct action, which is the strategic use of acts such as strikes, demonstrations, or sabotage to achieve a political or social end. It can be done with large or small groups of people. Direct action is most effective when carefully planned so that it focuses public attention on injustice The *Activist Handbook* advises that before we begin to protest an issue or problem, we understand how the system runs and find out whether it will be possible to change it from the inside. On the page titled "Why Direct Action," The Ruckus Society Web site (www.ruckus. org), explains what direct action is and why it works:

> There comes a moment in every struggle when the power of everyday people needs to be felt, and when the community can only attain victory by advancing their front line. That moment, if approached with creativity and vision, can be a transformative moment for the community and for the struggle itself. We see our purpose as increasing the capacity for vision, creativity and strategy in direct actions by impacted communities with the intention of changing history.

Direct Action

The idea of direct action emerged from Gandhi's work. Early in his career, Gandhi attempted to describe how his plans and actions differed from passive resistance, what was in Indian culture known as *dhurna*. Dhurna involved sitting in mourning or motionless, in the elements with no food or water. It was used to protest debtors who refused to pay debts and was intended to arouse the oppressor's sense of shame and evoke their sense of guilt. Gandhi understood, however, that what he was leading was not passive. Rather, he was advocating taking on the government in a very assertive, yet still nonviolent, manner. He rejected the idea that people might see this as weak. Further, "Gandhi knew that he and his comrades were intent on showing love and support to those who were persecuting them and would not turn to violence or brute force, no matter what. They were refraining from using force not because they were incapable of it but because they were instead exerting soul force, an even more powerful weapon" (Rynne, 2008, p. 40).

On the advice of his nephew, Gandhi joined two Indian words, *satya*, meaning truth, and *agraha*, meaning firmness, to coin the term *satyagraha*, or firmness in the truth. For Gandhi, civil disobedience was just one of the tools of satyagraha. Other forms of noncooperation involved strikes, boycotts, and work stoppages.

Gandhi thoroughly rejected *himsa*, or violence. As a proud Hindu, *ahimsa*, or nonviolence, was central to his religious beliefs. He also rejected violence based on his own personal observations and his study of history. Unlike the common myth, Gandhi saw ahimsa as an active force. "Ahimsa went beyond refusal to do no harm; it entailed doing good to those who did one harm" (Rynne, 2008, p. 58).

Gene Sharp (1973), one of the leading scholars on nonviolent direct action, developed a list of 198 forms of nonviolent action. He divided these into three categories, ranging from mildest to strongest: nonviolent protest and persuasion, noncooperation, and nonviolent intervention. Nonviolent protest and persuasion are generally symbolic actions that demonstrate peaceful opposition to a policy or law. This might include marches or parades, picketing, teach-ins, or vigils. The goal is to build a critical mass that will support changes in the policy or law. Noncooperation involves stronger action in that it requires participants' refusal to do things that are normally expected as a way to convince key decision makers to change a policy or law. Examples include refusal to pay taxes as a way to show disagreement with the government's military expenditures or refusal to work under unjust conditions.

Sharp's strongest category of nonviolent action is intervention. This is intended to interrupt an ongoing activity. An example is a sit-in, which disrupts a business or school from functioning. A strike or protest is intended to interrupt an ongoing activity or process of the opponent. Sharp also includes "psychological interventions," for example, self-inflicted fasting, in this category. Sharp asserted that these forms of direct action are effective because they diminish the power of the opponent (Conflict Research Consortium, 2003). As Martin Luther King Jr. explained in a 1963 speech, "Non-violent direct action seeks to create such a crisis and establish such creative tension that a community that has constantly refused to negotiate is forced to confront the issue. It seeks so to dramatize the issue that it can no longer be ignored."

Direct Action as a Teaching Tool

Training for Change provides training in using the principles and ideas of direct action in educational systems, both traditional schooling and other forms of learning. They defined direct education as that which "directly confronts and challenges the current system of injustice— which includes how people are taught. Rather than traditional education, which gives all the expertise to textbooks and teachers, direct education invites the expertise of the people themselves. Direct education is about liberation and empowerment—going to the direct source of wisdom: the group itself!"

Two key elements of direct action are risk-taking and accommodating different learning styles. While traditional education stresses reading, writing, and lectures as the major modes of learning, direct education recognizes that people learn in all sorts of different ways. Training is thus designed for a diversity of learning styles. TFC assumes that "deep learning is change, and change requires risk, and the facilitator's job is to invite risk and make it safe to risk." The idea is that any social change effort must involve risk-taking by all involved. Risk-taking is difficult, thus people must be trained to do it. Creativity can help us devise ways to make risk-taking less threatening and more fun and effective. Imagine a world in which police officers, judges, social workers—everyone!—were trained like this: trained to see that their work is about empowering each one of us, rather than controlling us. Learn more about using direct action as an educational tool at http://www.trainingforchange.org.

Key Qualities of a Peacemaking Culture

In addition, I follow Lin (2006) in that I believe peace education in any institution should be built on a pedagogy that includes reflectiveness, tranquility and silence, humility and simplicity, sensitivity, direct contact with nature and diverse peoples, caring, and creativity and imagination. In order to move toward a more peaceful world, all people must learn to be mindful in their intentions, thoughts, and actions, both in their lives and in their workplaces. Were each politician, corporate official, police officer, athlete, social worker (and on and on) to be trained to take time to think about their place in the world and how their actions impact others, we would be well on our way to peace. The hurried nature of our lives leads to burnout, apathy, and lack of focus, so taking time for silence and inner peace can make a big difference in addressing all forms of violence. Personally, my best and most creative ideas come when I'm alone, running. Peacemaking criminologist Richard Quinney noted the importance of personal reflection, or what he called witnessing. Quinney bore witness to systemic and structural violence, suffering, injustice, and thus contemplated the prospect of social justice (Quinney, 2001). Ultimately, "We as human beings must *be* peace if we are to live in a world free of crime" (Quinney, 1991, p. 11). We can incorporate reflective dialogue, or the process of telling our stories of personal and social relevance, into all institutions (Feuerverger, 2008, p. 129). Design conversation is a tool we can use to teach reflectiveness. Stokes (2008) described how design conversation benefits school systems. Design conversation is derived from systems thinking and emphasizes inclusivity and interconnectedness. Traditional conversation—in schools, workplaces, courtrooms, etc.—is dialectic, meaning two sides are presented against one another. Stokes (2008) explained that "if any innovation or change within a system is achieved as a result of dialectic conversation, it likely reflects a pre-conceived view of the dominant party" (p. 166). In other words, it's a power-over method that often reinforces a power-over structure. In contrast, design conversation creates a space where old concepts can be challenged and new ones can emerge. It is based on equity and valuing of diversity, care and respect, and critical consciousness (Jenlink, 2004). Similarly, Gibson (2006) noted the power of deliberative dialogue to help engage citizens to make social change in their communities and beyond.

Mindful Language

For reflectiveness to work, we must also adjust the way we understand certain terms that today have negative connotations. For instance, "activist" often conjures up images of rabble-rousers or crazy people chained to trees with extremist agendas. Instead, we can help people see that to be an activist means to be an active, engaged, and empowered citizen. Baumgardner and Richards (2005), in their book *Grassroots*, define activism as "consistently expressing one's values with the goal of making the world more just" (p. xix). Similarly, the word citizenship is often equated with boring and burdensome, instead of exciting, empowering, and community-building. Instead of seeing social justice as the domain of the far left, we can shift the conversation such that social justice is about fairness, opportunity, and freedom (Moore-Lappe, 2006). As Lin et al. (2008) explained, "Language creates reality . . . we should strive to use peaceful analogies, metaphors, and diction that promote peace" (p. xvi). For example, Clarke (2004) argued that we should "declare peace on terror." Katorsky (2006) asserted that the word "patriot" has come to be associated with acceptance of the status quo, but instead could describe those who speak out and act for the greater good. Gomes de Matos (2001) has created a list of principles for diplomatic communication to be carried out "constructively," all of which can be transferred to virtually all forms of communication. These include

- Avoidance of dehumanizing language
- Investment in handling differences constructively
- Emphasis on language with a potential for peace rather that language employed with a strategic agenda
- Focus on agreement rather than on polemic
- Avoidance of pompous language used to separate and hide

Humility

Humility helps us see that we are only one element in the universe, and that we can learn from all people and circumstances (Lin, 2006). Too often, the United States sees itself as exceptional, and thus refuses to acknowledge that others may know better or more effective means of structuring institutions (Lifton, 2003; Pease, 2009). This mentality is taught in schools (Loewen, 2005) and reinforced in all major institutions.

What if, instead of assuming our way is best and doing more of the same, we took an idea from a different country, let's say on how to train police, and instead of ridiculing it, we assumed *it* was the best. We brainstormed why it was a great idea and how it can help. Then we used that brainstorming to reform our training for police, keeping what we identified as the "pros" of that idea. Elbow (1986) explained that we are often taught to find flaws in every argument. To counter this, he uses an activity like I just described in classes, calling it "The Believing Game." Lin (2006) explained that she asks students to imagine how they can help create peace and always gets very creative responses, even some about how to restructure our society, such as having a Department of Peace instead of a Department of Defense, a Department of Economic Equality and Justice instead of a Department of Commerce, and a Department of Cultural Bridge-Building instead of a Department of State.

Listening

To shift from a dominator paradigm to a partnership paradigm, we need to practice what Moore-Lappe (2006) called "simply listening." She shared the example of the Communities Organized for Public Service (COPS) in San Antonio, Texas, that wanted to address the city's high unemployment rate, in particular for Hispanics. Rather than staging an angry protest, COPS members invited local corporate leaders to share their perspective and then actually listened. By listening, they discovered they shared an interest in expanding job training opportunities in the city. COPS went on to design an innovative job-training program and, having enlisted the input of corporate leaders, was able to get it passed unanimously by the city council. Organizations like the Public Conversations Project (www.publicconversations.org) offer training and assistance to communities, organizations, corporations, educational institutions, and others interested in learning how to bring people together to engage in constructive dialogue. From a sociological view, Project South (www.projectsouth.org) creates popular education tools and publishes research and curricula on grassroots organizing to help oppressed communities engage in social action that is liberating.

Sensitivity training can be built into all institutions. As Lin (2006) explained, "The heart that senses, feels, touches, is touched. Through learning with the heart, we develop a higher sense of sensitivity. This sensitivity is critical for fostering attributes of compassion, sympathy, and concern for social justice and equality" (p. 32). Increased sensitivity allows us to not just believe in peace, but to *live* it (Chopra, 2005; Hanh, 2005). Multicultural experience seems to enhance creativity (Leung, Maddox, Galinsky, & Chiu, 2008). "In short, multicultural experience may foster creativity by (a) providing direct access to novel ideas and concepts from other cultures, (b) creating the ability to see multiple underlying functions behind the same form, (c) destabilizing routinized knowledge structures, thereby increasing the accessibility of normally inaccessible knowledge, (d) creating a psychological readiness to recruit ideas from unfamiliar sources and places, and (e) fostering synthesis of seemingly incompatible ideas from diverse cultures (Westwood & Low, 2003, p. 173). An individual who has been exposed to different cultures may be able to spontaneously retrieve seemingly discrepant ideas from each culture and then juxtapose and integrate those ideas in novel ways (Chiu & Hong, 2005).

Service

In addition to simple training on sensitivity, why can't service learning opportunities be built into the way we train all professionals? Both in their college education or vocational preparation as well as part of on-the-job training. Service learning has long been utilized as a way to both engage students and for praxis (Jacoby, 1996). Service learning has been defined as "the integration of community service activities (as defined by the community) into the curriculum through intentional analytical processes such as journals, papers, and other expositional forms to enhance students' learning of course content" (Marullo & Edwards, 2000, p. 747). However, what makes service learning different from other pedagogical tools is that service learning is an experiential form of education. Education is experiential when academic knowledge is applied critically and in collaboration with communities to address salient problems.

Crews and Weigert (1999) noted in their edited volume *Teaching for Justice: Concepts and Models for Service-Learning in Peace Studies* that service helps enact the teachers-as-students, students-as-teachers model Freire envisioned. Service learning is ideally suited to helping participants understand and work toward positive peace, in that all kinds of opportunities are available to address interconnected social issues. Students who engage in service learning generally emerge with increased understanding and empathy. They are able to connect to one another and their community, to develop a sense of empathy and pride (Koliba, 2000), to acquire more finely tuned critical analysis and writing skills, and can better see connections between theory and practice (Alberle-Grass, 2000; Calderon & Farrell, 1996; Kuhn, 1995; Parker-Gwin, 1996; Roschelle, Turpin, & Elias, 2000; Smith, D., 2007). Alberle-Grass (2000) demonstrated that service learning may have a long-term impact on students. She found that students who engaged in service learning were more likely to enter careers in the nonprofit sector or in service and advocacy organizations. Finally, service learning can benefit community organizations by providing needed assistance and through the development of a larger network of supporters (Calderon & Farrell, 1996). Yet, as beneficial as service learning seems to be, it is not widely used in certain college academic programs like business, medicine, and criminal justice. Further, why can't police organizations, in addition to requiring training in the academy and by field officers, also require that recruits engage in some type of community service learning that enhances their understanding of local issues and responses to them? Why can't employees at nonprofits be required to engage in service learning to better understand the community issues that are closely related to the one in which they are employed? Can't athletes, as a condition of their participation in college or professional leagues, be required to not just volunteer or be philanthropic, but to truly engage with their community through service learning projects?

Concluding Thoughts

In conclusion, Lin et al. (2008) argued for a new paradigm of peace education, one that sees peace as an ongoing, attainable process built on the universal ethics of love, compassion, and forgiveness and directly linked to social justice. My hope is that this book helps us see how this new paradigm needs to be enacted in every societal institution and, importantly, that although there is still much work to be done, the seeds have indeed been planted.

Favorite Activities and Ideas for Teaching Peace and Justice

1. A good icebreaker: "The Blob": Ask people to pair up and find one thing they have in common. Then ask the pairs to move together and group up with another set of pairs so that the group of four finds something they all have in common. Continue until you are ready to stop or the class is one big group.
2. Another great icebreaker: Speed date for peace: Line everyone up in two rows, facing one another (so everyone is across from one other person). Ask a question and have each person very briefly discuss their response with the person across from them. Then have one row move down so that each person now has a new partner. Ask another question and repeat the activity until you are done with all the questions you'd like to ask. Then, discuss people's answers. Suggested questions include what song most makes you think of peace and why; what person most makes you think of peace and why? What would a peace superhero's powers be? What would s/he look like? What movie most makes you think of peace and why?
3. Develop a dictionary or Wikipedia-style resource on nonviolent vocabulary and terminology.

4. Revise famous quotes, movie titles (and plot summaries) or songs to focus on peace, not violence.
5. Use "This day in peace and justice history" timeline to discuss and celebrate significant achievements (available at http://www.salsa. net/peace/timeline/jan.html)
6. Brainstorm with your group ways you can use as many of Gene Sharp's 198 methods of nonviolence as possible (available at http://www.salsa.net/peace/genesharp.html)
7. Create a display to hang in the school, office, community center, etc. about famous peacemakers. Learn more about famous peacemakers at http://www.salsa.net/peace/faces/index.html
8. Discuss the meaning of famous quotes about peace. Display them publicly. Good sources of peace quotes are http://www.salsa.net/ peace/quotes.html and http://www.wagingpeace.org/menu/issues/peace-&-war/start/peace-quotes/
9. Use the Peace Corps Environmental Education in the Community guide to implement programs in your community. Available at http://multimedia.peacecorps.gov/multimedia/pdf/library/eec_full.pdf
10. Work with young girls using the Peace Corps Beyond the Classroom: Empowering Girls guide. Available at http://multimedia.peacecorps.gov/multimedia/pdf/library/empoweringgirls.pdf
11. Incorporate educational initiatives in any group or organization using the Peace Corps Nonformal Education manuals. Available at http://multimedia.peacecorps.gov/multimedia/pdf/library/M0042_nfemanual1.pdf and http://multimedia.peacecorps.gov/multimedia/pdf/library/M0042_nfemanual2.pdf
12. Utilize any of these lesson ideas to teach peace in any setting or group: http://www.yesmagazine.org/for-teachers/curriculum/connect-and-engage-teaching-peace
13. Have a "peace of cake" party (where people decorate desserts with messages of peace) or an international human rights potluck.
14. Organize a walk for human rights.
15. Host a peace/human rights fair that showcases local work and services related to human rights.
16. Host a film screening or peace/human rights film festival.
17. Make community art. Get canvases or large mural paper. Have everyone in the group contribute their vision of peace, with as many people coloring or painting at the same time as possible. Display prominently!

18. Play positive peace trivia—there are lots of great facts available online.
19. Chalk for peace—On September 21 (or any day!), use sidewalk chalk to create peace messages and drawings to beautify the area and spread messages of peace.
20. Sponsor a peace-essay contest for the school, organization, or community.
21. Adopt a Peace Corps volunteer: http://www.peacecorps.gov/wws/correspond/
22. Find an international pen pal and correspond to learn about someone different than you.
23. Help make peace while you travel! Take a group on a Volunteer for Peace trip: www.vfp.org. Other trips are available at http://www.peacework.org/
24. Take a course on peacemaking. Online courses available at the United States Institute for Peace (USIP—http://www.usip.org/education-training), the University for Peace (www.upeace.org), and a number of colleges and universities.
25. Adopt an area, street, or block and commit to keeping it clean and/or making it better for the entire community.
26. Sponsor a competition at your workplace/school/organization: Ask employees or students to team up, learn about a social issue in their community, and devise a plan to help address it. Reward the team that does the most to help.
27. Engage in an exchange program with another school/employer/organization for a day or as long as possible.
28. Research local nonprofits making a difference in your community. Invite a representative to speak to your group, host a donation drive, or group up to volunteer.
29. Create a peace/human rights book club.
30. Take a peace inventory of your community. Publish it on the Web, and include the many great resources available that can help effect positive peace.

Favorite Positive Peace Education Resources

Films

Amandla! A Revolution in Four-Part Harmony (2003)
> Presents the story of how music helped end apartheid in South Africa.

Capitalism: A Love Story (2009)
> Michael Moore's critique of the violence inherent in modern capitalism.

The Corporation (2003)
> Thoroughly demonstrates how corporations are like psychopaths and offers suggestions for a different way.

The End of Poverty? (2008)
> Highlights the role of colonization, military actions, and slavery in exploiting the developing world and creating and sustaining poverty.

Flow: For Love of Water (2008)
> Persuasively presents how politics, pollution, and human rights are intertwined in the global war for water.

Building a Peaceful Society, pages 143–148
Copyright © 2011 by Information Age Publishing
143

Food, Inc. (2008)
> Provides the scary details on how our food is made and the attendant environmental and human damage.

The Injustice System in America (2006)
> Focuses on the overrepresentation of minorities and nonviolent offenders in U.S. prisons.

Invisible Children (2003)
> Documents the devastating effects of Uganda's civil war and its use of child soldiers.

Into the Wild (2007)
> Based on Jon Krakauer's book; film beautifully shows that we are all interdependent.

Iraq for Sale: The War Profiteers (2006)
> Shows who is benefitting from the war in Iraq.

The Least of These (2009)
> Documents activists' efforts to reform Texas prisons.

Ladies First (2004)
> Demonstrates how Rwandan women are leading the country's healing process.

One Peace at a Time (2009)
> Examines ways to bring peace and human rights to the world's children.

Plan Columbia (2002)
> Documents the devastating environmental and human effects of the United States's drug war in Colombia.

Pray the Devil Back to Hell (2008/09)
> Chronicles the nonviolent movement of Christian and Muslim women to end the civil war and bring peace to Liberia.

Taking Root: The Vision of Wangari Maathai (2008)
> Dramatic story of Nobel Peace Prize Laureate's effort to plant trees to help the environment, protect human rights, and defend democracy.

Wal-mart: The High Cost of Low Price (2005)
> A thorough examination of how this behemoth perpetuates various forms of violence as well as resistance movements.

Books

Boulding, E. (2000). *Cultures of peace: The hidden side of history.* Syracuse, NY: Syracuse University Press.

Chomsky, N. (2010). *Hopes and Prospects.* Chicago: Haymarket Books.

Farmer, P. (2004). *Pathologies of power: Health, human rights, and the new war on the poor.* Berkeley, CA: University of California Press.

Freire, P. (2000). *Pedagogy of the oppressed.* New York: Continuum.

Galtung, J. (1996). *Peace by peaceful means: Peace and conflict, development and civilization.* Thousand Oaks, CA: Sage.

hooks, b. (1994). *Teaching to transgress: Education as the practice of freedom.* New York: Routledge.

Iadicola, P., & Shupe, A. (2003). *Violence, inequality and human freedom* (2nd Ed.). Oxford: Rowman & Littlefield.

Illich, I. (2000). *Deschooling society.* St. Paul, MN: Marion Boyars Publishers.

Jones, E., Haenfler, R., & Johnson, B. (2007). *The Better World Handbook.* Gabriola Island, BC, Canada: New Society.

Kappeler, V., & Potter, G. (2004). *The mythology of crime and criminal justice.* Waveland Press.

Klein, N. (2007). *The shock doctrine: The rise of disaster capitalism.* New York: Metropolitan Books.

Kohn, A. (1992). *No contest: The case against competition.* New York: Houghton Mifflin.

Kristof, N., & WuDunn, S. (2010). *Half the sky: Turning oppression into opportunity for women worldwide.* New York: Vintage.

Loeb, P. (2004). *The impossible will take a little while: A citizen's guide to hope in a time of fear.* New York: Basic.

Loeb, P. (2010). *Soul of a citizen: Living in conviction in challenging times.* New York: St. Martin's Griffin.

Louv, R. (2005). *Last child in the woods: Saving our children from nature-deficit disorder.* Chapel Hill, NC: Algonquin Books.

Luvmour, S., & Luvmour, J. (1990). *Everyone wins: Cooperative games and activities.* Gabriola Island, BC, Canada: New Society Publishers.

McGlynn, C., Bekerman, Z., Zembylas, M., & Gallagher, T. (Eds.). (2009). *Peace education in conflict and post-conflict societies: Comparative perspectives.* New York: Palgrave MacMillan.

Michalowski, R., & Kramer, R. (2006). *State-corporate crime: Wrongdoing at the intersection of business and government.* Rutgers, NJ: Rutgers University Press.

Norton, M. (2005). *365 ways to change the world.* New York: Free Press.

Pilisuk, M. (2007). *Who benefits from global violence and war: Uncovering a destructive system.* Westport, CT: Praeger.

Postman, N. (1971). Teaching as a subversive activity. *New York:* Delta.

Reiman, J. (2006). *The rich get richer and the poor get prison.* New York: Allyn and Bacon.

Rosenberg, M. (2003). *Nonviolent communication: A language of life.* Encinitas, CA: Puddledancer Press.

Rosenberg, M. (2004). *Raising children compassionately: Parenting the nonviolent communication way.* Encinitas, CA: Puddledancer Press.

Schirch, L. (1969). *The little book of peacebuilding.* PA: Good Books.

Smith, K. (2003). *Living out loud: Activities to fuel a creative life.* San Francisco: Chronicle Books.

Tifft, L., & Sutherland, D. (2008). *Handbook of restorative justice: A global perspective.* London: Routledge.

Tifft, L., & Sutherland, D. (2005). *Restorative justice: Healing the foundations of our everyday life.* Criminal Justice Press.

Timpson, W., Brantmeier, E., Kees, N., Cavanaugh, T., & McGlynn, C. (2009). *147 practical tips for teaching peace and reconciliation.* Atwood Publishing.

Weil, Z. (2003). *Above all, be kind: Raising a child in challenging times.* Gabriola Island, BC, Canada: New Society Publishers.

Zehr, H. (1990). *Changing lenses: A new focus for crime and justice.* Herald Press.

Zehr, H. (2002). *The little book of restorative justice.* Good Books.

Zelizer, C., & Rubenstein, R. (Eds.). (2009). *Building peace: Practical reflections from the field.* Kumarian Press.

Zirin, D. (2005). *What's my name, fool? Sports and resistance in the United States.* Chicago: Haymarket Books.

Web Sites

Amnesty International Human Rights Education Resources:
http://www.amnestyusa.org/educate/page.do?id=1102117

Educational materials, videos and more:
http://www.humanrights.com/#/home

Information and activism to end global hunger, disease, environmental damage and more:
www.thehungersite.com

Tools for helping communities make social change on a diversity of issues:
http://www.everyday-democracy.org/en/index.aspx

Provides stories about innovative ideas and good news:
www.gnn.com

Articles and materials related to school and societal reform:
www.rethinkignschools.org

Helping foreign countries through debt cancellation:
www.jubileeusa.org

Great ideas for all kinds of actions:
www.idea-a-day.com

Human rights information for young people:
http://www.youthforhumanrights.org/index.htm

Great information and ideas about all kinds of subjects:
http://www.yesmagazine.org/

Ideas for helping:
http://www.365act.com/

Ideas for teaching and supporting kindness:
http://www.actsofkindness.org/

Classroom information and activities related to human and civil rights:
http://www.tolerance.org/

International travel and peacemaking:
www.witnessforpeace.org

Direct Action tips and ideas:
www.ruckus.org

Direct Education training and information:
www.trainingforchange.org

Organizing to end exploitation of farmworkers:
www.ciw-online.org

Support for those taking creative approaches to end social injustice:
http://antiapathy.org/

Innovative ideas to solve personal and social problems:
http://www.whynot.net/

Database of creative, original ideas on all kinds of topics:
http://www.creativitypool.com/

Alternative media to help change our thinking:
http://www.worldchanging.com/

Alternate media source focused on women:
www.worldpulse.com

Ideas for innovations and creativity in business:
http://www.innovationtools.com/

Changing our thinking about peace through music:
http://www.newsongsforpeace.org/

Information, videos, and resources for environmental change:
www.storyofstuff.com

News source focused on global injustices:
www.newint.org

Documents corporate irresponsibility and demands accountability:
www.corpwatch.org

Activism to end poverty and militarism and to provide healthy food to those in need:
www.foodnotbombs.net

Tools and resources for popular education:
http://www.paulofreireinstitute.org/

Wonderful resources and links for peace and human rights education with children:
www.hrusa.org/store/EffectivePractices.doc

Peace curricula for incarcerated juveniles:
http://www.peacejam.org/education.aspx?pageName=PeaceJam%20Juvenile%20Justice#content

Curricula and materials for all educational levels:
www.efnv.org

Many kinds of positive peace programs:
http://www.transcend.org/

Curricula and readings from Colman McCarthy's class on nonviolence:
http://www.salsa.net/peace/conv/

References

100 Best Companies to Work for in 2007. (2007). Retrieved February 6, 2009, from http://money.cnn.com/magazines/fortune/bestcompanies/2007/snapshots/1.html

100 Best Companies to Work for in 2009. (2009). Retrieved February 6, 2009, from http://money.cnn.com/magazines/fortune/bestcompanies/2009/snapshots/22.html

Aall, P., Helsing, J., & Tidwell, A. (2007). Addressing conflict through education. In I. W. Zartman (Ed.), *Peace making in international conflict: Methods and techniques* (pp. 327–354). Washington, DC: U.S. Institute of Peace Press.

About the book. (n.d.). *The Corporation.* Retrieved June 21, 2010, from http://www.thecorporation.com/index.cfm?page_id=4

About the Happy Planet Index. (2009). Retrieved April 5, 2011 from http://www.happyplanetindex.org/

Abu-Nimer, M. (2004). Education for coexistence and Arab–Jewish encounters in Israel: Potential and challenges. *Journal of Social Issues, 60*(2), 405–422.

Adams, W. (2010, May 10). Norway builds the world's most humane prison. *Time.* Retrieved June 22, 2010, from http://www.time.com/time/magazine/article/0,9171,1986002,00.html?hpt=T2

Adarkar, A., & Keiser, D. (2007). The Buddha in the classroom: Toward a critical spiritual pedagogy. *Journal of Transformative Education, 5*(3), 246–261.

Adelman, M. (2003). The military, militarism, and the militarization of domestic violence. *Violence Against Women, 9*(9), 1118–1152.

Africa News. (2007, June 11). *Peace Institute, Refugee Commission launches peace education.* Retrieved April 12, 2010, from LexisNexis Academic database.

Agius, E., & Ambrosewicz, J. (2003). *Toward a culture of tolerance and peace.* Montreal, Quebec, Canada: International Bureau for Children's Rights.

Building a Peaceful Society, pages 149–177
Copyright © 2011 by Information Age Publishing
All rights of reproduction in any form reserved.

Ahladas, Y, & Sachs-Hamilton, B. (2008, April 21). Community Is no cliché: It works...the Burlington way. *Yes! Magazine.* Online edition. Retrieved April 5, 2011 from www.yesmagazine.org/issues/columns/2538

Alberle-Grasse, M. (2000). The Washington study-service year of Eastern Mennonite University: Reflections on 23 years of service learning. *American Behavioral Scientist, 43,* 848–857.

Albuquerque, C., & Paes-Machado, L. (2004). The hazing machine: The shaping of Brazilian military recruits. *Policing and Society, 14*(2), 175–192.

Alexander, G. (2007, April 23). The non-profit industrial complex: Is there such a thing as too much civil society? *American Enterprise Institute for Public Policy Research.* Retrieved August 19, 2010, from http://www.aei.org/article/25958

Alexander, N., & Carlson, T. (1999). Adventure-based learning in the name of peace. In L. Forcey & I. Harris (Eds.), *Peacebuilding for adolescents* (pp. 161–174). New York: Peter Lang.

Allard, S. (2009). *Out of reach: Place, poverty and the new American welfare state.* New Haven, CT: Yale University Press.

Alliance for Childhood. (2005, May). Ten steps for peace education. Retrieved June 15, 2010, from http://allianceforchildhood.org/ten_steps

Allport, G. (1954). *The nature of prejudice.* Reading, MA: Addison-Wesley.

Alvick, T. (1968). The development of views on conflict, war and peace among school children. *Journal of Peace Research, 5*(2), 171–195.

Amabile, T. (1985). Motivation and creativity: Effects of motivational orientation on creative writers. *Journal of Personality and Social Psychology, 48,* 393–399.

Amabile, T. (1996). *Creativity in context.* Boulder, CO: Westview Press.

Amabile, T., Barsade, S., Mueller, J., & Staw, B. (2005). Affect and creativity at work. *Administrative Science Quarterly, 50,* 367–403.

Amabile, T. M., Hennessey, B. A., & Grossman, B. S. (1986). Social influences on creativity: The effects of contracted-for reward. *Journal of Personality and Social Psychology, 50,* 14–23.

Amir, Y. (1998). Contact hypothesis in ethnic relations. In E. Weiner (Ed.), *The handbook of interethnic coexistence* (pp. 162–181). New York: Continuum Publishing.

Anderson, M. (1999). *Do no harm: How aid can support peace—or war.* Boulder, CO: Lynne Rienner.

Aronson, E. (2000). *Nobody left to hate: Teaching compassion after Columbine.* New York: Freeman.

Arthur, J. (1998). Proximate correlates of blacks' support for capital punishment. *Journal of Crime and Justice, 21,* 159–172.

Arthur, P. (1999). The Anglo-Irish peace process: Obstacles to reconciliation. In R. L. Rothstein (Ed.), *After the peace: Resistance and reconciliation* (pp. 85–109). Boulder, CO: Lynne Rienner.

Asmal, K., Asmal, L., & Roberts, R. (1997). *Reconciliation through truth: A reckoning of apartheid's criminal governance*. Cape Town, South Africa: David Phillips.

Astor, R., Vargas, L., Pitner, R., & Meyer, H. (1999). School violence: Research, theory, and practice. In J. Jenson & M. Howard (Eds.), *Youth violence: Current research and recent innovations* (pp. 139–171). Washington, DC: NASW Press.

Atkinson, M. (2009). Parkour, anarcho-environmentalism, and poiesis. *Journal of Sport and Social Issues, 33*(2), 169–194.

Avery, P., Johnson, D., Johnson, R., & Mitchell, J. (1999). Teaching an understanding of war and peace through structured academic controversies. In L. Oppenheimer, D. Bar-Tal, & A. Raviv (Eds.), *How children understand war and peace* (pp. 260–280). San Francisco: Jossey-Bass.

Axelrod, D. (2006, February 15). Freedom Project: Inmates find peace. *Yes! Magazine*. Online edition. Retrieved April 5, 2011 from www.yesmagazine.org/issues/10-most-hopeful-trends/freedom_project_inmates_find_peace

Ayers, W., Dohrn, B., & Ayers, R. (2001). *Zero tolerance: Resisting the drive for punishment*. New York: New Press.

Baker, M., Martin, D., & Pence, H. (2008). Supporting peace education in teacher education programs. *Childhood Education, 85*(1), 20–25.

Barak, G. (2005). A reciprocal approach to peacemaking criminology. *Theoretical Criminology, 9*(2), 131–152.

Barkan, S., & Cohn, S. (1994). Racial prejudice and support for the death penalty by whites. *Journal of Research in Crime and Delinquency, 31*(2), 202–209.

Bar-Tal, D. (1998). Societal beliefs in times of intractable conflict: The Israeli case. *International Journal of Conflict Management, 9*, 22–50.

Bar-Tal, D. (2007). Sociopsychological foundations of intractable conflicts. *American Behavioral Scientist, 50*, 1430–1453.

Bar-Tal, D., Halperin, E., & de Rivera, J. (2007). Collective emotions in conflict: Societal implications. *Journal of Social Issues, 63*, 441–460.

Bar-Tal, D., & Rosen, Y. (2009). Peace education in societies involved in intractable conflicts: Direct and indirect models. *Review of Educational Research, 79*, 557–575.

Batavick, L. (1997). Community-based family support and youth development: Two movements, one philosophy. *Child Welfare, 76*, 639–666

Baumgardner, J., & Richards, A. (2005). *Grassroots: A field guide for feminist activism*. New York: Farrar, Straus, & Giroux.

Baxi, U. (1997). Human rights education: The promise of the third millennium. In G. Andreopoulos & R. Claude (Eds.), *Human rights education for the twenty-first century* (pp. 142–154). Philadelphia: University of Pennsylvania Press.

Bazemore, G. (1997). *Balanced and restorative justice for juveniles: A framework for juvenile justice in the 21st century*. St. Paul: University of Minnesota Center for Restorative Justice and Peacemaking.

Bazemore, G., & Schiff, M. (2001). Understanding restorative community justice: What and why now? In G. Bazemore & M. Schiff (Eds.), *Restorative community justice: Repairing harm and transforming communities* (pp. 21–46). Cincinnati, OH: Anderson Publishing Co.

Beckett, K. *(1997). Making crime pay: Law and order in contemporary American politics.* New York: Oxford University Press.

Beckett, K., & Sasson, T. (2000). *The politics of injustice: Crime and punishment in America.* Thousand Oaks, CA: Pine Forge Press.

Beger, R. (2002). Expansion of police power in public schools and the vanishing rights of students. *Social Justice, 29,* 1.

Ben-Porat, A. (1998) .The commodification of football in Israel. *International Review for the Sociology of Sport, 33*(3), 267–277.

Ben-Porat, G., & Ben-Porat, A. (2004). (Un)bounded soccer: Globalization and localization of the game in Israel. *International Review for the Sociology of Sport, 39*(4), 421–436.

Berns, N. (2004). *Framing the victim: Domestic violence, media, and social problems.* New York: Aldine de Gruyter.

Bey, T., & Turner, G. (1995). *Making school a place of peace.* New York: Corwin.

Bickmore, K. (1999). Teaching conflict and conflict resolution in school. In L. Oppenheimer, D. Bar-Tal, & A. Raviv (Eds.), *How children understand war and peace* (pp. 233–259). San Francisco: Jossey-Bass.

Bilchik, S. (1998). *Guide for implementing the balanced and restorative justice model.* Washington, DC: Office of Juvenile Justice and Delinquency Prevention.

Blum, J., & Woodlee, Y. (2001, June 3). Trying to give kids a good scare: Many jails offer tours, but experts question their value. *The Washington Post,* p. C1.

Boulding,K. (1978). *Stable peace.* Austin, TX: University of Texas Press.

Bowen, N. K., & Bowen, G. L. (1999). Effects of crime and violence in neighborhoods and schools on the school performance of adolescents. *Journal of Adolescent Research, 14,* 319–342.

Boyes-Watson, C. (2005). *Seeds of change: Using peacemaking circles to build a village for every child.* Washington, DC: Child Welfare League of America.

Braithwaite, J. (1989). *Crime, shame, and reintegration.* New York: Cambridge University Press.

Braithwaite, V. (1999). Values and restorative justice in schools. Retrieved July 24, 2010, from http://crj.anu.edu.au/menus/PDFs/pubs.vb.values.pdf

Brauer, J., & Tepper-Marlin, J. (2009). Nonkilling economics. In J. Pim (Ed.), *Toward a nonkilling paradigm* (pp. 125–150). Honolulu: Center for Global Nonkilling.

Brett, R., & McCallin, M. (1996). *Children: The invisible soldiers.* Vaxjo, Sweden: Radda Barnen.

Brimmer, L. (1994). *Voices from the camps: Internment of Japanese Americans during World War II.* Danbury, CT: Franklin Watts.

Bronson, P., & Merryman, A. (2010, July 19). The creativity crisis. *Newsweek*, pp. 44–50.

Brown, E., & Morgan, W. (2008). A culture of peace via global citizenship education. *Peace Review: A Journal of Social Justice, 20*, 283–391.

Brown, S. (2009). *Play: How it shapes the brain, opens the imagination, and invigorates the soul.* New York: Avery.

Bruck, P., & Roach, C. (1993). Dealing with reality: The news media and the promotion of peace. In C. Roach (Ed.), *Communication and culture in war and peace* (pp. 71–95). Newbury Park, CA: Sage.

Bryant, D., Hanis, J., & Stoner, C. (1999). Special needs, special measures: Working with homeless and poor youth. In I. Harris & L. Forcey (Eds.), *Peacebuilding for adolescents: Strategies for educators and community leaders.* New York: Peter Lang.

Buerger, M. (1998). A tale of two targets: Limitations of community anticrime actions. In D. Karp (Ed.), *Community justice: An emerging field* (pp. 137–166). Lanham, MD: Rowman & Littlefield.

Buerger, M., Petrosino, A., & Petrosino, C. (1999). Extending the police role: Implications of police mediation as a problem-solving tool. *Police Quarterly, 2*(2), 125–149.

Bullard, S. (1996). *Teaching tolerance: Raising open-minded, empathetic children.* New York: Doubleday.

Burger, J. (1994). Keys to survival: Highlights in resilience research. *Journal of Emotional and Behavioral Problems, 3*(2), 6–10.

Cairns, E., & Roe, M. D. (Eds.). (2003). *The role of memory in ethnic conflict.* New York: Palgrave Macmillan.

Calderon, J ., & Farrell, B. (1996). Doing sociology: Connecting the classroom experience with a multiethnic school district. *Teaching Sociology, 26*, 46–53.

Caldicott, H. (2005). The nation that saved the world? In D. Church & G. Gendreau (Eds.), *Healing our planets, healing ourselves* (pp. 67–78). Santa Rosa, CA: Elite Books.

Calleja, J. (1994). Educating for peace in the Mediterranean: A strategy for peace building. In E. Boulding (Ed.), *Building peace in the Middle East: Challenges for states and civil society* (pp. 279–285). Boulder, CO: Lynne Rienner.

Campbell, D., & Campbell, K. (2010). Soldiers as police officers/police officers as soldiers: Role evolution and revolution in the United States. *Armed Forces & Society, 36*(2), 327–350.

Canadian Center for Peace Education. (n.d.). *Sports: When winning is the only thing, can violence be far away?* Retrieved May 26, 2010, from http://www.peace.ca/sports.htm

Carlin, J. (2007). *Invictus: Nelson Mandela and the game that made a nation.* New York: Penguin.

Carlton, E. (2001). *Militarism: Rule without law.* Aldershot, UK: Ashgate.

Casella, R. (2001). "Being down:" Challenging violence in urban schools. New York: Teachers College.

Center for Partnership Studies. (n.d.). *Family Policy.* Retrieved February 6, 2009, from http://www.partnershipway.org/html/family.htm

Chappell, A., & Lanza-Kaduce, L. (2010). Police academy socialization: Understanding the lessons learned in a paramilitary bureaucratic organization. *Journal of Contemporary Ethnography, 39*(2), 187–214.

Chiu, C-y., & Hong, Y. (2005). Cultural competence: Dynamic processes. In A. Elliot & C. S. Dweck (Eds.), *Handbook of motivation and competence* (pp. 489–505). New York: Guilford Press.

Christie, N. (1971). *Hvis Skolen ikke Fantes* (If school did not exist). Oslo: Universitetsforlaget.

Christie, N. (1994). *Crime control as industry.* London: Routledge.

Chopra, D. (2005). *Peace is the way.* New York: Harmony Books.

Clarke. K. (2004, August). Declare peace on terror. *U.S. Catholic, 69*(8), 35.

Clarke-Habibi, S. (2005). Transforming worldviews: The case of education for peace in Bosnia and Herzegovina. *Journal of Transformative Education, 3*(1), 33–56.

Coalition to Stop the Use of Child Soldiers. (2008). *Child soldiers: Global report, 2008.* Retrieved August 16, 2010, from http://www.childsoldiersglobalreport.org/

Cohen, S. (1980). *Folk devils and moral panics: The creation of the mods and rockers* (New ed.). Oxford, UK: Martin Robertson.

Collier, P. (2010, February 18). How to fix Haiti's fixers. Retrieved May 30, 2010, from http://www.foreignpolicy.com/articles/2010/02/18/how_to_fix_haitis_fixers?print=yes&hidecomments=yes&page=full

Combs, M., & Comer, J. (1984). Race and capital punishment: A longitudinal analysis. *Phylon, 43*(4), 350–359.

Conflict Research Consortium. (2003). *Article summary of "Nonviolent Action in Acute Interethnic Conflicts" by Gene Sharp.* Retrieved August 16, 2010, from http://www.beyondintractability.org/articlesummary/10538/

Cooper, P. (1965). The development of the concept of war. *Journal of Peace Research, 2*(1), 1–17.

Coppola, A. (2007, October 22). *Making strides without taking steps.* Corrections. com. Retrieved August 19, 2010, from http://www.corrections.com/articles/16914-making-strides-without-taking-steps

Couper, D. (1994, March). *Seven seeds for policing.* Retrieved September 9, 2010, from http://findarticles.com/p/articles/mi_m2194/is_n3_v63/ai_15353031/?tag=content;col1

Covell, K., Rose-Krasnor, L., & Fletcher, K. (1994). Age difference in understanding peace, war and conflict resolution. *International Journal of Behavioral Development, 19*(4), 871–883.

Cox, S. (2008, May 20). *Problems with drug resistance education.* Retrieved May 20, 2010, from http://war-on-drugs.suite101.com/article.cfm/why_dare_flunked

Craft, A. (2003). The limits to creativity in education: Dilemmas for the educator. *British Journal of Educational Studies, 51*(2), 113–127.

Cretu, T. (1988). Peace and its most obvious meanings in preschool children's drawings. *Revue Roumaine des Sciences Sociales-Serie de Psychologie, 32,* 97–99.

Crews, G., & Tipton, J. (2001). *A comparison of public schools and prison security measures: Too much of a good thing?* Retrieved January 8, 2001, from http://www.kci.org/publication/articles/school_security_measures.html

Crews, R., & Weigert, K. (Eds.). (1999). *Teaching for justice: Concepts and models for service-learning in peace studies.* Herndon, VA: American Association for Higher Education.

Crone, J. (2011). *How can we solve social problems?* Scarborough, Ontario, Canada: Nelson.

Crook, W. (2001). Trickle-down bureaucracy: Does the organization affect client responses to programs. *Administration in Social Work, 26*(1), 27–59.

Cropley, A. (2001). *Creativity in education & learning.* London: Kogan-Page.

Dacey, J. (1989). *Fundamentals of creative thinking.* Lexington, MA: Lexington Press.

Dalai Lama. (2005). Compassion in action. In D. Church & G. Gendreau (Eds.), *Healing our planets, healing ourselves* (pp. 61–66). Santa Rosa, CA: Elite Books.

Dale, C., & Kalob. D. (2006, May). Embracing social activism: Sociology in the service of social justice and peace. *Humanity & Society, 30*(2), 121–152.

Davis, R. (2009). Brooklyn mediation field test. *Journal of Experimental Criminology, 5*(1), 25–39.

Dellas, M., & Gaier, E. (1970). Identification of creativity: The individual. *Psychological Bulletin, 73,* 55–73.

Dellasega, C. (2005). *Mean girls grown up: Adult women who are still queen bees, middle bees, and afraid-to-bees.* New York: Wiley.

Deutsch, M. (1993). Educating for a peaceful world. *American Psychologist, 48*(5), 510–517.

Deutsch, M. (2000). Justice and conflict. In M. Deutsch & P. T. Coleman (Eds.), *The handbook of conflict resolution: Theory and practice* (pp. 41–64). San Francisco: Jossey-Bass.

Deutsch, M. (2005). Cooperation and conflict: A personal perspective on the history of the social psychological study of conflict resolution. In M. West, D. Tjosvold, & K. Smith (Eds.), *The essentials of teamworking: International perspectives* (pp. 1–36). New York: John Wiley.

Dewey, J. (1902). *The child and the curriculum.* University of Chicago Press.

Dewey, J. (1933). *How we think: A restatement of the relation of reflective thinking to the educative process.* New York: D. C. Heath.

DiGiulio, R. (1999). Nonviolent interventions in secondary schools: Administrative perspectives. In L. Forcey & I. Harris (Eds.), *Peacebuilding for adolescents* (pp. 195–212). New York: Peter Lang.

DiGiulio, R. (2001). *Educate, medicate, or litigate? What teachers, parents and administrators must do about student behavior.* Thousand Oaks, CA: Sage.

Dohrenwend, B., Levav, I., Shrout, P., Schwartz, S., Naveh, G., Link, B. et al. (1992, February 21). Socioeconomic status and psychiatric disorders: The causation-selection issue. *Science, 255*(5047), 946–952.

Dokoupil, T. (2010, May 28). "Zero Tolerance" trouble in New York. *Newsweek.* Retrieved July 25, 2010, from http://www.newsweek.com/2010/05/28/zero-tolerance-trouble-in-new-york.html

Dowler, K. (2003). Media consumption and public attitudes toward crime and justice: The relationship between fear of crime, punitive attitudes, and perceived police effectiveness. *Journal of Criminal Justice and Popular Culture 10*(2), 109–126.

Drew, N. (2000). *Peaceful parents, peaceful kids.* New York: Kensington Books.

DuBois, M. (1997). Human rights education for the police. In G. Andreopoulos & R. Claude (Eds.), *Human rights education for the twenty-first century* (pp. 310–333). Philadelphia: University of Pennsylvania Press.

Durkheim, E. (1933). *The division of labor in society.* New York: Free Press.

Edwards, P. (2008, May 4). Criminals see gold at Olympics. *The Star.* Retrieved August 15, 2010, from http://www.thestar.com/News/World/article/421229

Eisenberger, R., & Cameron, J. (1996). Detrimental effects of reward: Reality or myth? *American Psychologist, 51,* 1153–1166.

Eisler, R. (n.d. a). *The four cornerstones.* Center for Partnership Studies. Retrieved August 22, 2010, from http://www.partnershipway.org/about-cps/foundational-concepts/four-cornerstones

Eisler, R. (n.d. b). *The real wealth of nations public policy initiative: A strategy to advance healthy economic priorities.* Retrieved June 14, 2010, from http://www.rianeeisler.com/documents/9-20publicplicyRWNtwo-pager-1.pdf

Eisler, R. (1987). *The chalice and the blade.* San Francisco: HarperCollins.

Eisler, R. (1993). Roles of women and men: Integrating the public and the private. In P. Juviler & B. Gross (Eds.), *Human rights for the twenty-first century: Foundations for responsible hope* (pp. 245–262). New York: M. E. Sharpe.

Eisler, R. (2000). *Tomorrow's children.* Boulder, CO: Westview.

Eisler, R. (2007). *The real wealth of nations: Creating a caring economics.* San Francisco, CA: Berrett-Koehler.

Elbow, P. (1986). *Embracing contraries.* New York: Oxford University Press.

Elhance, A. P., & Ahmar, M. (1995). Nonmilitary CBMs. In M. Krepon & A. Sevak (Eds.), *Crisis prevention, confidence building and reconciliation in South Asia* (pp. 131–151). New York: St. Martin's Press.

Elias, R. (1986). *The politics of victimization: Victims, victimology, and human rights.* New York: Oxford University Press.

Elikann, P. (1999). Superpredators: The demonization of our children by the law. New York: Perseus.

Engel, B. (1984). Between feeling and fact: Listening to children. *Harvard Education Review, 54*, 304–314.

Enloe, C. (2000). *Maneuvers: The international politics of militarizing women's lives.* Berkeley: University of California Press.

Ericson, R., & Carriere, K. (1994). The fragmentation of criminology. In D. Nelken (Ed.), *The futures of criminology.* London: Sage.

Erickson, D. (2010, May 17). At this prison graduation, the focus is on knowing the effects of their crimes. *Wisconsin State Journal.* Retrieved June 22, 2010, from http://host.madison.com/wsj/news/local/crime_and_courts/article_8e99eef6-6204-11df-9f92-001cc4c03286.html

European Commission on Sport. (2009, July 3). *Study on money laundering through the football sector.* Retrieved August 25, 2010, from http://ec.europa.eu/sport/news/news789_en.htm

Eysenck, H. (1997). Creativity and personality. In M. Runco (Ed.), *The creativity research handbook,* (Vol. 1, pp. 41–66). Creskill, NJ: Hampton Press.

Farmer, P. (1996, Winter). On suffering and structural violence: A view from below. *Daedalus, 125*(1), 261–282.

Farmer, P. (2004). *Pathologies of power: Health, human rights, and the new war on the poor.* Berkeley: University of California Press.

Feagin, J., & Vera, H. (2001). *Liberation sociology.* Boulder, CO: Westview.

Feinburg, S., & Mindess, M. (1994). *Eliciting children's full potential: Designing and evaluating developmentally-based programs for young children.* Pacific Grove, CA: Brooks/Cole.

Feist, G. J. (1998). A meta-analysis of the impact of personality on scientific and artistic creativity. *Personality and Social Psychological Review, 2*, 290–309.

Feldman, D., & Benjamin, A. (2006, September). Creativity and education: An American retrospective. *Cambridge Journal of Education, 36*(3), 319–336.

Fellman, G. (1998). *Rambo and the Dalai Lama: The compulsion to win and its threat to human survival.* Albany: State University of New York Press.

Ferrucci, P. (2006). *The power of kindness: The unexpected benefits of leading a compassionate life.* New York: Penguin.

Feurverger, G. (2008). Teaching about peaceful coexistence. In J. Lin, E. Brantmeier, & C. Bruhn (Eds.), *Transforming education for peace* (pp. 129–142). Charlotte, NC: Information Age.

Finckenauer, J. (1982). *Scared straight and the panacea phenomenon.* Englewood Cliffs, NJ: Prentice-Hall.

Finley, L. (2004a). Teaching peace in higher education: Overcoming the challenges to addressing structure and methods. *Online Journal of Peace and Conflict Resolution, 5*(2).

Finley, L. (2004b). Militarism goes to school. *Essays in Education, 4.*

Finley, L. (2006). Examining school searches as systemic violence. *Critical Criminology, 14*, 117–135.

Finley, L. (2008). *Hawking hits on the information highway: The challenge of online drug sales for law enforcement.* New York: Peter Lang.

Finley, L., & Finley, P. (2004). *Piss off!* Monroe, ME: Common Courage.

Finley, L., & Finley, P. (2006). *The sport industry's war on athletes.* Westport, CT: Praeger.

Finley, L. L. (2010). Where's the peace in this movement?: A domestic violence advocates reflections on the movement. *Contemporary Justice Review, 13*(1), 57–69.

Florida, R. (2004). *The rise of the creative class and how it is transforming work, leisure, community, and everyday life.* New York: Basic.

Flowers, N., & Shiman, D. (1997). Teacher education and human rights vision. In G. Andreopoulos & R. Claude (Eds.), *Human rights education for the twenty-first century* (pp. 161–175). Philadelphia: University of Pennsylvania Press.

Flynn, M. (2010, February 4). *Student-led group pinpoints solutions to youth violence.* Retrieved June 10, 2010, from http://oaklandnorth.net/2010/02/04/heal-the-streets-workshop/

Fogarty, B. (2000). *War, peace, and the social order.* Boulder, CO: Westview.

Fong, T. (2006). The effects of emotional ambiguity on creativity. *Academy of Management Journal, 49,* 1016–1030.

Forcey, L., & Harris, I. (1999). Introduction. In L. Forcey & I. Harris (Eds.), *Peacebuilding for adolescents* (pp. 1–14). New York: Peter Lang.

Ford, R. (2003). Saying one thing, meaning another: The role of parables in police training. *Police Quarterly, 6,* 84–110.

Fortune, D., Thompson, J., Pedlar, A., & Yuen, F. (2010). Social justice and women leaving prison: Beyond punishment and exclusion. *Contemporary Justice Review, 13*(1), 19–33.

Fountain, S. (1999). *Peace education in UNICEF* (Working Paper Series, Programme Division, Education Section). New York: UNICEF.

Förster, J., Friedman, R. S., & Liberman, N. (2004). Temporal construal effects on abstract and concrete thinking: Consequences for insight and creative cognition. *Journal of Personality and Social Psychology, 87,* 177–189.

Fredrickson, B. (2001). The role of positive emotions in positive psychology: The broaden-and-build theory of positive emotions. *American Psychologist, 56,* 218–226.

Freire, P. (1974). *Pedagogy of the oppressed.* New York: Seabury Press.

Freire, P. (1983). The banking concept of education. In H. Giroux & D. Purpel (Eds.), *The hidden curriculum and moral education.* Berkeley, CA: Mc-Cutchan Publishing Corporation.

Friedman, R., & Förster, J. (2001). The effects of promotion and prevention cues on creativity. *Journal of Personality and Social Psychology, 81,* 1001–1013.

Friedrich, P., & Gomes de Matos, F. (2009). Nonkilling linguistics. In J. Pim (Ed.), *Toward a nonkilling paradigm* (pp. 219–240). Honolulu: Center for Global Nonkilling.

Fritz, R. (1994). *The path of least resistance.* New York: Butterworth-Heinemann.

Fromm, E. (1973). *The anatomy of human destructiveness.* New York: Holt.

Fuller, J. (1998). *Criminal justice: A peacemaking perspective.* Boston: Allyn & Bacon.

Gallagher, S. (2008). The American prison: Open for business? *Peace Review: A Journal of Social Justice, 20,* 376–379.

Galtung, J. (1984). *There are alternatives.* Nottingham, UK: Spokesman Books.

Galtung, J. (1996). *Peace by peaceful means: Peace and conflict, development and civilization.* Thousand Oaks, CA: Sage.

Gardner, H. (1983). *Frames of mind. The theory of multiple intelligences.* New York: BasicBooks.

Gardner, H. (1999a). *The disciplined mind: What all students should understand.* New York: Simon & Schuster.

Gardner, H. (1999b). *Intelligence reframed.* New York: Basic.

Gardner Feldman, L. (1999). The principle and practice of "reconciliation" in German foreign policy: Relations with France, Israel, Poland and the Czech Republic. *International Affairs, 75,* 333–356.

Garland, D. (1990). *Punishment and modern society.* University of Chicago Press.

Gaskew, T. (2009). Peacemaking criminology and counterterrorism: Muslim Americans and the war on terror. *Contemporary Justice Review, 12*(3), 345–366.

Gawande, A. (2009, March 30). Hellhole. *The New Yorker.* Retrieved June 22, 2010, from http://www.newyorker.com/reporting/2009/03/30/090330fa_fact _gawande

Georgiadis, K., & Syrigos, A. (2009). *Olympic truce: Sport as a platform for peace.* Retrieved May 26, 2010, from www.olympictruce.com

Gibson, C. (2006). Citizens at the center: A new approach to civic engagement. Retrieved June 21, 2010, from www.civicengagement.org/agingsociety/links/Citizens_Center.pdf

Gierycz, D. (1997). Education on the human rights of women as a vehicle for change. In G. Andreopoulos & R. Claude (Eds.), *Human rights education for the twenty-first century* (pp. 96–118). Philadelphia: University of Pennsylvania Press.

Gil, D. (1996). Preventing violence in a structurally violent society: Mission impossible. *American Journal of Orthopsychiatry, 66,* 77–84.

Gil, D. (1999). Understanding and overcoming social-structural violence. *Contemporary Justice Review, 2,* 23–35.

Gilliom, J. (2005). Resisting surveillance. *Social Text, 23,* 71–83.

Gillmor, D. (2004). *We the media: Grassroots journalism by the people, for the people.* Sebastopol, CA: O'Reilly Media.

Gilmore, R. (2007). In the shadow of the shadow state. In INCITE! Women of Color Against Violence (Eds.), *The Revolution will not be funded.* Cambridge, MA: South End Press.

Giroux, H. (2009, April 20). Ten years after Columbine. *Counterpunch.* Retrieved July 25, 2010, from http://www.counterpunch.org/giroux04212009.html

Giulianotti, R., & Robertson, R. (Eds.). (2007a). *Globalization and sport.* Malden, MA: Blackwell.

Giulianotti, R., & Robertson, R. (2007b). Sport and globalization: Transnational dimensions. *Global Networks, 7,* 107–112.

Glenny, M. (2008). *McMafia: A journey through the global criminal underworld.* New York: Random House.

Glissman, B. (2010). *Chief: Anti-violence effort helps.* Retrieved May 27, 2010, from http://www.omaha.com/article/20100513/NEWS01/705139852

Goleman, D. (1995). *Emotional intelligence.* New York: Bantam.

Gomes de Matos, F. (2001). Applying the pedagogy of positiveness to diplomatic communication. In J. Kurbalija & H. Slavik (Eds.), *Language and diplomacy.* Msida, Malta: DiploProjects.

Goodhand, J. (2006). *Aiding peace? The role of NGOs in armed conflict.* Boulder, CO: Lynne Rienner.

Goodman, A. (2009, October 2). Sportswriter Dave Zirin on Obama's Olympic error. *Democracy Now!* Retrieved August 16, 2010, from http://www.democracynow.org/2009/10/2/sportswriter_dave_zirin_on_obamas_olympic

Greene, M. (1995). *Releasing the imagination: Essays on education, the arts, and social change.* San Francisco: Jossey-Bass.

Groff, L., & Smoker, P. (n.d.). *Creating global-local cultures of peace.* Retrieved June 15, 2010, from http://www.gmu.edu/programs/icar/pcs/smoker.htm

Haarr, R. (2001). The making of a community policing officer: The impact of basic training and occupational socialization on police recruits. *Police Quarterly, 4*(4), 402–433.

Hakvoort, I. (1996). Children's conceptions of peace and war: A longitudinal study. *Journal of Peace Psychology, 2,* 1–15.

Haliburton may be culprit in oil rig explosion. (2010, April 30). *Huffington Post.* Retrieved August 22, 2010, from http://www.huffingtonpost.com/2010/04/30/halliburton-may-be-culpri_n_558481.html

Hall, R. (1993). How do children think and feel about war and peace: An Australian study. *Journal of Peace Research, 30*(2), 181–196.

Hammer, M. (2005). *Assessment of the impact of the AFS study abroad experience.* New York: AFS International.

Hammond, W., Haegerich, T., & Saul, J. (2009). The public health approach to youth violence and child maltreatment prevention at the Centers for Disease Control and Prevention. *Psychological Services, 6*(4), 253–263.

Hanh, T. (2005). *Keeping the peace: Mindfulness and public service.* Berkeley, CA: Parallax Press.

Harris, I. (1999). Types of peace education. In L. Oppenheimer, D. Bar-Tal, & A. Raviv (Eds.), *How children understand war and peace* (pp. 299–317). San Francisco: Jossey-Bass.

Harris, I. (2007). Peace education in a violent culture. *Harvard Educational Review, 77*(3), 350–354.

Harris, I., & Morrison, M. (2003). *Peace education* (2nd ed.). Jefferson, NC: Mc-Farland & Co.

Harman, A. (2001). Room with a view: An "open" prison in the Swiss Alps. *Corrections Technology and Management, 5*(2), 32–36.

Hayes, D. (2004). Understanding creativity and its implications for schools. *Improving Schools, 7*(3), 279–286.

Hayner, P. B. (1999). In pursuit of justice and reconciliation: Contributions of truth telling. In C. J. Arnson (Ed.), *Comparative peace processes in Latin America* (pp. 363–383). Stanford, CA: Stanford University Press.

Hennessey, B., & Amabile, T. (1998). Reality, intrinsic motivation, and creativity. *American Psychologist, 53,* 674–675.

Hernandez, A. (1998). *Peace in the streets: Breaking the cycle of gang violence.* Washington, DC: Child Welfare League of America.

Hill, C. (2010, June 8). Dear American aristocracy, it's time to show your face. Retrieved June 21, 2010, from http://uspoverty.change.org/blog/category/income_inequality

Hill, S., & Beger, R. (2009). A paramilitary policing juggernaut. *Social Justice, 36*(1), 25–40.

Hilliard, R. (2001). *Media, education, and America's counter-culture revolution.* Westport, CT: Ablex.

Hirsh-Pasek, K., & Golinkoff, R. (2003). *Einstein never used flash cards.* New York: Rodale.

Hoffman, M. L. (2000). *Empathy and moral development: Implications for caring and justice.* New York: Cambridge University Press.

Hofstetter, A. (2010, January). Can sports bring world peace? *The Atlantic.* Retrieved May 29, 2010, from http://www.theatlantic.com/magazine/archive/2010/01/can-sports-bring-world-peace/7872/

Holtzman, L. (2000). *Media messages.* Armonk, New York: M. E. Sharpe.

hooks, b. (1994). *Teaching to transgress: Education as the practice of freedom.* New York: Routledge.

Human Rights. (2010). *Amnesty International.* Retrieved August 15, 2010, from http://www.amnestyusa.org/human-rights/page.do?id=1031002

Human Rights Watch. (2003). *Ill-equipped: U.S. prisons and offenders with mental illness.* Retrieved April 5, 2011 from http://www.hrw.org/en/reports/2003/10/21/ill-equipped

Human Rights Watch. (2006). "No blood, no foul": Soldiers accounts of detainee abuse in Iraq. *Human Rights Watch, 18*(3), 1–55.

Human Rights Watch. (2008). Beijing Olympics basics. Retrieved August 16, 2010, from http://china.hrw.org/press/faq/beijing_olympics_basics

Iadicola, P., & Shupe, A. (1999). *Violence, inequality, and human freedom.* Dix Hills, NY: General Hall.

Ierley, A., & Ivker, C. (2002). *Restoring School Communities -Restorative Justice in Schools Program: Spring 2002 Report Card.* Boulder, CO: School Mediation Center.

Ikeda, D. (2001). *For the sake of peace: Seven paths to global harmony, a Buddhist perspective.* Santa Monica, CA: Middleway Press.

Illich, I. (1970). *Deschooling society.* New York: Harper and Row.

Illich, I. (2000). *Deschooling society.* London: Marion Boyars Publishers Ltd.

Institute for Economics & Peace. (2010a). 2010 discussion paper. *Global Peace Index.* Retrieved June 18, 2010, from www.visionofhumanity.org

Institute for Economics & Peace. (2010b). 2010 methodology, results, and findings. *Global Peace Index.* Retrieved June 18, 2010, from www.visionofhumanity.org

Iram, Y. (2006). Culture of peace: Definition, scope, and application. In Y. Iram (Ed.), *Educating toward a culture of peace* (pp. 3–12). Greenwich, CT: Information Age.

Irvin, R. (2009). Review of *Uncharitable.* Retrieved August 19, 2010, from http://www.uncharitable.net/

Jackson, P. (1983). The daily grind. In H. Giroux & D. Purpel (Eds.), *The hidden curriculum and moral education.* Berkeley, CA: McCutchan Publishing Corporation.

Jackson, N., & Shaw, M. (2005). *Subject perspectives on creativity: A preliminary synthesis.*York, UK: An Imaginative Curriculum Study for The Higher Education Academy. Retrieved February 4, 2008, from http://www.palatine.ac.uk/files/1004.pdf

Jacoby, B. (1996). *Service learning in higher education: Concepts and practices.* San Francisco: Jossey-Bass.

James, S., Johnson, J., Raghavan, C., Lemos, T., Barakett, M., & Woolis, D. (2003). The violent matrix: A study of structural, interpersonal, and intrapersonal violence among a sample of poor women. *American Journal of Community Psychology, 31*(1/2), 129–141.

Jenkins, T. (2007). Rethinking the unimaginable: The need for teacher education in peace education. *Harvard Educational Review, 77*(3), 366–369, 372.

Jenlink, P. (2004). Discourse ethics in the design of educational systems: Considerations for design praxis. *Systems Research and Behavioral Science,21*(3), 237–249.

Jennings, T. (2009, April 30). Prison reform back on Richardson's agenda. *New Mexico Independent.* Retrieved June 22, 2010, from http://newmexicoindependent.com/24774/prison-reform-back-on-gov-bill-richardsons-agenda

Johnson, D. (2009). Anger about crime and support for punitive criminal justice policies. *Punishment & Society, 11*(1), 51–66.

Johnson, D., & Johnson, R. (2005). Essential components of peace education. *Theory Into Practice, 44*(4), 280–292.

Jones, E., Haenfler, R., & Johnson, B. (2007). *The better world handbook.* Gabriola Island, BC, Canada: New Society Publishers.

Joseph Rountree Foundation. (n.d.). *An evaluation of the implementation and effectiveness of an initiative in restorative cautioning.* Retrieved May 29, 2010, from www.jrf.org.uk

Jurik, N. (2005). *Bootstrap dreams: U.S. microenterprise development in an era of welfare reform. Ithaca*, NY: Cornell University Press.

Jurik, N., Cavendar, G., & Cowgill, G. (2009). Resistance and accommodation in a post-welfare social service agency. *Journal of Contemporary Ethnography, 38(1)*, 25–51.

Kappeler, V., Blumberg, M., & Potter, G. (2000). *The mythology of crime and criminal justice* (3rd ed.). Chicago: Waveland Press.

Karstedt, S. (2002). Emotions and criminal justice. *Theoretical Criminology, 6*(3), 299–317.

Katel, P. (2008, February 8). Fighting crime. *Congressional Quarterly Researcher, 18*(6), 121–144.

Katorsky, B. (2006). *Patriots act: Voices of dissent and the risk of speaking out.* Guilford, CT: Lyons Press.

Katz, J., (Performer) & Jhally, S. (Director) (1999). *Tough Guise* [motion picture]. Northampton, MA: Media Education Foundation.

Kaufman, E. (1997). Human rights education for law enforcement. In G. Andreopoulos & R. Claude, (Eds.), *Human rights education for the twenty-first century* (pp. 278–295). Philadelphia: University of Pennsylvania Press.

Kaye, M. (1997). The role of the truth commissions in the search for justice, reconciliation and democratization: The Salvadorean and Honduran cases. *Journal of Latin American Studies, 29*, 693–716.

Keim, M. (2003) *Nation building at play: Sport as a tool for integration in post-apartheid South Africa.* Aachen, Germany: Meyer & Meyer.

Kelley, L. (2010, June 19). *The pay gap affects men too.* Retrieved June 21, 2010, from http://uspoverty.change.org/blog/category/income_inequality

Kelling, G., & Wilson, J. (1982, March). Broken windows: The police and neighborhood safety. *The Atlantic.* Retrieved April 5, 2011 from http://www.theatlantic.com/magazine/archive/1982/03/broken-windows/4465/

Kern, J., Gunja, F., Cox, A., Rosenbaum, M., Appel. J., & Verma, A. (2006, January). Making sense of student drug testing: Why educators are saying no. *Drug Policy Alliance.* Retrieved August 19, 2010, from http://www.drugpolicy.org/docUploads/drug_testing_booklet.pdf

Killingbeck, D. (2001). The role of television news in the construction of school violence as a "moral panic." *Journal of Criminal Justice and Popular Culture, 8*(3), 186–202.

Kivel, P. (1999). *Boys will be men: Raising our sons for courage, caring, and community.* Gabriola Island, BC, Canada: New Society.

Kleiman, P. (2008, August). Toward transformation: Conceptions of creativity in higher education. *Innovations in Education and Teaching International, 45*(3), 209–217.

Klein, M. (2007). Peace education and Paulo Freire's method: Toward the democratization of teaching and learning. *Convergence, 40*(1–2), 187–203.

Klein, N. (2007). *The shock doctrine: The rise of disaster capitalism.* New York: Metropolitan Books.

Kohn, A. (1990). Fun and fitness without competition. *Women's Sports and Fitness*. Retrieved May 27, 2010, from http://www.alfiekohn.org/miscellaneous/compsports.htm

Kohn, A. (2004). *What does it mean to be well educated?* Boston: Beacon Press.

Koliba, C. (2000). Moral language and networks of engagement: Service-learning and civic education. *American Behavioral Scientist, 43*, 825–838.

Kostelny, K. (2004). What about the girls? *Cornell International Law Journal, 37*, 505–512.

Kraska, P. (1994). The police and military in the post–Cold War era: Streamlining the state's use of force entities in the drug war. *Police Forum, 4*, 1–8.

Kraska, P. (1999, Winter). Militarizing criminal justice: Exploring the possibilities. *Journal of Political and Military Sociology, 27*(2), 205–215.

Kraska, P., & Cubellis, L. (1997). Militarizing Mayberry and beyond: Making sense of American paramilitary policing. *Justice Quarterly, 14*(4), 607–629.

Kriesberg, L. (1998a). Coexistence and the reconciliation of communal conflicts. In E. Weiner (Ed.), *The handbook of interethnic coexistence* (pp. 182–198). New York: Continuum.

Kriesberg, L. (1998b). Intractable conflicts. In E. Weiner (Ed.), *The handbook of interethnic coexistence* (pp. 332–342). New York: Continuum.

Krishnamurti, J. (1981). *Education and the significance of life*. New York: Harper and Row.

Kuhn, G. (1995). The other curriculum: Out-of-class experiences associated with student leaning and personal development. *Journal of Higher Education, 66*(2), 123–155.

Kupermintz, H., & Salomon, G. (2003). Lessons to be learned from research on peace education in the context of intractable conflict. *Theory Into Practice, 44*(4), 293–302.

Lam, T., & Chiu, C. (2002). The motivational function of regulatory focus in creativity. *Journal of Creative Behavior, 36*, 138–150.

Lanier, M., & Henry, S. (2004). *Essential criminology* (2nd ed.). Boulder, CO: Westview.

Lederach, J. (1998). Beyond violence: Building sustainable peace. In E. Weiner (Ed.), *The handbook of interethnic coexistence* (pp. 236–245). New York: Continuum.

Leonard, A. (2010). *The story of stuff: How our obsession with stuff is trashing the planet, our communities, and our health—and a vision for change*. New York: Free Press.

Lerner, J., & Antieau, M. (2010, April 20). Chicago's $1.3 million experiment in democracy. *Yes! Magazine*. Retrieved April 7, 2011 from www.yesmagazine.org/people-power/chicagos-1.3million-experiment-in-democracy

Leung, A. K., Maddox, W. W., Galinsky, A. D., & Chiu, C-y. (2008). Multicultural experience enhances creativity. *American Psychologist, 63*(3), 169–181.

Liebenberg, I., & Zegeye, A. (1998). Pathway to democracy? The case of the South African Truth and Reconciliation process. *Social Identities, 4,* 541–558.

Lifton, R. (2003). *Superpower syndrome.* New York: Thunder's Mouth Press.

Lin, J. (2006). *Love, peace, and wisdom in education.* Lanham, MD: Rowman & Littlefield.

Lin, J. (2008). Constructing a global ethic of universal love, forgiveness and reconciliation: The role of peace education in the 21st century. In J. Lin & C. Bruhn (Eds.), *Transforming education for peace: Educators as peacemakers* (pp. 301–316). Greenwich, CT: Information Age Publishing.

Lin, J., Brantmeier, E., & Bruhn, C. (2008). *Transforming education for peace.* Charlotte, NC: Information Age.

Lindle, J. (2008). School safety: Real or imagined fear? *Educational Policy, 22*(1), 28–44.

Link, B., Lennon, M., & Dohrenwend, B. (1993). Socioeconomic status and depression: The role of occupations involving direction, control, and planning, *American Journal of Sociology, 98,* 1351–1387.

Lintott, J. (2004). Teaching and learning in the face of school violence. *Georgetown Journal on Poverty Law and Policy, 11,* 553–580.

Lipsey, M. (1992). Juvenile delinquency treatment: A meta-analytic inquiry. In T. C. Cook, H. Cooper, D. S. Cordray, H. Harmann, L. V. Hedges, R. L. Light et al. (Eds.), *Meta-analysis for explanation* (pp. 83–127). New York: Russell Sage.

Loewen, J. (2005). *Lies my teacher told me: Everything your American history textbook got wrong.* New York: The New Press.

Lomax, A. (2005). The *real* American gulag. *Counterpunch.* Retrieved August 15, 2010, from http://wwww.counterpunch.org/lomax06162005.html

Lozada, C. (2010, February 28). Obama's beer summit vs. Obama's health-care summit. *Washington Post.* Retrieved September 7, 2010, from http://www.washingtonpost.com/wp-dyn/content/article/2010/02/26/AR2010022603136.html

Lundman, R. (1993). *Prevention and the control of juvenile delinquency* (2nd ed.). New York: Oxford University Press.

Lurenco, O. (1999). Toward a positive conception of peace. In L. Oppenheimer, D. Bar-Tal, & A. Raviv (Eds.), *How children understand war and peace* (pp. 91–108). San Francisco: Jossey-Bass.

Lutz, C. (2002). Making war at home in the United States: Militarization and the current crisis. *American Anthropologist, 104,* 723–735.

Machel, G. (2001). *The impact of war on children.* Cape Town, South Africa: David Philip.

Madriz, E. (2001). Terrorism and structural violence. *Social Justice, 28*(3), 45–46.

Males, M. (1996). *Scapegoat generation.* Monroe, ME: Common Courage.

Males, M. (1999). *Framing youth: 10 myths about the next generation.* Monroe, ME: Common Courage.

Males, M. (2004, June). With a Drug Czar like John Walters, who needs Osama? *Youth Today.* Retrieved June 4, 2010, from http://home.earthlink.net/~mmales/yt-walt.htm

Males, M. (2006, September). Whatever sells. *Youth Today.* Retrieved June 4, 2010, from http://home.earthlink.net/~mmales/yt-sells.htm

Maran, R. (1997). Teaching human rights in the universities: Paradoxes and prospects. In G. Andreopoulos & R. Claude (Eds.), *Human rights education for the twenty-first century* (pp. 194–208). Philadelphia: University of Pennsylvania Press.

Marsick, V., Sauquet, A., & Yorks, L. (2006). Learning through reflection. In M. Deutsch, P. Coleman, & E. Marcus (Eds.), *The handbook of conflict resolution: Theory and practice* (pp. 486–506). San Francisco: Jossey-Bass.

Marsick, V., & Watkins, K (1990). *Informal and incidental learning in the workplace.* New York: Routledge.

Marullo, S. (1993). *Ending the cold war at home: From militarism to a more peaceful world order.* New York: Lexington Books.

Marullo, S., & Edwards, B. (2000.) Editor's Introduction: Service-learning pedagogy as universities' responses to troubled times. *American Behavioral Scientist, 43,* 746–755.

Maslow, A. (1970). *Motivation and personality* (3rd ed.). London: HarperCollins.

McCarthy, C. (2002). *I'd rather teach peace.* Maryknoll, NY: Orbis.

McCully, A., O'Doherty, M., & Smyth, P. (1999). The speak your piece project: Exploring controversial issues in Northern Ireland. In L. Forcey & I. Harris, (Eds.), *Peacebuilding for adolescents* (pp. 119–138). New York: Peter Lang.

McElrea, F. (1998, November). Roles of community and government. Retrieved May 25, 2010, from http://www.restorativejustice.org/10fulltext/mcelrea8/view

McKay, S., & Mazurana, D. (2004). *Where are the girls? Girls in fighting forces in Northern Uganda, Sierra Leone, and Mozambique: Their lives during and after war.* Montréal, Canada: International Centre for Human Rights and Democratic Development.

Meintjes, G. (1997). Human rights education as empowerment: Reflections on pedagogy. In G. Andreopoulos & R. Claude (Eds.), *Human rights education for the twenty-first century* (pp. 64–79). Philadelphia: University of Pennsylvania Press.

Merryfinch, L. (1981). Militarization/civilization. In W. Chapkis (Ed.), *Loaded questions: Women in the military.* Amsterdam: Transnational Institute.

Meyer, J. (2002). It is a gift from the Creator to keep us in harmony: Original (versus alternative) dispute resolution on the Navajo Nation. *International Journal of Public Administration, 25,* 1379–1414.

Michalowski, R. (1985). *Order, law and crime: An introduction to criminology.* New York: McGraw-Hill.

Miller, A. (2002). *For your own good: Hidden cruelty in child-rearing and the roots of violence.* New York: Farrar, Straus & Giroux.

Miller, T., Lawrence, G., McKay, J., & Rowe, D. (2001). *Globalization and sport: Playing the world.* London: Sage.

Milward, H., & Provan, K. (1993. The hollow state: Private provision of public services. In H. Ingram & S. Smith (Eds.), *Public policy for democracy* (pp. 222–237). Washington, DC: Brookings.

Mirsky, L. (2003, May 20). *SaferSanerSchools: Transforming school culture with restorative practices.* International Institute for Restorative Practices. Retrieved June 21, 2010, from http://www.iirp.org/iirpWebsites/web/uploads/article_pdfs/ssspilots.pdf

Mirsky, L. (2004, April 27). Restorative justice practices of Native American, First Nation, and other indigenous people of North America: Part One. *Restorative Practices E-Forum.* Retrieved August 19, 2010, from http://www.realjustice.org/uploads/article_pdfs/natjust1.pdf

Moller, F. (2008). Imaging and remembering peace and war. *Peace Review: A Journal of Social Justice, 20,* 100–106.

Moore-Lappe, F. (2006). *Getting a grip: Clarity, courage, and creativity in a world gone mad.* San Francisco: Creative Commons.

Moyers, B. (2010, April 2). *American inequality.* Retrieved June 21, 2010, from http://www.pbs.org/moyers/journal/04022010/profile4.html

Mukherjee, J. (2007). Structural violence, poverty, and the AIDS pandemic. *Society for International Development, 50*(2), 115–121.

Munro, B. (2009, June). *Sport for peace and reconciliation: Young peacemakers in the Kakuma refugee camp and Mathare slums in Kenya.* Retrieved May 26, 2010, from www.mysakenya.org

Nadelman, E. (1993). *Cops across borders: The internationalization of U.S. criminal law enforcement.* University Park: University of Pennsylvania Press.

Nash, P. (1999). Disturbing the peace: Multicultural education, transgressive teaching, and independent school culture. In L. Forcey & I. Harris (Eds.), *Peacebuilding for adolescents* (pp. 227–235). New York: Peter Lang.

Nava, R. (2001). *Holistic education: Pedagogy of universal love.* Brandon, VT: Foundation for Educational Renewal.

Nelson, L., Van Slyck, M., & Cardella, L. (1999). Peace and conflict curricula for adolescents. In L. Forcey & I. Harris (Eds.), *Peacebuilding for adolescents* (pp. 91–117). New York: Peter Lang.

Nicholl, C. (1999). *Toolbox for implementing restorative justice and advancing community policing.* Washington, DC: U.S. Department of Justice, Office of Community Oriented Policing Services.

Noddings, N. (2004). *Happiness and education.* Cambridge, MA: Cambridge University Press.

Noddings, N. (2005). *The challenge to care in schools: An alternative approach to education* (2nd ed.). New York: Teachers College Press.

Noddings, N. (2006). *Philosophy of Education.* Boulder, CO: Westview.

Noddings, N. (2007). *What our schools should teach*. Cambridge, MA: Cambridge University Press.

Noe, N. (2008). Hope for peace: Against all odds. In J. Lin, E. Brantmeier, & C. Bruhn (Eds.), *Transforming education for peace* (pp. 143–161). Charlotte, NC: Information Age.

Noguera, P. (1996). *Reducing and preventing violence: An analysis of causes and an assessment of successful programs*. Retrieved June 21, 2010, from http://www.inmotionmagazine.com/pedro3.html

Norval, A. (1998). Memory, identity and the (im)possibility of reconciliation: The work of the Truth and Reconciliation Commission in South Africa. *Constellations, 5*, 250–265.

Norval, A. (1999). Truth and reconciliation: The birth of the present and the reworking of history. *Journal of African Studies, 25*, 499–519.

Nussbaum, M. (2003). *Upheavals of thought, the intelligence of emotions*. Cambridge, MA: Cambridge University Press.

O'Brien, E. (1997). Community education for law, democracy, and human rights. In G. Andreopoulos, & R. Claude, (Eds.), *Human rights education for the twenty-first century* (pp. 416–435). Philadelphia: University of Pennsylvania Press.

Offering Boston's gangs alternatives to violence. (1992, November 16). *New York Times*. Retrieved August 19, 2010, from http://www.nytimes.com/1992/11/16/us/offering-boston-s-gangs-alternatives-to-violence.html

Ogi, A. (2005, October 21). Sports are a tool for global social change. *Christian Science Monitor*. Retrieved May 29, 2010, from http://www.csmonitor.com/2005/1021/p09s03-coop.html

O'Hear, M. (2009). Rethinking drug courts: Restorative justice as a response to racial injustice. *Stanford Law and Policy, 20*(2), 463–500.

O'Kane, M. (1991/1992, Winter). Peace: The overwhelming task. *Veterans for Peace Journal, 19*(3).

Okhuysen, G., Galinsky, A., & Uptigrove, T. (2003). Saving the worst for last: The effect of time horizon on the efficiency of negotiating benefits and burdens. *Organizational Behavior and Human Decision Processes, 91*, 269–279.

Oppenheimer, L, Bar-Tal, D., & Raviv, A. (1999). Introduction: Understanding peace, conflict, and war. In L. Oppenheimer, D. Bar-Tal, & A. Raviv (Eds.), *How children understand war and peace* (pp. 1–24). San Francisco: Jossey-Bass.

Otto, N., & Lupton, A. (2009). *Give peace a deadline*. Austin, TX: Greenleaf.

Page, J. (2007). Teaching peace to the military. *Peace Review: A Journal of Social Justice, 19*, 571–577.

Paige, G. (2009). *Nonkilling global political science*. Honolulu: Center for Global Nonkilling.

Palast, G. (2000, December 4). Florida's flawed "voter cleansing" system. *Salon*. Retrieved August 8, 2010, from http://www.salon.com/news/politics/feature/2000/12/04/voter_file

Pallotta, D. (2008). *Uncharitable: How restraints on nonprofits undermine their potential.* Medford, MA: Tufts University Press.

Palmer, P. (1998). *The courage to teach: Exploring the inner landscape of a teacher's life.* San Francisco: Jossey-Bass.

Panera Bread Co. opens non-profit restaurant where customers can pay what they want. (2010, May 19). *New York Daily News.* Retrieved June 19, 2010, from http://www.nydailynews.com/lifestyle/food/2010/05/19/2010-05-19_panera_bread_co_opens_nonprofit_restaurant_where_customers_can_pay_what_the_wan.html

Parenti, C. (1999). *Lockdown America: Police and prisons in the age of crisis.* London: Verso.

Parker-Gwin, R. (1996.) Connecting service to learning: How students and communities matter. *Teaching Sociology, 24,* 97–101.

Parr, T. (2004). *The peace book.* New York: Little, Brown Young Readers.

Peak, K., & Glensor, R. (2004). *Community policing and problem solving practices and strategies* (4th ed.). Upper Saddle River, NJ: Prentice Hall.

Pease, D. (2009). *The new American exceptionalism.* Minneapolis: University of Minnesota Press.

Pepinsky, H. (2006). Peacemaking in the classroom. *Contemporary Justice Review, 9*(4), 427–442.

Pepinsky, H., & Quinney, R. (1991). *Criminology as peacemaking.* Bloomington: Indiana University Press.

Petrosino, A., Turpin-Petrosino, C., & Buehler, J. (2003). Scared straight and other juvenile awareness programs for preventing juvenile delinquency: A systematic review of the randomized experimental evidence. *The Annals of the American Academy of Political and Social Science, 589,* 41–62.

Petrosino, A., Turpin-Petrosino, C., & Finckenauer, J. (2000). Well-meaning programs can have harmful effects! Lessons from experiments of programs such as scared straight. *Crime & Delinquency, 46*(3), 354–379.

Pettigrew, T., & Tropp, L. (2000). Does intergroup contact reduce prejudice? Recent meta-analytic findings. In S. Oskamp (Ed.), *Reducing Prejudice and Discrimination* (pp. 93–114). Mahwah, NJ: Lawrence Erlbaum Associates.

Pilisuk, M. (2001). Globalism and structural violence. In D. Christie, R. Wagner, & D. Winter (Eds.), *Peace, conflict, and violence: Peace psychology for the 21st century.* Englewood Cliffs, NJ: Prentice Hall. Available online at http://academic.marion.ohio-state.edu/dchristie/Peace%20Psychology%20Book_files/Chapter%2013%20-%20Globalism%20%26%20Structural%20Violence%20(Pilisuk).pdf

Pilisuk, M. (2008). *Who benefits from global violence and war?* Westport, CT: Greenwood.

Piven, F., & Cloward, R. (1977). *Poor people's movements: How they succeed, why they fail.* New York: Pantheon.

Plimpton, G. (1999, June 14). Muhammad Ali: The greatest. *Time.* Retrieved August 25, 2010, from http://www.time.com/time/magazine/article/0,9171,991256,00.html

Pollard, C. (2000). *Restorative justice and police complaints.* International Institute for Restorative Practices. Retrieved July 25, 2010, from http://www.iirp.org/article_detail.php?article_id=NDk5

Pont-Brown, M., & Krumboltz, J. (1999). Countering school violence: The rise of conflict resolution programs. In L. Forcey, & I. Harris (Eds.), *Peace-building for adolescents* (pp. 35–55). New York: Peter Lang.

Pope sets up Vatican sports department. (2004, August 3). *Fox News.* Retrieved August 25, 2010, from http://www.stclementsports.com/article2.pdf

Postman, N. (1971). *Teaching as a subversive activity.* New York: Delta.

Postman, N. (1996). *The end of education: Redefining the value of school.* New York: Vintage.

Pranis, K., Stuart, B., & Wedge, M. (2003). *Peacemaking circles: From crime to community.* St. Paul, MN: Living Justice Press.

Pratt, J. (2000). Emotive and ostentatious punishment: Its decline and resurgence in modern society. *Punishment and Society, 2*(4), 417–439.

Prevention Institute. (2006, June). *Creating safe environments: Violence prevention strategies and programs.* Retrieved June 5, 2010, from *www.preventioninstitute.org/component/jlibrary/article/id.../127.html*

Price, R., & Dunnigan, C. (1995). *Toward an understanding of aboriginal peacemaking.* Victoria, BC, Canada: University of Victoria Institute for Dispute Resolution.

Prothrow-Stith, D., & Spivak, H. (2003). *Murder is no accident: Understanding and preventing youth violence in America.* San Francisco, CA: Jossey-Bass.

Putnam, R. (2001). *Bowling alone: The collapse and revival of American community.* Carmichael, CA: Touchstone Books

Quadagno, J. (1999). *Aging and the Life Course.* New York: McGraw Hill.

Quadagno, J., & Fobes, C. (1995, May). The welfare state and the cultural reproduction of gender: Making good girls and boys in the Job Corps. *Social Problems, 42,* 171–190.

Quaglia, R. (2000). Making an impact on student aspirations: A positive approach to school violence. *NASSP Bulletin, 84,* 56–60.

Quinney, R. (1991). The way of peace: On crime, suffering and service. In H. Pepinsky & R. Quinney (Eds.), *Criminology as peacemaking* (pp. 3–13). Bloomington: Indiana University Press.

Quinney, R. (2001). Foreword. In R. Sheldon (Ed.), *Controlling the dangerous classes: A critical introduction to the history of criminal justice* (pp. ix–x). Boston: Allyn & Bacon.

Radomski, C. (2008). Building peace in the family: American host families of Muslim exchange students post 9/11. In J. Lin, E. Brantmeier, & C. Bruhn (Eds.), *Transforming education for peace* (pp. 23–44). Charlotte, NC: Information Age.

Reardon, B. (1995). *Education for human dignity: Learning about rights and responsibilities.* Philadelphia: University of Pennsylvania Press.

Reardon, B. (1997). Human rights as education for peace. In G. Andreopoulos & R. Claude (Eds.), *Human rights education for the twenty-first century* (pp. 21–34). Philadelphia: University of Pennsylvania Press.

Redden, J. (2000). *Snitch culture.* Venice, CA: Feral House.

Reddy, M., Borum, R., Vossekuil, B., Fein, R., Berglund, J. & Modzeleski, W. (2001). Evaluating risk for targeted violence in schools: Comparing risk assessment, threat assessment, and other approaches. *Psychology in the Schools, 38*(2), 157–172.

Reick, D. (n.d.). *How to create a more creative staff.* Retrieved January 27, 2009, from http://www.directcreative.com/how-to-create-a-more-creative-staff.html

Reiman, J. (2000) *The rich get richer and the poor get prison: Ideology, class, and criminal justice* (6th ed.) New York: Allyn & Bacon

Right to Play. (2000, September 8). *Sport and peace: Social inclusion, conflict prevention, and peacebuilding.* Retrieved June 21, 2010, from www.righttoplay.com/International/.../Final_Report_Chapter_6.pdf

Ritzer, G. (1996). *The McDonaldization of society: An investigation into the changing character of contemporary social life.* Thousand Oaks, CA: Sage.

Robertson, R. (1992). *Globalization: Social theory and global culture.* New York: Russell Sage.

Robinson, M. (2000). Active learning in criminal justice: 25 examples. *Journal of Criminal Justice Education, 11*(1), 65–78.

Rodriguez, D. (2007). The political logic of the non-profit industrial complex. In INCITE! Women of Color Against Violence (Eds.), *The Revolution will not be funded.* Cambridge, MA: South End Press.

Rojas, P. (2007). Are the cops in our heads and hearts? In INCITE! Women of Color Against Violence (Eds.), *The Revolution will not be funded.* Cambridge, MA: South End Press.

Roschelle, A., Turpin, J., & Elias, R. (2000). Who learns from service learning? *American Behavioral Scientist, 43,* 839–847.

Rose, N. (1995). Gender, race, and the welfare state: Government work programs from the 1930s to the present. *Feminist Studies, 19*(2), 318–343.

Rosenberg, M. (2004). *Raising children compassionately: Parenting the nonviolent communication way.* Encinitas, CA: PuddleDancer Press.

Rosenberg, M. (n.d.). Anger and domination systems. Retrieved May 25, 2010, from http://www.cnvc.org/en/what-nvc/articles-writings/anger-and-domination-systems/anger-and-domination-systems

Ross, R. (1996). *Returning to the teachings.* Toronto: Penguin Books.

Rousseau, N., & Rousseau, S. (1999). Dr. King's triplets: Racism, materialism, and militarism. In L. Forcey & I. Harris (Eds.), *Peacebuilding for adolescents* (pp. 17–32). New York: Peter Lang.

Ruggiero, V. (2005). Criminalizing war: Criminology as ceasefire. *Social and Legal Studies, 14*(2), 239–257.

Runco, M., & Richards, R. (Eds.). (1997). *Eminent creativity, everyday creativity and health.* Greenwich, CT: Ablex Publishing Co.

Runyan, D. K., Hunter, W. M., Socolar, R., Amaya-Hackson, L., English, D., Landsverk, J., et al. (1998). Children who prosper in unfavorable environments: The relationship to social capital. *Pediatrics, 101.*

Rynne, T. (2008). *Gandhi & Jesus: The saving power of nonviolence.* Maryknoll, NY: Orbis Books.

Sa'ar, R. (2004, August 22). Government's financial neglect may cause collapse of Galilee communities. Available online at: www.haaretz.com

Saleeby, D. (1992). *The strengths perspective in social work practice.* New York: Longman.

Salomon, G. (2004). A narrative-based view of coexistence education. *Journal of Social Issues, 60*(2), 273–287.

Sanzen, P. L. (1991). The role of education in peacemaking. In H. E. Pepinsky & R. Quinney (Eds.), *Criminology as peacemaking* (pp. 239–244). Bloomington: Indiana University Press.

Sax, L., Keup, J., Gilmartin, S., Stolzenberg, E., & Harper, C. (2002). *Findings from the 2002 Administration of Your First College Year (YFCY): National Aggregates* (Monograph). Los Angeles: UCLA, Higher Education Research Institute.

Scharf, A., & Bagat, R. (2007). Arts and peace education: The Richmond Youth Peace Project. *Harvard Educational Review, 77*(3), 391–393.

Schor, J. (2010). *Plenitude: The new economics of true wealth.* New York: Penguin.

Scripps J. (1999, October 27). Prison tour serves as a wake-up call. *The Forum, 1.*

Seaton, E. (2000). Exposing the invisible: Unraveling the roots of rural boys' violence in schools. *Journal of Adolescent Research, 22*(3), 211–218.

Seita, J. (2000). In our best interest: Three necessary shifts for child welfare workers and children. *Child Welfare, 79(1),* 77.

Selman, R. (1980). *The growth of interpersonal understanding.* New York: Academic Press.

Shalala, D. (2001). *Youth violence: A report of the Surgeon General.* Retrieved August 15, 2010, from http://mentalhealth.samhsa.gov/youthviolence/surgeongeneral/SG_Site/home.asp

Sharp, G. (1973). *The methods of nonviolent action.* Boston: Porter-Sargent.

Shein, F. (2009, November 21). SWAT raids: Knock, knock-you're dead. Retrieved June 1, 2010, from http://www.examiner.com/x-28964-Anchorage-Conservative-Examiner~y2009m11d21-SWAT-Raids-Knock-Knock-Youre-Dead

Sheldon, R. (2001). *Controlling the dangerous classes: A critical introduction to the history of criminal justice.* Boston: Allyn & Bacon.

Sherman, L. (2003). Reason for emotion: Reinventing justice with theories, innovations, and research. *Criminology, 41*(1), 1–38.

Sherman, L., Gottfredson, D., MacKenzie, D., Eck, J., Reuter, P., & Bushway, S. (1997). *Preventing Crime: What works, what doesn't, what's promising. A report to the United States Congress*. College Park, MD: University of Maryland, Department of Criminology and Criminal Justice.

Shields, D., & Bredemeier, B. (1996). Sport, militarism, and peace. *Peace and Conflict: Journal of Peace Psychology, 2,* 369–383.

Shiver, D. W., Jr. (1995). *An ethic for enemies: Forgiveness in politics*. New York: Oxford University Press.

Shutts, S. (2009, September 22). Costa Rica creates Department of Peace. *Yes! Magazine*. Retrieved April 6, 2011 from www.yesmagizine.org/peace-justice/costa-rica-creates-department-of-peace

Singer, P. (2005). *Children at war.* NewYork: Pantheon.

Sins of the secular missionaries. (2000, January 29). Retrieved August 19, 2010, from http://www.friends-partners.org/CCSI/resource/sins.htm

Skiba, R., & Peterson, R. (1999, January). The dark side of zero tolerance. *Phi Delta Kappan, 80,* 372–382.

Sloane, S. (2002). *A Study of the effectiveness of Alternatives to Violence workshops in a prison system*. Retrieved June 22, 2010, from http://www.sfu.ca/cfrj/fulltext/sloane.pdf

Smith, A. (2007). Introduction. In INCITE! Women of Color Against Violence (Eds.), *The revolution will not be funded*. Cambridge, MA: South End Press.

Smith, D. (2007, October 26). How community colleges can work for world peace. *Chronicle of Higher Education, 54*(9), B30.

Smith, M. (1996). Strategies to reduce school violence: The New Mexico Center for Dispute Resolution. In A. Hoffman (Ed.), *Schools, violence and society* (pp. 253–264). NewYork: Praeger.

Smoker, P. (1969, July/August). Social research for social anticipation. *American Behavioral Scientist, XII*(6), 7–13.

Snook, C. (2002). Oregon's "Bully Bill": Are we needlessly repressing student speech in the. name of school safety? *Willamette Law Review, 38,* 657–728.

Solomon, B. (2006). Traditional and rights-informed talk about violence: High school educators' discursive production of student violence. *Youth & Society, 37*(3), 251–286.

Solnit, R. (2009). *A paradise built in hell: The extraordinary communities that arise in disaster*. New York: Viking.

Sorek, T. (2003). Arab football in Israel as an "integrative enclave." *Ethnic and Racial Studies, 26*(3), 422–450.

Sperber, M. (2001). *Beer and circus: How big-time college sports is crippling undergraduate education*. New York: Holt.

Staub, E., Pearlman, L. A., Gubin, A., & Hagengimana, A. (2005). Healing, reconciliation, forgiving and the prevention of violence after genocide or mass killing: An intervention and its experimental evaluation in Rwanda. *Journal of Social and Clinical Psychology, 24*(3), 297–334.

Sternberg, R., & Gordeeva, T. (1996). The anatomy of impact: What makes an article influential? *Psychological Science, 7,* 69–75.

Stokes, H. (2008). Design conversation: An instrument of peace education. In J. Lin, E. Brantmeier, & C. Bruhn (Eds.), *Transforming education for peace* (pp. 163–184). Charlotte, NC: Information Age.

Sugden, J. (2006). Teaching and playing sport for conflict resolution and co-existence in Israel. *International Review for the Sociology of Sport, 41*(2), 221–240.

Sugden, J., & Tomlinson, A. (1999). *Great balls of fire: How big money is hijacking world football.* Edinburgh: Mainstream Publishing.

Sullum, J. (2003). *Saying yes: In defense of drug use.* New York: Tarcher.

Sun, Y. (2003). A comparison of police field training officers' and nontraining officers' conflict resolution styles: Controlling versus supportive strategies. *Police Quarterly, 6*(1), 22–50.

Talbot, M. (2000, Fall). No justice, no peace: Lawyers and judges who practice dharma. Retrieved May 24, 2010, from http://www.contemplativemind. org/programs/law/nojustice.html

Thibault, L. (2009). Globalization of sport: An inconvenient truth. *Journal of Sport Management, 23,* 1–20

Tifft, L. (2000). Social justice and criminologies: A commentary. *Contemporary Justice Review, 1,* 43–52.

Tifft, L. (2002). Crime and peace: A walk with Richard Quinney. *Crime and Delinquency, 48,* 243–262.

Tifft, L., & Sullivan, D. (2001). A needs-based social harms approach to defining crime. In S. Henry & M. Lanier (Eds.), *What is crime? Controversies over the nature of crime and what we should do about it* (pp. 179–203). Lanham, MD: Rowan and Littlefield.

Thoits, P. (1981). Undesirable life events and psychophysiological distress: The impact of an income maintenance experiment. *American Sociological Review, 46*(1), 97–109.

Thrash, R. (2008, June 6). Bullies, beware: This school teaches peace. *St. Petersburg Times,* Retrieved April 6, 2011 from www.tampabay.com/news/ education/k12/article606675.ece

Toews, B. (2006). *The little book of restorative justice for people in prison.* Beaverton, OR: Good Books.

Tomlinson, A., & Young, C. (2006). Culture, politics, and spectacle in the global sports events. An introduction. In A. Tomlinson & C. Young (Eds.), *National identity and global sports events* (pp. 1–14). Albany: State University of New York Press.

Transparency International. (2008, August 7). *Red card: Time to expel corruption from the game.* Retrieved August 16, 2010, from http://www.transparency .org/news_room/in_focus/2008/corruption_in_sports

Triplett, W. (2004, May 14). Gangs. *Congressional Quarterly Researcher, 14*(18), 421–444.

Ulbrich, P., Warheit, G., & Zimmerman, R. (1989). Race, socioeconomic status, and psychological distress: An examination of differential vulnerability. *Journal of Health and Social Behavior, 30,* 131–146.

United for a Fair Economy. (2010). *State of the dream 2010: Drained*. Boston: United for a Fair Economy. Retrieved June 18, 2010, from www.faireconomy.org

Unnever, J., Cullen, F., & Fisher, B. (2005). Empathy and public support for capital punishment. *Journal of Crime and Justice, 28*(1), 1–34.

Urban, K. (1991). On the development of creativity in children. *Creativity Research Journal, 4*, 177–191.

Van Slyk, M., & Stern, M. (1999). A developmental approach to the use of conflict resolution interventions with adolescents. In L. Forcey & I. Harris. *Peacebuilding for adolescents: Strategies for educators and community leaders* (pp. 177–194). New York: Peter Lang.

Vargas, J. (2007, July 23). Binary America: Split in two by a digital divide. *Washington Post*. Retrieved June 21, 2010, from http://www.washingtonpost.com/wp-dyn/content/article/2007/07/22/AR2007072201278.html

Varney, W. (2000). Playing with "war fare." *Peace Review, 12*(3), 385–391.

Vidmar, N. (2001) Retribution and revenge. In S. Sanders, & V. Hamilton (Eds.), *Handbook of justice research in law* (pp. 31–63). New York: Kluwer Academic/Plenum.

Vogt, W. (1997). *Tolerance and education: Learning to live with diversity and difference*. Thousand Oaks, CA: Sage.

Vriens, L. (1999). Children, war, and peace. In L. Oppenheimer, D. Bar-Tal, & A. Raviv (Eds.), *How children understand war and peace* (pp. 17–58). San Francisco: Jossey-Bass.

Vygotsky, L. (1978). The role of play in development. In M. Cole (Ed.), *Mind in society* (pp. 92–104). Cambridge, MA: Harvard University Press.

Wade, M. (2008, November 14). India's Commonwealth Games facilities on track, insists premier. *Sydney Morning Herald*. Retrieved August 15, 2010, from http://www.smh.com.au/news/world/matt-wade/2008/11/14/1226318850279.html

Walgrave, L., & Bazemore, G. (1999). Reflections on the future of restorative justice for juveniles. In G. Bazemore, & L. Walgrave (Eds.), *Restorative juvenile justice: An exploration* (pp. 359–370). Monsey, NY: Willow Tree Press.

Walker, S. (2001.) Police accountability: The role of citizen oversight. Belmont, CA: Wadsworth.

Walker, S., Archbold, C., & Herbst, L. (2002). *Mediating citizen complaints against police officers: A guide for police and community leaders*. Washington, DC: Government Printing Office.

Wals, A. (1999). Stop the violence: Conflict management in an inner-city junior high school through action research and community problem solving. In L. Forcey, & I. Harris, (Eds.), *Peacebuilding for adolescents* (pp. 239–262). New York: Peter Lang.

Watts, I., & Erevelles, N. (2004) These deadly times: Reconceptualizing school violence by using critical race theory and disability studies. *American Educational Research Journal, 41*(2), 271–299.

Weber, C. (2006, May). An activist and a scholar: Reflections of a feminist sociologist negotiating academia. *Humanity & Society, 30*(2), 153–166.

Weil, P. (2003). *The art of living in peace: Guide to education for a culture of peace.* Zurich: UNESCO Publishing.

Well-Strande, H., & Tjeldvoll, A. (2003). Creativity, curricula, and paradigms. *Scandinavian Journal of Educational Research, 47*(3), 359–372.

Werner, E, & Smith, R. (1992). *Overcoming the odds.* Ithaca, NY: Cornell University Press.

Wertheim, L. J. (2004, June 14). The whole world is watching. *Sports Illustrated, 100*(24),72–86.

Wessells, M. (1997). Child soldiers. *Bulletin of the Atomic Scientists, 53*(6), 32–39.

Wessells, M. (2005). Child soldiers, peace education, and postconflict reconstruction for peace. *Theory Into Practice, 4*(4), 363–369.

Wessells, M., & Monteiro, C. (2004). Healing the wounds following protracted conflict in Angola: A community-based approach to assisting war-affected children. In U. P. Gielen, J. Fish, & J. G. Draguns (Eds.), *Handbook of culture, therapy, and healing* (pp. 321–341). Mahwah, NJ: Lawrence Erlbaum Associates, Inc.

Westerbeek, H., & Smith, A. (2003). *Sport business in the global marketplace.* Hampshire, UK: Palgrave Macmillan.

Westwood, R., & Low, D. (2003). The multicultural muse: Culture, creativity and innovation. *International Journal of Cross Cultural Management, 3*(2), 235–259.

Where your income tax $ really goes. (2010, February). *War Resisters League.* Retrieved June 18, 2010, from http://www.warresisters.org/

White, D. (2006.) A conceptual analysis of the hidden curriculum of police training in England and Wales. *Policing and Society, 16*, 386–404.

White, R. (2001). Restorative community justice: Community building approaches in juvenile justice. *Australian Institute of Criminology.* Retrieved August 19, 2010, from http://www.aic.gov.au/events/aic%20upcoming%20events/2001/~/media/conferences/outlook4/white.ashx

White, R. (2003).Communities, conferences, and restorative social justice. *Criminal Justice, 3*(2), 139–160.

Winfield, B. (1999). Community-based service: Re-creating the beloved community. In L. Forcey, & I. Harris (Eds.), *Peacebuilding for adolescents* (pp. 289–307). New York: Peter Lang.

Wink, W. (1992). Engaging the powers: Discernment and resistance in a world of domination. Minneapolis, MN: Fortress Press.

Wink, W. (1999). *The powers that be: Theology for a new millennium.* New York: Galilee Trade.

Wong, L. (1998). Disrupted journeys: Women, welfare and workfare. *Dissertation Abstracts International, Section B: The Sciences and Engineering, 58*(9-B), 5–27.

Woolford, A., & Ratner, R. (2010). Disrupting the informal-formal justice complex: On the transformative potential of civil mediation, restorative justice and reparations politics. *Contemporary Justice Review, 13*(1), 27–40.

Worman, D. (2006, April 9). Ultimate peace in the Middle East. *Al-Jazeera.* Retrieved April 29, 2010, from http://english.aljazeera.net/sport/2009/04/200942161555516370.html

Worman, D. (2009, April 17). Building peace in the Middle East. *Al-Jazeera.* Retrieved July 26, 2010, from http://english.aljazeera.net/sport/2009/04/20094161491338189.html

Wozniak, J. (2002). Toward a theoretical model of peacemaking criminology: An essay in honor of Richard Quinney. *Crime and Delinquency, 48*(2), 204–231.

Yablon, Y. (2007). Cognitive rather than emotional modification in peace education programs. *Journal of Moral Education, 36*(1), 51–65.

Yazzie, R. (1994). Life comes from it: Navajo justice concepts. *New Mexico Law Review, 24,* 175–190.

Yazzie, R. (2000, September 30). Navajo justice. *Yes! Magazine.* Retrieved August 19, 2010, http://www.yesmagazine.org/issues/is-it-time-to-close-the-prisons/navajo-justice

Young, J. (1971). *The drugtakers.* London: Paladin.

Zehr, H. (1990). Changing lenses: A new focus for crime and justice. Ages and limitations. *Journal of Moral Education, 36*(1), 51–65.

Zehr, H., & Mika, H. (1998). Fundamental concepts of restorative justice. *Contemporary Justice Review, 1,* 47–55

Ziller, R., Moriarty, D., & Phillips, S. (1999). The peace personality. In L. Oppenheimer, D. Bar-Tal, & A. Raviv (Eds.), *How children understand war and peace* (pp. 78–90). San Francisco: Jossey-Bass.

Zinn, H. (2007). *A power governments cannot suppress.* San Francisco: City Lights Books.

Zirin, D. (2005). *What's my name, fool? Sports and resistance in the United States.* Chicago: Haymarket Books.

Zirin, D. (2007). *Welcome to the terrordome.* Chicago: Haymarket Books.

Zirin, D. (2010, March 10). The South Africa World Cup: Invictus in reverse. *Huffington Post.* Retrieved August 16, 2010, from http://www.huffingtonpost.com/dave-zirin/the-south-africa-world-cu_b_493802.html

Zogby Poll: Americans favor rehabilitation. (2006, February 15–18). *The Peace Alliance.* Retrieved June 22, 2010, from http://www.thepeacealliance.org/content/view/139/68/

Zohar, D., & Marshall, I. (2000). *Connecting with our spiritual intelligence.* New York: Bloomsbury.

Zoppi, I., & Yaeger, A. (2008). Transforming teaching warfare into peace. In J. Lin, E. Brantmeier, & C. Bruhn (Eds.), *Transforming education for peace* (pp. 283–300). Charlotte, NC: Information Age.